OXFORD WORLD'S CLASSICS

SELECTED JOURNALISM

OSCAR WILDE was born in Dublin in 1854, the son of an eminent surgeon and a poetess who wrote under the pseudonym 'Speranza'. He was educated at Trinity College, Dublin and Magdalen College, Oxford where he achieved a double first and won the Newdigate Prize for Poetry. Unable to take up an academic career, Wilde began writing professionally as a means of making a living. In October 1881 the entrepreneur Richard D'Oyly Carte offered him a lecture tour of America. This led to a short period of employment as a lecturer. Wilde's career as a journalist began late in 1884 with the publication of a number of letters to the editor of the *Pall Mall Gazette* on the subject of dress. Wilde's employment as a reviewer by the paper followed in February 1885 and initiated a five-year career as a full-time professional journalist and editor.

In the late 1880s, Wilde began publishing his critical essays and short stories and cut down on his reviewing work although he continued to publish in periodicals. The notoriety of *The Picture of Dorian Gray* (1891) was swiftly followed by the tremendous success of Wilde's social comedies, *Lady Windermere's Fan* (1892), *A Woman of No Importance* (1893), *An Ideal Husband* (1895), and *The Importance of Being Earnest* (1895). However, this success was to prove short-lived after Wilde's libel action against the Marquess of Queensberry in 1895 resulted in a two-year prison sentence for gross indecency. When he was released from prison, Wilde lived on the Continent in self-imposed exile but continued to write, producing *The Ballad of Reading Gaol* (1898) and his confessional letter *De Profundis* (1905). He died in Paris in 1900.

ANYA CLAYWORTH is a Teaching Fellow in the School of English at the University of St Andrews. She has been working in the field of Wilde's journalism for over ten years and has written a number of articles on the subject.

OXFORD WORLD'S CLASSICS

*For over 100 years Oxford World's Classics have brought
readers closer to the world's great literature. Now with over 700
titles—from the 4,000-year-old myths of Mesopotamia to the
twentieth century's greatest novels—the series makes available
lesser-known as well as celebrated writing.*

*The pocket-sized hardbacks of the early years contained
introductions by Virginia Woolf, T. S. Eliot, Graham Greene,
and other literary figures which enriched the experience of reading.
Today the series is recognized for its fine scholarship and
reliability in texts that span world literature, drama and poetry,
religion, philosophy and politics. Each edition includes perceptive
commentary and essential background information to meet the
changing needs of readers.*

OXFORD WORLD'S CLASSICS

OSCAR WILDE

Selected Journalism

Edited with an Introduction and Notes by
ANYA CLAYWORTH

OXFORD
UNIVERSITY PRESS

OXFORD
UNIVERSITY PRESS

Great Clarendon Street, Oxford OX2 6DP

Oxford University Press is a department of the University of Oxford.
It furthers the University's objective of excellence in research, scholarship,
and education by publishing worldwide in

Oxford New York

Auckland Bangkok Buenos Aires Cape Town Chennai
Dar es Salaam Delhi Hong Kong Istanbul Karachi Kolkata
Kuala Lumpur Madrid Melbourne Mexico City Mumbai Nairobi
São Paulo Shanghai Taipei Tokyo Toronto

Oxford is a registered trade mark of Oxford University Press
in the UK and in certain other countries

Published in the United States by
Oxford University Press Inc., New York

Selection and editorial material © Anya Clayworth 2004

The moral rights of the author have been asserted

Database right Oxford University Press (maker)

First published as an Oxford World's Classics paperback 2004

British Library Cataloguing in Publication Data

Data available

Library of Congress Cataloging in Publication Data

Data available

0–19–280412–X

1

Typeset in Ehrhardt
by RefineCatch Limited, Bungay, Suffolk
Printed in Great Britain by
Clays Ltd, St Ives plc

ACKNOWLEDGEMENTS

This edition aims to give an insight into the different kinds of material that Wilde published in periodicals during his career as a journalist. The anthology therefore presents reviews, letters to the editor, drama criticism, and social comment from four of Wilde's major periodical publishers. It avoids well-known pieces of work published by Wilde in periodicals such as the critical essays and 'The Canterville Ghost', concentrating instead on showcasing a body of neglected journalistic work.

I owe, as ever, an enormous debt of gratitude to my partner Alex Hale for encouraging me to begin this project and keeping faith with it and with me. This edition is for him and for our first child Felix (who gestated alongside it) with all my love. I am indebted to Merlin Holland for his continued support for and interest in my work. John Sutherland provided inspiration at just the right time when he pointed out the importance of playing to one's strengths. Other academics and Wildeans whose work has inspired my own and who have contributed in one way or another to this volume are John Stokes, Ian Small, Russell Jackson, Joseph Bristow, Josephine Guy, Don Mead, and Bob Langenfeld.

Among friends at the School of English, St Andrews University who helped out in various ways were Douglas Dunn, Tom Jones, Sara Lodge, Phillip Mallett, Susan Manly, Andrew Murphy, Philip Parry, Malcolm Phillips, Rhiannon Purdie, and Susan Sellers. I am also grateful to the staff of the National Library of Scotland.

The support of friends and family has proved invaluable to this project. Love and thanks go to the Clayworths, Boyles, Hales, Thursfields, and to Claire Hider. Special thanks to Judith Luna, who has been the best editor an editor could ask for, kindly, humorous, patient, and generous with her experience.

ANYA CLAYWORTH

St Andrews, 2003

CONTENTS

INTRODUCTION

> To know the vintage and quality of a wine one need not drink
> the whole cask. It must be perfectly easy in half an hour to say
> whether a book is worth anything or worth nothing. Ten minutes
> are really sufficient, if one has the instinct for form. Who wants
> to wade through a dull volume?[1]

Oscar Wilde is well known as a wit and as the author of dazzling
society comedies and the controversial novel *The Picture of Dorian
Gray* (1891). However, what is less well known is that Wilde spent
much of his life working as a journalist. His work began appearing in
the periodical press as early as 1876 with the publication of some of
his poems in the *Irish Monthly* and *The Month and Catholic Review*.
He worked full-time as a journalist between 1885 and 1890. During
these years, Wilde produced more than seventy reviews for the *Pall
Mall Gazette* alone. As well as a large number of reviews of books,
plays, and social events, he published all kinds of work in periodicals.
Periodicals provided the first point of publication for his critical
essays, short stories, and *The Picture of Dorian Gray*.[2] In addition he
used the press as a way of communicating with the public, responding to criticism of his views on issues such as women's dress and
morality in art through the letters pages. By the time his final article
was published in *The Daily Chronicle* in 1898, Wilde had contributed
to over fifty different periodicals, as well as having held the post of
editor of *The Woman's World* for three years.

Wilde was therefore a journalist, in some sense, for nearly the
whole of his writing career. His careers as a dramatist and novelist
which receive so much critical attention are, ironically, markedly
shorter. The reason for the lack of attention paid to the journalism is
due partly to our perception of Wilde as a writer. The idea of Wilde
sitting at a desk working at reviewing books with titles like *How to be
Happy Though Married* is at odds with our received view of him. We

[1] Oscar Wilde, 'The True Function and Value of Criticism I', *The Nineteenth
Century*, 28 (1890), 123–47 (p. 137).
[2] *The Picture of Dorian Gray* first appeared in an American periodical, *Lippincott's
Monthly Magazine*, in July 1890.

like to see him as the lackadaisical genius, summing 'up all systems in a phrase, and all existence in an epigram'.[3] The literary value of the journalism has also been questioned. As writing was Wilde's only source of income, he has suffered under the bias (justified or not) against the professional author who earns money for occasional pieces, a bias that became increasingly prevalent in discussions of literary culture in the twentieth century.[4]

In contrast to the journalism of Walter Pater and Matthew Arnold which holds an important place in the canon of their work, Wilde's journalism has, until now, remained marginal. Although there are some pieces which are ephemeral because of their explicit topicality, the majority of his journalism shows Wilde to be exploring a catholic variety of subjects while also formulating the writing practices and ideas which would stand him in such good stead later on. We may casually wonder what Wilde thought of contemporary cookery, famous stage performers, major literary figures, the changes in the status of women in the 1880s, or the cosmopolitan culture of London. The journalism can show us that and more, with the odd witticism thrown in for good measure.

Journals and Journalism

Wilde's career in journalism came about as the result of a series of failures and fortuitous coincidences. Although Wilde had graduated from Oxford University in 1879 with a double first and had won the prestigious Newdigate Prize for Poetry, his prospects did not look good. Despite some assiduous efforts, he had failed to find himself an academic post and could not therefore follow the model of his mentors, Walter Pater and John Ruskin, and move into the academic community. He also failed to follow another of his writer models, Matthew Arnold, into a career as a School Inspector. Wilde thus arrived in London with no real means of financial support apart from a very small income from some land in Ireland. He set about getting himself known by people of influence in London by presenting himself as a prototypical aesthete. His wit and charm soon got

---

[3] *The Complete Letters of Oscar Wilde*, ed. Merlin Holland and Rupert Hart-Davis (London, 2002), 729. Hereafter referred to as *Letters*.

[4] For further discussion of this bias against the professional author, see John Carey, *The Intellectuals and the Masses* (London, 1992).

him noticed and he became a minor celebrity known for his excesses of dress and sharp tongue. His celebrity status paid off in 1881 when the entrepreneur Richard D'Oyly Carte invited him to do a lecture tour of America in connection with the D'Oyly Carte Company production of Gilbert and Sullivan's operetta *Patience*.

The lecture tour came at just the right time as Wilde's forays into professional writing had at this point flopped. His first play, *Vera; Or, The Nihilists* (1880), proved more difficult to sell than he had anticipated and his first poetry volume, *Poems* (1881), was dogged by accusations of derivativeness. Wilde's lecturing brought in a new source of income and introduced him as a personality to an American audience. The success of the American tour led to further lecturing engagements in Britain where he talked about his experiences in America but also about another subject close to his heart, reform of women's dress. Serious debates about women's clothing were under way at this time and commentators like Wilde's friend E. W. Godwin advocated innovations such as less constrictive garments and lighter underwear. The *Pall Mall Gazette* reported on Wilde's lecture on dress reform on 2 October 1884, including his idea for suspending all clothing from the shoulders rather than the hips and thereby abolishing the need for a corset. Two letters responding to the report were published on 3 and 7 October. Wilde wrote in with his own point of view on 14 October and again on 11 November 1884. These were his first two publications in the *Pall Mall Gazette*.[5]

It is likely that Wilde's appointment to the *Pall Mall Gazette* as a reviewer followed on from his letters to the editor about dress. He had had no contact with the paper prior to the correspondence and seems to have had no social connections that would have created an opening for him. His appointment at the *Gazette* was ostensibly merely a piece of good fortune but it was a piece of good fortune which came at a useful time as Wilde had married and was about to start a family. The pressures upon him to find a stable source of income had therefore become much more immediate. Wilde's first review for the paper appeared on 21 February 1885, only three months after his letters on dress, and he worked regularly for the *Gazette* until 1890.

[5] See 'Woman's Dress', below, pp. 3–5.

Pall Mall Gazette

The *Pall Mall Gazette* was a daily evening penny newspaper established in February 1865. Its content was diverse and included news,
comment, reviews, and feature articles. Initially it was owned by
George Smith of the publishers, Smith, Elder and Co., and was edited
by Frederick Greenwood, who modelled it on the *Anti-Jacobin*, a
paper founded to combat radical views in the late eighteenth century.[6]
When Wilde came to work for the newspaper, its editor was the controversial figure William Thomas Stead.[7] Stead aimed the *Gazette* at
an audience he called the 'political and literary classes' and used it as a
means for campaigning on Irish politics, divorce, and other social
issues.[8] Indeed, Stead was imprisoned in 1885 when undertaking an
investigation into child prostitution for the paper, the so-called
'Maiden Tribute of Babylon' campaign that resulted in the raising of
the legal age of consent.[9] While Stead's reasons for taking on his
campaigns were supposedly to ensure the greater good, there was a
consequence to his actions which only served to help him: his paper's
circulation increased enormously. After the week-long 'Maiden
Tribute' campaign, circulation of the *Pall Mall Gazette* soared
suddenly from the usual 20,000–30,000 copies to 100,000.[10]

It was partly this rise in circulation that drove Matthew Arnold to
put into print his objections to the kind of popular sensational journalism that the *Gazette* was promulgating, a journalism he labelled
pejoratively the 'new journalism'. In a famous article for *The Nineteenth Century* in 1887, Arnold noted: 'We have had opportunities of
observing a new journalism which a clever and energetic man has
lately invented. It has much to recommend it; it is full of ability,
novelty, variety, sensation, sympathy, generous instincts; its one

---

[6] For more detailed information about the *Pall Mall Gazette*, see Laurel Brake,
Subjugated Knowledges: Journalism, Gender and Literature in the Nineteenth Century
(Basingstoke, 1994), 93.

[7] William Thomas Stead (1849–1912), editor of the *Pall Mall Gazette* (1883–90) and
founder of the *Review of Reviews* in 1890.

[8] W. T. Stead, 'The *Pall Mall Gazette*', *Review of Reviews*, 7 (1893), 139–54 (p. 146).

[9] For a fuller discussion of Stead's case, see Roy Hattersley, 'Skill for Scandal',
Guardian, 16 Oct. 1999; Raymond L. Schults, *Crusader in Babylon: W. T. Stead and the
Pall Mall Gazette* (Lincoln, Nebr., 1972).

[10] Brake, *Subjugated Knowledges*, 94.

great fault is that it is *feather-brained*.'[11] Although Arnold never named the *Pall Mall Gazette* directly in the article, it was clear that it was the *Gazette* he was referring to when he described this 'new' 'feather-brained' journalism and that the 'clever and energetic man' who had invented it was Stead. By positing the existence of this 'new journalism' Arnold suggested that the paper was not of the same cultural value as 'literature' or 'criticism', an idea Wilde himself would later take up in his critical essays.

Wilde began working for the *Pall Mall Gazette* only shortly before Stead's 'Maiden Tribute' campaign began. He was thus working at the cutting edge of the 'new journalism' during the paper's period of greatest notoriety and popularity. Other writers who reviewed for the paper at the same time included George Bernard Shaw and H. G. Wells. Wilde's first review was of James McNeill Whistler's 'Ten O'Clock Lecture' (pp. 6–8). He wrote more than seventy reviews for the *Gazette*, which mostly appeared anonymously (in line with the conventions of the paper). Wilde was given a wide range of material to review, from books about marriage to biographies of Charles Dickens, to poetry and song in celebration of socialism. He expressed a correspondingly wide range of views. Marriage was 'the one subject on which all women agree and all men disagree' (p. 10), Dickens was a man with a 'fascinating, tyrannous personality' (p. 18), and socialism had 'the attraction of a wonderful personality' (p. 34). Wilde seems to have had little or no choice in what he was given although he did occasionally review work by friends and acquaintances such as Walter Pater, Whistler, and Algernon Swinburne. He reviewed a great deal of poetry for the paper, gaining his own irregular column, 'The Poet's Corner', in September 1886. Wilde's reviews were often reprinted in the weekly version of the *Pall Mall Gazette*, the *Pall Mall Budget*.

As well as his anonymous reviewing work for the journal, Wilde also occasionally provided signed work. One of his most telling signed pieces is his review of J. A. Froude's historical novel *The Two Chiefs of Dunboy*, which appeared signed with his initials 'O.W.' in April 1889. The review is heavily critical of the British government's actions in Ireland, suggesting that the government had ruled Ireland 'with a stupidity that is aggravated by good intentions' (p. 36). The

[11] Matthew Arnold, 'Up to Easter', *The Nineteenth Century*, 21 (1887), 629–43 (p. 638).

year 1889 was a landmark in Irish history, not least because it saw
the continuation of the Parnell Commission which was investigating
the activities of the Home Rule Party leader, Charles Stewart
Parnell. In December 1889 Parnell was publicly shamed when he
was cited as co-respondent in the divorce case of Captain and Kitty
O'Shea. The coverage of this event in the *Pall Mall Gazette* played a
key role in his downfall. For Wilde to speak out at this particular
time was in effect for him to nail his colours to a rather controversial
mast. However, the content of the *Pall Mall Gazette* at the same time
as this review was published shows that the paper shared the views
on Ireland espoused by Wilde. The striking similarity between the
rhetoric of Wilde's review and the position of the *Gazette* towards
Ireland must at least cast doubt over whether the views expressed in
this review belong to Wilde personally or whether they merely
reflect his conformity to editorial policy on Ireland.[12]

Wilde continued to write for the *Pall Mall Gazette* on a regular
basis until May 1890 when his final review for the paper was published.[13] There is no clear indication of why Wilde left the paper at
this point. His essays and *The Picture of Dorian Gray* may have
brought him a certain amount of critical success and notoriety but his
financial position did not improve substantially until 1892 when he
began to earn well from the society comedies. There was therefore no
financial impetus for him to leave the *Gazette* behind. He may have
wanted to shift the emphasis of his career away from journalism and
the reception of his essays in particular may have convinced him that
this was possible. It is equally possible, however, that with Stead's
departure from the *Pall Mall Gazette* to set up the *Review of Reviews*
in December 1889, Wilde's work for the paper simply dried up.

The Dramatic Review

Shortly after Wilde began work at the *Pall Mall Gazette* in 1885, his
first review for *The Dramatic Review* appeared. *The Dramatic
Review: A Journal of Theatrical, Musical and General Criticism* was a
weekly journal which began publication in February 1885. It was

---

[12] For further discussion of this point, see Anya Clayworth, 'Revising a Recalcitrant
Patriot: Oscar Wilde's Irish Reviews Reconsidered', *Forum for Modern Language Studies*,
38 (2002), 252–60.
[13] Oscar Wilde, 'Primavera', *Pall Mall Gazette* (24 May 1890), 3.

originally priced at threepence but the price was reduced in June 1886 to a penny in an effort to increase circulation. The journal was edited by Edwin Paget Palmer and was designed to appeal to 'all who find in dramatic art one of the serious interests in life, who take rational pleasure in the English stage of the present, and who look forward with intelligent hope to the English stage of the future'.[14] The journal consisted of feature articles about the theatre, reviews of current productions at home and abroad, backstage news, and small ads for actors. From the outset, Palmer made signed journalism a feature of *The Dramatic Review* so all the major articles were signed with a facsimile of the author's signature.[15] In this way, Palmer supported the move towards signed work begun by periodicals like *The Fortnightly Review* and *The Nineteenth Century* in the 1860s and asked his journalists to take responsibility for their own opinions.

Palmer assembled a mix of contributors for *The Dramatic Review* from experienced dramatic critics like William Archer to the less well known George Bernard Shaw as music critic.[16] Wilde began working for *The Dramatic Review* in March 1885. Although Wilde's name was relatively unknown in theatrical reviewing, half of his eight reviews took the leader position in the journal, underlined by his distinctive signature. His first article for the journal, 'Shakespeare on Scenery' (pp. 44–7), imagined Shakespeare's response to the fashion for archaeologically accurate productions of his work in the 1880s. Archaeological realism was a popular theatrical practice of the time and this popularity is reflected in most of Wilde's reviews which concentrate at least in part on judging the historical accuracy of a performance. He admires, for example, the costumes of the Oxford University Dramatic Society because 'their archaeological accuracy gave us, immediately on the rise of the curtain, a perfect picture of the time' (p. 51).

Wilde's arguments about archaeological realism owe a great deal to E. W. Godwin, who, as a theatrical designer, went to considerable

[14] Anon., 'Introductory', *The Dramatic Review* (1 Feb. 1885), 3.

[15] As John Stokes notes, though, not all contributors to the journal signed their work entirely truthfully. The drama critic Edward Aveling, for example, used the name 'Alec Nelson'. See John Stokes, 'Wilde's World: Oscar Wilde and Theatrical Journalism in the 1880s', in Joseph Bristow, ed., *Wilde Writings: Contextual Conditions* (Toronto, 2003), 41–58.

[16] William Archer (1856–1924), dramatic critic and popularizer of the plays of Henrik Ibsen.

lengths to establish the historical context of the plays he was producing. It seems more than a coincidence that Wilde reviewed three
famous productions involving Godwin: an outdoor performance of
As You Like It at Coombe House, a private performance of Percy
Bysshe Shelley's controversial play *The Cenci*, and a presentation of
John Todhunter's *Helena in Troas* in the circular arena at Hengler's
Circus. Wilde's approval for historically accurate productions in
these reviews was also probably influenced by the context. With the
exception of the editor's column, 'Notes by Ignotus', *The Dramatic
Review* largely took a stance in favour of archaeological realism.

   Most of Wilde's reviews for *The Dramatic Review* concern Shakespearian revivals. He reviewed Henry Irving's *Hamlet* as well as
Oxford University student productions of *Henry IV* and *Twelfth
Night*. This is not necessarily a reflection of Wilde's specific interest
in Shakespeare but probably more of an indication of theatrical
trends of the time. Shakespeare was very popular with audiences and
gave theatres the opportunity to build spectacular sets such as Herbert Beerbohm Tree's famously expensive interior of the tomb of
Juliet for *Romeo and Juliet*. Wilde's reviews of Shakespeare also
proved a fruitful resource for him. He reused ideas from them for an
article for *The Nineteenth Century* entitled 'Shakespeare and Stage
Costume' in 1885 and then rewrote them into 'The Truth of Masks'
for his 1891 volume of essays, *Intentions*.

   Reviews were not, however, Wilde's only contribution to *The
Dramatic Review*. The journal also published his decadent poem
'The Harlot's House' and 'Sonnet, On the Recent Sale by Auction of
Keats's Love Letters'.[17] Wilde's work for the journal therefore
reflects the diversity of his writing at this time; he was both poet and
journalist. The 'Sonnet, On the Recent Sale by Auction of Keats's
Love Letters' appeared after a seven-month hiatus in Wilde's contributions to *The Dramatic Review*. This rather patchy pattern of
work for the journal can be explained by Edwin Palmer's financial
problems at the time which meant that he could not pay his contributors. George Bernard Shaw noted in his diary that he was not paid
for his work for the journal after the autumn of 1885.[18] Unlike Shaw,

----

[17] 'The Harlot's House', *The Dramatic Review* (11 Apr. 1885), 167. 'Sonnet, On the
Recent Sale by Auction of Keats's Love Letters', *The Dramatic Review* (23 Jan. 1886),
249.
[18] *Bernard Shaw: The Diaries 1885–1887*, ed. Stanley Weintraub (London, 1986), 53.

who continued to contribute to *The Dramatic Review* despite not being paid, Wilde seems to have been unable to commit himself to the journal without promise of payment, hence his temporary suspension of work. Wilde's final review for the journal appeared on 22 May 1886 and shortly afterwards there was a steep increase in his publications in the *Pall Mall Gazette*. It is possible that his anxiety about the financial stability of *The Dramatic Review* deterred him from further work for the journal.

The Court and Society Review

A further source of income was *The Court and Society Review*. This was a sixpenny weekly magazine edited by Alsager Vian. It began publication in July 1884 under the title *Orange Blossoms, A Marriage Chronicle and Social Review*, and became *The Court and Society Journal* in July 1885 before taking the title *The Court and Society Review* in October 1885. It was a miscellaneous publication, providing illustrated serial fiction, book reviews, society gossip, and, perhaps slightly oddly, sporting tips. In a column called 'What to Back' tips were provided for 'the chief immediate events in the world of sport' which were 'intended to lead to judicious hedging'.[19] The journal's title and content suggest that it was intended for a high-society audience who would be keen to know the society news but who might also want to read the latest fiction by the most fashionable of authors. Wilde's first publication in *The Court and Society Review* was his story 'The Canterville Ghost', which appeared in two parts with illustrations by F. H. Townsend in February and March 1887.[20] The story appeared signed with Wilde's name, as did 'Lord Arthur Savile's Crime', which was published in the journal in three parts in May 1887, again with illustrations by Townsend.[21] Wilde's final contribution to the journal, a poem 'Un amant de nos jours', also appeared signed.[22] In contrast, Wilde's reviewing work for the journal was always anonymous.

Wilde's contributions to *The Court and Society Review* are eclectic

---

[19] Anon., 'What to Back', *The Court and Society Review*, 4 (1887), 380.

[20] Oscar Wilde, 'The Canterville Ghost', *The Court and Society Review*, 4 (1887), 183–6, 207–11.

[21] Oscar Wilde, 'Lord Arthur Savile's Crime', *The Court and Society Review*, 4 (1887), 447–50, 471–3, 495–7.

[22] Oscar Wilde, 'Un amant de nos jours', *The Court and Society Review*, 5 (1887), 587.

in their subject matter, as this selection shows. He wrote on topics as diverse as the role of Americans in British society, the contemporary biographical article, and the mistakes made by American Board-School children when asked general knowledge questions. In addition to these subjects, Wilde reviewed a number of plays for the journal including a production of *The Winter's Tale* at the Lyceum Theatre, an exhibition of the caricaturist Harry Furniss at the Gainsborough Gallery, and a lecture given by the American social radical Courtland Palmer. He also published a short note encouraging readers to raise funds for the new wing at Great Ormond Street Children's Hospital.

Wilde's pattern of work for *The Court and Society Review* and his letters to the journal's editor Alsager Vian suggest a different way of working from any of his other periodical work shown here. Rather than having a prescribed role as drama critic as he had for *The Dramatic Review* or as book reviewer as he was for the *Pall Mall Gazette*, here we see Wilde in a role more akin to a freelance journalist. He offered Vian articles and reviews instead of being given books to write about, as he was by the staff at the *Pall Mall Gazette*. For example, Wilde wrote to Vian on 13 April 1887 suggesting he write 'an article called "The Child Philosopher" . . . on Mark Twain's amazing and amusing record of the answers of American children at a Board-School'.[23] A week later, Vian had published the article.

Wilde's essays for *The Court and Society Review*, such as his response to Twain's article, are particularly interesting because they show his growing independence from the stimulus of a review task and his ability to spot the potential for unsolicited pieces. 'The Child Philosopher' (pp. 77–80) is also a good example of Wilde's grasp of the importance of topicality in journalistic work. Mark Twain's article describing the erroneous responses of American schoolchildren to general knowledge questions had only been published in the April issue of *The Century Magazine* but Wilde was in the process of getting himself commissioned to write about it only a few weeks later. Even the content of his articles exploited topicality by reflecting current events. 'The American Invasion' (pp. 66–9) mentions recent arrivals in London such as Buffalo Bill and the actress Cora Urquhart. Buffalo Bill's Wild West Show came to Britain for the first

[23] *Letters*, p. 296.

time in 1887 for Queen Victoria's Golden Jubilee and Urquhart had just made her début at the Haymarket Theatre. Wilde's final piece for *The Court and Society Review* appeared in December 1887 just as his editorship of *The Woman's World* gathered pace. *The Court and Society Review* folded in June 1888.

The Woman's World

The Woman's World was a shilling monthly magazine published by Cassell and Co. Thomas Wemyss Reid, the general manager of the company, founded the magazine in order to appeal to the new potential audience of financially empowered women created by changes in the status of women in the 1880s. Educational reforms such as the foundation of 'ladies'' colleges like Girton College together with changes in the law such as the Married Woman's Property Act of 1882 led to women having an increasingly active place in nineteenth-century society. More women began seeking careers and goals outside the family and home and professions such as medicine and teaching began to open their doors to this newly qualified workforce. In this way, women began to have independent financial spending power, a spending power which publishers recognized and tried to exploit. *The Woman's World* first appeared under the title *The Lady's World* in November 1886. After only six months of issues, Reid began negotiations with Wilde to take over as editor. Reid sent out some copies of the magazine to Wilde for his opinion and Wilde responded with a long, detailed letter in April 1887. In it, Wilde suggested that *The Lady's World* was 'too feminine and not sufficiently womanly' and that the magazine should 'deal not merely with what women wear, but with what they think, and what they feel'.[24] In May 1887 negotiations were concluded and Wilde began work on the reconstruction of *The Lady's World*.

Although his first issue was not to be published until November 1887, Wilde began writing to potential contributors immediately. He approached a mixture of his society contacts and well-known female literary figures, highlighting to them the value of his magazine as 'an organ through which women of culture and position will be able to find expression for their views'.[25] By September 1887, however,

---

[24] *Letters*, p. 297.   [25] Ibid. 302.

Wilde had realized an essential problem about his project, the title of the magazine. The terms 'lady' and 'woman' had become politicized due to the ongoing debates about the status of women and the rise of the so-called 'New Woman'.[26] As a result, some of the women he approached objected so strongly to the use of the word 'lady' that they refused to be associated with the magazine at all. Wilde's friend, the novelist Dinah Craik, offered the solution of changing the name of the magazine to the more acceptable title, *The Woman's World*. Wilde had to work hard to persuade Reid that this was the best idea and wrote to him stressing the importance of the new name to his contributors. He noted: 'For our magazine there is a definite opening and a definite mission, but without an alteration in the title it will not be able to avail itself of its opportunity.'[27] Finally, in September 1887, Reid agreed and the first edition to appear under Wilde's editorship, November 1887, appeared under the new title, *The Woman's World*.

The content of *The Woman's World* consisted of fiction, poetry, essays, reviews, and fashion. Although there were contributions by notable supporters of women's suffrage which set forth radical views on the status of women, there were also articles which offered opposing views. For example, in November 1888 Wilde published an article by the well-known women's campaigner Millicent Garrett Fawcett advocating the female vote and then, six months later, a response from Lucy Garnett which argued that women lacked the emotional control to vote logically.[28] Garnett's article is so vituperative in its tone that it seems irrational alongside Fawcett's elegant prose. Wilde, however, was willing for both sides of the contemporary debates about the status of women to be represented in his magazine.

Cassell and Co. exploited Wilde's celebrity status by advertising his editorship of the paper well in advance and unusually by emblazoning his name on the front cover.[29] Wilde's contribution to the magazine's content was a column, 'Literary and Other Notes', in

---

[26] 'New Woman' was the name the press gave to women who espoused feminist views or who sought careers in the newly opened professions of medicine and teaching in the 1880s. For further discussion of the 'New Woman', see John Sloan, *Oscar Wilde* (Oxford, 2003).

[27] *Letters*, p. 318.

[28] For further discussion of these two articles, see Katherine Ksinan, 'Wilde as Editor of *Woman's World*: Fighting a Dull Slumber in Stale Certitudes', *English Literature in Transition*, 41 (1998), 408–26.

[29] Editors for Cassell and Co. habitually remained anonymous, even if they were celebrities in their own right.

which he examined the latest publications relevant to women readers as well as social events, charity work, and current affairs. This column replaced the gossip section in *The Lady's World*, perhaps indicating the seriousness of Wilde's intention when he claimed that the magazine would appeal to 'those who have university training' and act as a forum for them to put forward their views on 'life and things'.[30] His taste in reviewing material was diverse. As well as considering collections of women's poetry such as Mrs Sharp's ground-breaking *Women's Voices*, Wilde also gave his attention to memoirs of women of achievement such as the Italian actress Adelaide Ristori and Emily Ruete, the first Arab woman to write her autobiography.

Wilde's early columns for the magazine were long, detailed, and wide in scope. However, as time went on, they became shorter until they ceased altogether between March and December 1888. The hiatus in Wilde's column seems to have been in part due to his disillusion with the content. In a letter to Reid of October 1888, Wilde suggested that 'there are many things in which women are interested about which a man really cannot write'.[31] His idea that he write only on literary subjects was obviously one supported by Reid because Wilde's later columns such as 'A Note on Some Modern Poets' and 'Some Literary Notes' are devoted solely to reviews of current literature. The later columns also see Wilde broadening his selections to include more works by male authors such as the poets W. E. Henley and W. B. Yeats.

At least initially, Wilde's editorship of *The Woman's World* was successful. However, circulation began dropping, and in October 1888 there was an internal review of the magazine.[32] The general editor at Cassell and Co., John Williams, suggested that the serial, Constance Fletcher's *The Truth about Clement Ker*, should be abandoned in favour of short stories and that Wilde's column should be broadened in its appeal.[33] While Wilde agreed with some of the changes, he did point out that, as far as he was concerned, the real problem with the magazine was that it was too expensive and advised

---

[30] *Letters*, p. 301.

[31] *Letters*, p. 363.

[32] The circulation figures for *The Woman's World* are not known because the magazine's archive was destroyed by fire in World War II.

[33] *Letters*, p. 363.

that the price be reduced to sixpence or sevenpence.[34] Articles by his sub-editor, Arthur Fish, recollecting Wilde's time as an editor have put forward an idea of Wilde as a 'Pegasus in harness' who lacked commitment to the magazine.[35] This has in turn led to the widely held view that Wilde's lackadaisical attitude was responsible for the failure of *The Woman's World*. While this view seems to be borne out by the absence of Wilde's column for seven issues, it is worth bearing in mind Wilde's achievements at *The Woman's World*. He succeeded in rebranding and reconstructing his magazine and ensuring its survival for three years in a notoriously volatile and competitive marketplace.[36] After Wilde resigned in August 1889 and his final contributions appeared in October 1889, *The Woman's World* only survived another year.

'Day after Day, All the Year Round'

When Wilde came to work as a journalist, he was following a well-established route for a writer in the 1880s. Many aspiring writers such as George Bernard Shaw and H. G. Wells began their careers in journalism. Wilde's brother Willie also worked as a professional journalist in London.[37] The 1880s saw the heyday of the periodical, which, much like today, catered to an enormous variety of tastes and markets, from the publishers' journals such as *Macmillan's Magazine*, to reviews like *The Edinburgh Review*, to satirical papers like *Punch*. The advantages of working in journalism for a writer at the start of his career were clear. Where the returns on a book published by a relatively unknown writer could prove uncertain (as the returns on Wilde's *Poems* proved to be), commissioned journalism always paid on receipt of goods.[38] Depending on the status of the journalist, an article for a monthly magazine such as *The Nineteenth Century*

---

[34] *Letters*, p. 363. For further discussion of the expenses associated with *The Woman's World*, see Anya Clayworth, '*The Woman's World*: Oscar Wilde as Editor', *Victorian Periodicals Review*, 30 (1997), 84–101.

[35] Arthur Fish, 'Oscar Wilde as Editor', *Harper's Weekly* (4 Oct. 1913), 18–20 (p. 18).

[36] *The Lady's Review*, which aspired to some of the same enlightened views on the subject of women's issues as *The Woman's World*, foundered in under a year.

[37] Willie Wilde was a drama critic for *Punch* and *Vanity Fair*, wrote leaders for *The Daily Telegraph* and, later on, highly regarded articles for *The Daily Chronicle* about the Parnell Commission.

[38] Wilde's agreement for *Poems* required him to pay all the costs of publication and to give 10 per cent of the profits to his publisher.

usually paid about a guinea per page. It was therefore possible, once established, for a journalist like Wilde to earn a reasonable and regular salary writing for the periodical press. George Bernard Shaw, for example, who recorded his journalistic income in minute detail, noted a healthy salary of £800 for a year's work in 1895.[39]

Perhaps the biggest advantage of a career in journalism for a writer starting out like Wilde was the training that it offered in the profession of writing. It is no coincidence that Wilde's ability to identify niches in the market and fill them and his knowledge of what his work was worth in the marketplace improved dramatically after his time as a journalist. Journalism inherently involved skills of topicality and negotiation and Wilde became increasingly adept at using those skills in the late 1880s, after he had spent five years working full-time in the periodical world. When he sent 'The Portrait of Mr W. H.' to *Blackwood's Edinburgh Magazine* in April 1889, Wilde pressed the editor hard and succeeded in getting it published by July.[40] He earned £28. 15s. for the piece, a figure that the editor noted was 'somewhat beyond *Maga*'s [*Blackwood's Edinburgh Magazine*] usual scale'.[41] As well as being paid over the odds, Wilde also negotiated the retention of copyright for the story. This too went against the usual practice of the magazine but allowed him to reprint the story as he chose and thus potentially to continue to earn money for it every time it appeared in print. In addition, Wilde began negotiations with the publisher of the magazine, fruitless though they turned out to be, to publish more of his work in book form. Once he had an opening with Blackwood's he did not hesitate to exploit it. Wilde's negotiations with publishers in the early 1880s show nothing of this business savvy.

Despite the advantages of money and training, the life of a journalist like Wilde in the 1880s was not always an easy one. The sheer volume of work could be overwhelming, as Walter Besant suggests in his account of a journalist's daily routine in *The Pen and the Book*:

He finds on his desk two or three books waiting for review: a MS sent him for an opinion: a book of his own to go on with—possibly the life of some

[39] Michael Holroyd, *Bernard Shaw. Volume I: 1856–1898: The Search for Love* (London, 1988), 216.

[40] See also Horst Schroeder, *Oscar Wilde, 'The Portrait of Mr W. H.': Its Composition, Publication and Reception* (Braunschweig, 1984).

[41] *Letters*, p. 401.

dead and gone worthy for a series: an article which he has promised for a magazine: a paper for the Dictionary of National Biography: perhaps an unfinished novel to which he must give three hours of absorbed attention. This goes on, day after day, all the year round.[42]

Besant's account is to a certain extent borne out by Wilde's work schedule. Take, for example, a week in May 1887. As well as publishing a review of seven works for the *Pall Mall Gazette* and an article, 'Should Geniuses Meet?', in *The Court and Society Review*, Wilde was also preparing his story 'Lord Arthur Savile's Crime' for its appearance in *The Court and Society Review*.[43] In addition, he was writing reams of formulaic letters to potential contributors to *The Woman's World*.

The work which filled Wilde's weeks was likely at times to be utter drudgery. Often journalists were given no choice in the material that they had to review or write about, so their output frequently did not exploit their specialisms or interests. This seems to have been the case at the *Pall Mall Gazette*. George Bernard Shaw eventually resigned as a reviewer for the paper because he could no longer stand to review books which he had not chosen and which he judged to be worse than his own unpublished work. Before he left, Shaw wrote furiously to the sub-editor at the *Gazette*: 'Why condemn me to read things that I can't review—that no artistic conscience can survive the reviewing of!'[44] Although Wilde seems to have had more patience with the mundanity of his journalistic life than Shaw, he did write wryly to an unknown correspondent in 1885, 'The best work in literature is always done by those who do not depend upon it for their daily bread', perhaps reflecting on his own working life at the time.[45]

Frustration at the dullness of the work could also be complicated by uncertainty, as H. G. Wells found when two of his periodical outlets suddenly dropped his work:

There was a sudden fall in my income. Abruptly the *National Observer* changed hands. Mr Vincent [the new editor] thought my articles queer

---

[42] Walter Besant, *The Pen and the Book* (London, 1899), 24.

[43] Oscar Wilde, 'A Batch of Novels', *Pall Mall Gazette* (2 May 1887), 11. Oscar Wilde, 'Should Geniuses Meet?', *The Court and Society Review*, 4 (1887), 413–14. Oscar Wilde, 'Lord Arthur Savile's Crime', *The Court and Society Review*, 4 (1887), 447–50.

[44] Holroyd, *Bernard Shaw*, 214.

[45] *Letters*, p. 265.

wild ramblings and wound them up at once. At the same time the *Pall
Mall Gazette* stopped using my articles. The literary editor, Marriott
Watson, always a firm friend of mine, was away on holiday and his tem-
porary successor did not think very much of my stuff.[46]

Wells's experiences are characteristic of the conditions of such work
during this period; journalists were always subject to the mercurial
nature of editors.

Another potential disadvantage for the jobbing journalist was the
widespread practice of anonymity in periodical publishing. Most of
Wilde's work for both the *Pall Mall Gazette* and *The Court and
Society Review* appeared anonymously. An editorial 'we', for
example, habitually prefaced his review comments in both periodicals. So, Wilde notes of *How to be Happy Though Married* in the *Pall
Mall Gazette* that 'we strongly recommend this book as one of the
best of wedding presents' (p. 11), and of Routledge's editions of
Honoré de Balzac in English, 'We fear Mr Routledge's edition will
not do' (p. 15). In this way Wilde was able to invoke the collective
authority of the periodical rather than his own perhaps more dubi-
ous authority as an individual reviewer. The editorial 'we' also pre-
vented recrimination from angry reviewed authors and gave him the
opportunity to be more frank than he may have been willing to be
under his own name. The downside to all this was that Wilde's work
went unattributed and therefore uncelebrated.

However, Wilde did successfully turn this potential disadvantage
to his advantage. Anonymity allowed him, for example, to publish
more than one piece of his writing in an issue of a periodical without
it being apparent. For example, on 13 April 1887, Wilde published a
note about fundraising for Great Ormond Street Children's Hospital, an essay entitled 'The American Man', and a review of William
Gillette's play, *Held by the Enemy*, all in the same issue of *The Court
and Society Review*.[47] Wilde was thus able to maximize his output per
issue and increase his income. By signing some pieces of work and
not others, he presented himself as a *writer* who published in periodicals rather than a jobbing journalist reviewing a ragbag of publications at the behest of an editor. This in turn allowed him to maintain

[46] H. G. Wells, *Experiment in Autobiography: Discoveries and Conclusions of a Very
Ordinary Brain Since 1866*, Vol. II (London, 1934), 516.
[47] See *The Court and Society Review*, 4 (1887), 337, 341–3, 357.

his public persona as an aesthete not in hock to the sordid everyday transactions of the journalistic world.

'I have merely to do with literature'

For Wilde journalism was a mixed blessing. It brought in the money that he needed to support his family and burgeoning social life but set him at odds with the way in which he wanted to present himself to the public. Even while he was still working full-time in the profession he tried to insist upon his difference from other hack writers. In a letter responding to a request for a description of himself in the mid-1880s, Wilde noted that he wrote 'only on questions of literature and art—am hardly a journalist'.[48] Once his career as a full-time professional journalist was safely over, he attempted (in a way reminiscent of Matthew Arnold's 1887 attack on the *Pall Mall Gazette*) to distance himself from hack journalism by disparaging its claims to be literature. As Gilbert remarks in Wilde's essay, 'The True Function and Value of Criticism' (1890): 'As for modern journalism, it is not my business to defend it. It justifies its own existence by the survival of the vulgarest. I have merely to do with literature'; Wilde reiterated this point once more in 'The Soul of Man Under Socialism' in 1891.[49]

Wilde's journalism sheds light on a number of the writing practices he used throughout his *œuvre*, including self-plagiarism. It is a well-documented fact that Wilde moved material, at times only thinly disguised, between pieces. Editors of the later works such as *The Picture of Dorian Gray* and the society comedies have exhaustively investigated the movement of ideas between these texts. But the movement and development of ideas from Wilde's journalism to his later works is also noteworthy.[50] Indeed, the idea of reusing material in different forums probably originated as a result of Wilde's work in the periodical marketplace. The pressure to produce material in order to earn money may well have inclined him to take short cuts and recycle good material where he could.

There are clear examples of this strategy within the journalistic

---

[48] *Letters*, p. 293.

[49] 'The True Function and Value of Criticism I', 129.

[50] Ian Small and Josephine Guy look at some examples of self-plagiarism originating in the journalism in *Oscar Wilde's Profession* (Oxford, 2000).

œuvre itself. In his review, 'Dinners and Dishes', for the *Pall Mall Gazette* on 7 March 1885, Wilde notes:

A man can live for three days without bread, but no man can live for one day without poetry, was an aphorism of Baudelaire's . . . Who indeed, in these degenerate days, would hesitate between an ode and an omelette, a sonnet and a salmi? (p. 8)

In his column, 'Literary and Other Notes', for *The Woman's World* of January 1888, Wilde remarks:

The most perfect and the most poisonous of all modern French poets once remarked that a man can live for three days without bread, but that no one can live for three days without poetry . . . I fancy that most people, if they do not actually prefer a salmi to a sonnet, certainly like their culture to repose on a basis of good cookery, and as there is something to be said for this attitude, I am glad to see that several ladies are interesting themselves in cookery classes. (pp. 119–20)

The similarities between these two pieces are undeniable. However, this is not the end of the self-borrowing as Wilde goes on to borrow from 'Literary and Other Notes'. The reference to Baudelaire as 'the most perfect and the most poisonous of all modern French poets' is itself reworked in a review of Algernon Charles Swinburne's *Poems and Ballads* (1889) for the *Pall Mall Gazette* on 27 June 1889. Wilde notes: 'Mr Swinburne once set his age on fire by a volume of very perfect and very poisonous poetry' (p. 40). The phrase is slightly different and it is applied to a new subject: Wilde uses it here to refer to Swinburne's scandalous first volume of *Poems and Ballads* published in 1866.

It is likely that Wilde thought he could get away with this three-fold self-borrowing because of the different audiences that these two periodicals attracted. The *Pall Mall Gazette* was a daily penny newspaper and *The Woman's World* an expensive monthly woman's magazine and so they were aimed at completely different target audiences. Wilde could probably have counted on the fact that not many of his readers would have read both or indeed remember the turns of phrase after three years. His resolve to recycle his ideas may also have been strengthened by the fact that his two reviews for the *Pall Mall Gazette* were published anonymously and his authorship of them was therefore always deniable.

As well as transferring material from journal to journal Wilde also began developing ideas in his journalistic work which he would reuse as the cornerstone of some of his later work. Ian Small has noted in his edition of Wilde's short fiction that one of the things that distinguishes Wilde's fairy-tales from other nineteenth-century moral children's fiction is the reversal in the relationship between child and adult. In the fairy-tales, Small notes, 'the narrative focus is always the child's perception of a good parent, and not the parent's perception of a good child'.[51] So the role of the child in 'The Selfish Giant' (1888) is to 'educate the giant into the art of good parenting'.[52] Small treats this very much as part of the strategy of the reversal of norms or expectations that we see throughout Wilde's work and which we have seen on a small scale even in his construction of jokes. However, the idea that underpins Wilde's approach to his fairy-tales comes from the journalism.

On 23 March 1887 Wilde published an essay entitled 'The American Invasion' in *The Court and Society Review* (pp. 66–9). The essay is an amusing piece that looks at Americans in London society and analyses their successes and failures. American women, Wilde notes, 'have one grave fault—their mothers', who, he says, are 'dull, dowdy, or dyspeptic'. The dullness of American parents in general, though, cannot, Wilde suggests, be blamed on their children, who 'spare no pains at all to bring up their parents properly, and to give them a suitable, if somewhat late, education'. He goes on to develop this idea, stating with characteristic wit that American children 'are always ready to give to those who are older than themselves the full benefits of their inexperience'. 'Parents', he quips, 'should be seen, not heard.' He remarks in conclusion that the system whereby children educate their parents has not been as successful as it could have been. However, Wilde still insists that this is no reflection on the children because 'the material with which the children had to deal was crude and incapable of real development'.

Wilde returns to the idea of children educating adults in another essay for *The Court and Society Review*, 'The Child Philosopher', published on 20 April 1887 (pp. 77–80). As we have seen, this essay was written in response to an article by Mark Twain that Wilde had read in *The Century Magazine* highlighting the amusing mistakes

---

[51] Oscar Wilde, *Complete Short Fiction*, ed. Ian Small (Harmondsworth, 1994), p. xiii.
[52] Ibid., p. xii.

made by American Board-School children.[53] To Wilde, though, the children's mistakes are not evidence of poor teaching or lack of study but are 'full of the richest suggestion and pregnant with the very highest philosophy'. 'No wonder', he notes, echoing his previous month's essay, 'that the American child educates its father and mother, when it can give us such luminous definitions as the following: *Republican*, a sinner mentioned in the Bible'. At the end of the essay, Wilde again insists upon the child's ability to educate the adult. He states, 'the utterances of the child-philosopher will be treasured by the scientific historian as the best criticism upon modern education, the best epigram upon modern life'.

This almost Blakean idea of the child educating the adult is further developed as the mainstay for the fairy-tales. The children who enter the garden of the Selfish Giant show him his selfishness in keeping his garden for himself. When the Giant picks up the child who cannot reach the tree and places him in it, he learns to appreciate the beauty of his garden and the children themselves and is finally rewarded by a place in Paradise. The Little Dwarf in 'The Birthday of the Infanta' (1889) teaches a lesson to children and adults alike about laughing at those less fortunate than oneself. When the Little Dwarf sees himself in a mirror for the first time and realizes that he has been an object of ridicule not entertainment, he dies of a broken heart. Wilde's moral message is clear when the spoiled Infanta remarks at the end of the story, 'For the future let those who come to play with me have no hearts.'[54]

The fairy-tales were not, however, the only beneficiary of ideas from the journalism. Even the society comedies contain ideas first rehearsed by Wilde in his articles: the juxtaposition of triviality and seriousness that would later underpin Wilde's most famous work, *The Importance of Being Earnest*, has its first outing in periodicals. The play turns on the idea that the trivial is important whereas the serious is trivial. So Gwendolen and Cecily want to marry a man called Ernest, not someone who loves them or who has a stable background that can make them happy. As Wilde told Robert Ross of the play in 1895, 'It is exquisitely trivial, a delicate bubble of fancy, and it has its philosophy—that we should treat all the trivial things

---

[53] Mark Twain, 'English as She is Taught', *The Century Magazine* (Apr. 1887), 932–6.
[54] *Complete Short Fiction*, ed. Small, 114.

of life very seriously, and all the serious things with sincere and studied triviality.'[55]

Treating the 'trivial things of life very seriously' is a feature of Wilde's approach to his journalism from as early as 1885. In an anonymous review entitled 'Dinners and Dishes' in the *Pall Mall Gazette* of 7 March 1885 Wilde observes that the 'British cook is a foolish woman, who should be turned, for her iniquities, into a pillar of that salt which she never knows how to use' (p. 9). By alluding to the biblical fate of Lot's wife (turned into a pillar of salt for disobeying God's command not to look back on the destruction of Sodom), Wilde implies that the British cook has committed an equivalent series of immoral acts. However, the British cook's immoral acts extend only to her (and he does specify that the cook is a woman) relatively trivial faults as previously exposed by Wilde:

Her entire ignorance of herbs, her passion for extracts and essences, her total inability to make a soup which is anything more than a combination of pepper and gravy, her inveterate habit of sending up bread poultices with pheasants,—all these sins and many others are ruthlessly unmasked by the author. (p. 9)

These are hardly sins on the scale of those perpetrated by Lot's wife but Wilde treats them as such, giving the cook a suitably hyperbolical yet culinary punishment.

By 1888 though, Wilde begins to spell out his juxtaposition of triviality and seriousness in more familiar terms. When describing American girls in his essay 'The American Invasion' in *The Court and Society Review*, Wilde notes that 'they never talk seriously, except to their dressmakers, and never think seriously, except about amusements' (p. 68). Wilde then repeats the idea in a review of W. E. Henley's *A Book of Verses* (1888) for his column in *The Woman's World* of December 1888. He finishes off his section on Henley with the epigram: 'If he took himself more seriously his work would become trivial' (p. 146). By suggesting *if* 'he took himself more seriously', Wilde implies that Henley (with whom he had a complex friendship and rivalry) does not take himself seriously enough and is, therefore, under the terms of the juxtaposition, trivial. This

---

[55] Anon., 'Mr Oscar Wilde on Mr Oscar Wilde', *St James's Gazette* (18 Jan. 1895). This article was probably a collaboration between Ross and Wilde and is reprinted in *More Letters of Oscar Wilde*, ed. Rupert Hart-Davis (Oxford, 1985), 189–96 (p. 196).

judgement is borne out by Wilde's professed admiration in the review for 'the very lightness and slightness of so much of the work'. As the epigram is so ambiguous, though, it may be hard for the reader to tell whether Wilde approves of Henley's work or not. Henley clearly thought Wilde was praising him as he wrote to thank him for the review afterwards.

As Wilde himself noted in a review of W. G. Wills's play *Olivia* for *The Dramatic Review*: 'It is only the unimaginative who ever invent. The true artist is known by the use he makes of what he annexes, and he annexes everything' (p. 54). While he did not annex everything, the extent to which Wilde used his journalistic work serves to underline, by his own definition, his status as a 'true artist'. It may have only taken him ten minutes 'to say whether a book is worth anything or worth nothing' but Wilde's journalism provided him with a legacy of material which he would exploit for the rest of his literary career.[56]

[56] 'The True Function and Value of Criticism I', 137.

NOTE ON THE TEXTS

Much of the manuscript material related to Wilde's journalism has been destroyed and I have not managed to locate any manuscripts relevant to the pieces published. I have therefore taken the texts from their first published source and have retained each periodical's house style. This accounts for some variations in spelling, punctuation, italicization, and grammar between the pieces. The only modifications made to Wilde's published punctuation for this edition have been the replacement of double quotation marks with single ones and the removal of full-stops after titles such as 'Mr'.

I have chosen examples from Wilde's four main periodical publishers in order to present a representative sample of his work during his most prolific period as a journalist. The reviews and essays reprinted here reflect Wilde's developing views on a wide variety of topics including women's dress, Irish politics, contemporary trends in staging, and British cookery. The material has been arranged by periodical and then chronologically. Identification of Wilde as author of the anonymous works is largely based on Robert Ross's 1908 editions of the journalism and on Stuart Mason's *Bibliography of Oscar Wilde*. While these sources are not exhaustive, they remain for the time being the best resource for identifying Wilde's journalistic *œuvre*. It is hoped that John Stokes and Russell Jackson's forthcoming editions of the complete journalism for the Oxford English Texts project will supplement and complement this edition.

SELECT BIBLIOGRAPHY

Nineteenth-Century Journalism

The following volumes are useful as a general starting point for the study of nineteenth-century journalism: Walter Houghton, ed., *The Wellesey Index to Victorian Periodicals* (London, 1966); Alvin Sullivan, ed., *British Literary Magazines: The Victorian and Edwardian Age 1837–1913* (London, 1984); J. Don Vann and Rosemary T. Van Arsdel, eds., *Victorian Periodicals: A Guide to Research I* (New York, 1978); J. Don Vann and Rosemary T. Van Arsdel, eds., *Victorian Periodicals: A Guide to Research II* (New York, 1989); Cynthia L. White, *Women's Magazines 1693–1968* (London, 1970).

Biography

Probably the most important text for learning about Wilde's life is the latest edition of his letters: *The Complete Letters of Oscar Wilde*, ed. Merlin Holland and Rupert Hart-Davis (London, 2002). Richard Ellmann's biography, despite its flaws, remains the best to date: Richard Ellmann, *Oscar Wilde* (London, 1987). For correction of Ellmann's errors, see Horst Schroeder, *Additions and Corrections to Ellmann's Wilde* (Braunschweig, 2002). For a transcript of Wilde's prosecution of the Marquess of Queensberry, see Merlin Holland, ed., *Irish Peacock and Scarlet Marquess* (London, 2003).

Wilde's Journalism

Relatively little has been written on Wilde's journalism and there are, as yet, no book-length studies of the material. Key resources for study of the journalism are Stuart Mason's *Bibliography of Oscar Wilde* (London, 1914), Robert Ross's two volumes (Vols. XIII and XIV) containing most of Wilde's periodical output in his *Collected Works of Oscar Wilde* (London, 1908), and Karl Beckson's *The Oscar Wilde Encyclopedia* (New York, 1998). There is as yet no definitive edition of the journalism. It is hoped that the Oxford English Texts editions will fill that niche. John Stokes has published a number of articles on aspects of the journalism, including his excellent essay 'Wilde the Journalist', in Peter Raby, ed., *The Cambridge Companion to Oscar Wilde* (Cambridge, 1997). Stokes's essay on Wilde's work at *The Dramatic Review* is also very insightful: John Stokes, 'Wilde's World: Oscar Wilde and Theatrical Journalism in the 1880s', in Joseph Bristow, ed., *Wilde Writings: Contextual Conditions* (Toronto, 2003). Josephine Guy and Ian Small devote a chapter of their groundbreaking study, *Oscar Wilde's Profession* (Oxford, 2000), to the journalism. There is some discussion of nineteenth-century journalism and Wilde's periodical contributions in John Sloan's *Oscar Wilde* (Oxford, 2003).

There have been a few articles attributing anonymous reviews to Wilde: Oskar Wellens, 'A Hitherto Unnoticed Review by Wilde', *Notes and Queries*, 41 (1994), 364; Kevin H. O'Brien, 'Oscar Wilde: An Unsigned Book Review', *Notes and Queries*, 30 (1983), 312–15; John Stokes, 'Wilde on Dostoevsky', *Notes and Queries*, 27 (1980), 215–16. An unpublished, incomplete review by Wilde in manuscript form is reprinted and discussed by Anya Clayworth and Ian Small, eds., ' "Amiel and Lord Beaconsfield": An Unpublished Review by Oscar Wilde', *English Literature in Transition 1880–1920*, 39 (1996), 284–97.

The Woman's World

Wilde's time as editor of *The Woman's World* has received more critical attention than most other aspects of his journalistic *œuvre*. See Laurel Brake, *Subjugated Knowledges: Journalism, Gender and Literature in the Nineteenth Century* (Basingstoke, 1994); Arthur Fish, 'Oscar Wilde as Editor', *Harper's Weekly* (4 Oct. 1913), 18–20; Arthur Fish, 'Memories of Oscar Wilde—Some Hitherto Unpublished Letters', *Cassell's Weekly* (2 May 1923), 215–16; Simon Nowell-Smith, *The House of Cassell 1848–1958* (London, 1958); Katherine Ksinan, 'Wilde as Editor of *Woman's World*: Fighting a Dull Slumber in Stale Certitudes', *English Literature in Transition*, 41 (1998), 408–26; Stephanie Green, 'Oscar Wilde's *The Woman's World*', *Victorian Periodicals Review*, 30 (1997), 102–18; Anya Clayworth, '*The Woman's World*: Oscar Wilde as Editor', *Victorian Periodicals Review*, 30 (1997), 84–101.

The Pall Mall Gazette

The following book-length studies and articles are useful in relation to the study of the *Pall Mall Gazette*. There is limited information about Wilde in some of these titles: Matthew Arnold, 'Up to Easter', *The Nineteenth Century*, 21 (1887), 629–43; Raymond L. Schults, *Crusader in Babylon: W. T. Stead and the Pall Mall Gazette* (Lincoln, Nebr., 1972); J. W. Robertson Scott, *The Story of the 'Pall Mall Gazette'* (Oxford, 1950); J. W. Robertson Scott, *The Life and Death of a Newspaper* (London, 1952); W. T. Stead, 'The *Pall Mall Gazette*', *Review of Reviews*, 7 (1893), 139–54. A more detailed study of Wilde's engagement with Irish politics in his reviews for the *Pall Mall Gazette* is provided by Anya Clayworth, 'Revising a Recalcitrant Patriot: Oscar Wilde's Irish Reviews Reconsidered', *Forum for Modern Language Studies*, 38 (2002), 252–60.

Further Reading in Oxford World's Classics

Sloan, John, *Oscar Wilde* (Authors in Context).

Wilde, Oscar, *Complete Poetry*, ed. Isobel Murray.

—— *Complete Shorter Fiction*, ed. Isobel Murray.

—— *The Importance of Being Earnest and Other Plays*, ed. Peter Raby.

—— *Oscar Wilde: The Major Works*, ed. Isobel Murray.

—— *The Picture of Dorian Gray*, ed. Isobel Murray.

—— *The Soul of Man and Prison Writings*, ed. Isobel Murray.

A CHRONOLOGY OF OSCAR WILDE

1854   (16 October) Oscar Fingal O'Flahertie Wills Wilde is born in Dublin, the second son of a leading oculist and antiquarian Sir William Wilde and poet Jane Francesca Elgee (Speranza).

1864–71   Wilde is sent away to Portora Royal boarding school in Enniskillen.

1871–4   Reads Classics at Trinity College, Dublin under the guidance of Professor J. P. Mahaffy.

1874   Wins the Berkeley Gold Medal for Greek. He moves to England in October to study Greats at Magdalen College, Oxford.

1875   Visits Italy with Mahaffy. Wilde's first piece of published journalism, a poem 'Chorus of Cloud Maidens', appears in the *Dublin University Magazine*.

1876   Death of Sir William Wilde. Wilde takes a first class degree in Classical Moderations.

1877   Visits Greece with Mahaffy and returns via Rome. Reviews the first exhibition at the Grosvenor Gallery for the *Dublin University Magazine*.

1878   Wins the Newdigate Prize for his poem, 'Ravenna', and takes a first class degree in Literae Humaniores.

1879   Settles in London.

1880   Privately publishes his first play, *Vera; Or, the Nihilists*, and circulates it around potential producers and friends.

1881   *Poems* is published partly at Wilde's expense. Arrangement of his lecture tour of America through Richard D'Oyly Carte.

1882   Tours America and Canada with lectures on 'The English Renaissance of Art' and 'The House Beautiful'.

1883   Spends three months in Paris writing his new play, *The Duchess of Padua*. Begins a lecture tour of Britain. The first production of *Vera* in America fails.

1884   Marries Constance Lloyd and settles in Tite Street, Chelsea. Engages in correspondence with the *Pall Mall Gazette* on the subject of women's dress.

1885   Wilde's first review for the *Pall Mall Gazette* appears in February and he begins to write regularly for the paper. His first piece for *The Dramatic Review*, 'Shakespeare on Scenery', is published in March. Cyril Wilde is born on 5 June.

1886   Meets his friend and literary executor Robert Ross. In May Wilde's last piece is published in *The Dramatic Review*. Vyvyan Wilde is born on 3 November.

1887   Begins to publish in *The Court and Society Review* with 'Lord Arthur Savile's Crime' and then more general articles. Thomas Wemyss Reid approaches Wilde to edit *The Woman's World* in April. Wilde's first number as editor appears in November. His last piece for *The Court and Society Review* appears in December.

1888   *The Happy Prince and Other Tales* is published in May.

1889   In June Wilde's final contributions appear in *The Woman's World* and his name is removed from the cover in November 1889. 'The Portrait of Mr W. H.' is published in *Blackwood's Edinburgh Magazine*, 'Pen, Pencil and Poison' in *The Fortnightly Review*, and 'The Decay of Lying' in *The Nineteenth Century*.

1890   The first version of *The Picture of Dorian Gray* is published in *Lippincott's Monthly Magazine* and 'The True Function and Value of Criticism' in *The Nineteenth Century*. Wilde's final review for the *Pall Mall Gazette* is published.

1891   *The Duchess of Padua* is produced in New York under the new title *Guido Ferranti*. Wilde meets Lord Alfred Douglas. Publishes a revised book version of *The Picture of Dorian Gray*, a book version of his essays under the title *Intentions*, and two volumes of stories, *Lord Arthur Savile's Crime and Other Stories* and *A House of Pomegranates*. 'The Soul of Man Under Socialism' is published in *The Fortnightly Review*. Begins work on *Salomé*.

1892   George Alexander produces *Lady Windermere's Fan* at the St James' Theatre. *Salomé* is denied a licence.

1893   *Salomé* is published in French in Paris. Herbert Beerbohm Tree produces *A Woman of No Importance* at the Haymarket Theatre. *Lady Windermere's Fan* is published.

1894   *Salomé* is published in English translation with illustrations by Aubrey Beardsley. *The Sphinx* and *A Woman of No Importance* are published.

1895   *An Ideal Husband* is produced by Lewis Waller at the Haymarket Theatre. *The Importance of Being Earnest* begins in February, produced by George Alexander at the St James' Theatre. In April Wilde's prosecution of the Marquess of Queensberry for criminal libel begins. The case fails and Wilde is arrested for gross indecency. His first trial fails because the jury cannot reach an agreement but at the second trial Wilde is found guilty and sentenced to two years' hard labour. In November Wilde is declared bankrupt.

1896   Wilde's mother dies. The first production of *Salomé* is mounted in Paris.

1897   Composes the letter to Alfred Douglas now known as *De Profundis*. On his release on 19 May, he heads directly for exile on the Continent. Writes to *The Daily Chronicle* in May to protest about the prison conditions of children.

1898   Moves to Paris. *The Ballad of Reading Gaol* is published. Constance dies in April and Wilde is refused access to his children.

1899   *The Importance of Being Earnest* and *An Ideal Husband* published by Leonard Smithers.

1900   (30 November) Dies after a serious illness.

SELECTED JOURNALISM

PALL MALL GAZETTE

WOMAN'S DRESS[1]

MR OSCAR WILDE, who asks us to permit him 'that most charming of all pleasures, the pleasure of answering one's critics,' sends us the following remarks:—

The 'Girl Graduate'* must of course have precedence, not merely for her sex, but for her sanity: her letter is extremely sensible. She makes two points: that high heels are a necessity for any lady who wishes to keep her dress clean from the Stygian mud* of our streets, and that without a tight corset 'the ordinary number of petticoats and etceteras' cannot be properly or conveniently held up. Now it is quite true that as long as the lower garments are suspended from the hips, a corset is an absolute necessity; the mistake lies in not suspending all apparel from the shoulders. In the latter case a corset becomes useless, the body is left free and unconfined for respiration and motion, there is more health, and consequently more beauty. Indeed, all the most ungainly and uncomfortable articles of dress that fashion has ever in her folly prescribed, not the tight corset merely, but the farthingale, the vertugadin, the hoop, the crinoline, and that modern monstrosity the so-called 'dress improver'* also, all of them have owed their origin to the same error, the error of not seeing that it is from the shoulders, and from the shoulders only, that all garments should be hung.

And as regards high heels, I quite admit that some additional height to the shoe or boot is necessary if long gowns are to be worn in the street; but what I object to is that the height should be given to the heel only, and not to the sole of the foot also. The modern high-heeled boot is, in fact, merely the clog of the time of Henry VI,* with the front prop left out, and its inevitable effect is to throw the body forward, to shorten the steps, and consequently to produce that want of grace which always follows want of freedom. Why should clogs be despised? Much art has been expended on clogs. They have been

[1] 14 October 1884. A letter to the editor in response to criticism of his ideas about dress reform.

made of lovely woods, and delicately inlaid with ivory, and with mother of pearl. A clog might be a dream of beauty, and, if not too high or too heavy, most comfortable also. But if there be any who do not like clogs, let them try some adaptation of the trouser of the Turkish lady, which is loose round the limb, and tight at the ankle. The 'Girl Graduate,' with a pathos to which I am not insensible, entreats me not to apotheosise 'that awful, befringed, beflounced, and bekilted divided skirt.' Well, I will acknowledge that the fringes, the flounces, and the kilting do certainly defeat the whole object of the dress, which is that of ease and liberty; but I regard these things as mere wicked superfluities, tragic proofs that the divided skirt is ashamed of its own division. The principle of the dress is good, and, though it is not by any means perfection, it is a step towards it. Here I leave the 'Girl Graduate,' with much regret, for Mr Wentworth Huyshe.* Mr Huyshe makes the old criticism that Greek dress is unsuited to our climate, and the, to me, somewhat new assertion that the men's dress of a hundred years ago was preferable to that of the second part of the seventeenth century, which I consider to have been the exquisite period of English costume. Now, as regards the first of these two statements, I will say, to begin with, that the warmth of apparel does not really depend on the number of garments worn, but on the material of which they are made. One of the chief faults of modern dress is that it is composed of far too many articles of clothing, most of which are of the wrong substance; but over a substratum of pure wool, such as is supplied by Dr Jaeger* under the modern German system, some modification of Greek costume is perfectly applicable to our climate, our country, and our century. This important fact has been already pointed out by Mr E. W. Godwin in his excellent, though too brief, handbook on Dress, contributed to the Health Exhibition.* I call it an important fact because it makes almost any form of lovely costume perfectly practicable in our cold climate. Mr Godwin, it is true, points out that the English ladies of the thirteenth century abandoned after some time the flowing garments of the early Renaissance in favour of a tighter mode, such as northern Europe seems to demand. This I quite admit, and its significance; but what I contend, and what I am sure Mr Godwin would agree with me in, is that the principles, the laws of Greek dress, may be perfectly realized, even in a moderately tight gown with sleeves: I mean the principles of suspending all apparel from the shoulders, and of relying for beauty of effect, not on the stiff ready-made ornaments of the modern milliner—the bows where there should be no bows, and the flounces where there should be no flounces—but on the exquisite play of light and line that one gets from rich and rippling folds. I am not proposing any antiquarian revival of an ancient costume, but trying merely to point out the right laws of dress, laws which are dictated by art and not by archæology, by science and not by fashion; and just as the best work of art in our days is that which combines classic grace with absolute reality, so from a continuation of the Greek principles of beauty with the German principles of health will come, I feel certain, the costume of the future.

And now to the question of men's dress, or rather to Mr Huyshe's claim of the superiority, in point of costume, of the last quarter of the eighteenth century over the second quarter of the seventeenth. The broad-brimmed hat of 1640 kept the rain of winter and the glare of summer from the face; the same cannot be said of the hat of one hundred years ago, which, with its comparatively narrow brim and high crown, was the precursor of the modern 'chimney-pot:' a wide turned-down collar is a healthier thing than a strangling stock, and a short cloak much more comfortable than a sleeved overcoat, even though the latter may have had 'three capes;' a cloak is easier to put on and off, lies lightly on the shoulder in summer, and, wrapped round one in winter, keeps one perfectly warm. A doublet, again, is simpler than a coat and waist-coat; instead of two garments we have one; by not being open, also, it protects the chest better. Short loose trousers are in every way to be preferred to the tight knee-breeches which often impede the proper circulation of the blood; and, finally, the soft leather boots which could be worn above or below the knee, are more supple, and give consequently more freedom, than the stiff Hessian which Mr Huyshe so praises. I say nothing about the question of grace and picturesqueness, for I suppose that no one, not even Mr Huyshe, would prefer a macaroni to a cavalier, a Lawrence to a Vandyke, or the third George to the first Charles;* but for ease, warmth, and comfort this seventeenth century dress is infinitely superior to anything that came after it, and I do not think it is excelled by any preceding form of costume. I sincerely trust that we may soon see in England some national revival of it.

MR WHISTLER'S TEN O'CLOCK[1]

LAST night, at Prince's Hall, Mr Whistler* made his first public
appearance as a lecturer on art, and spoke for more than an hour with
really marvellous eloquence on the absolute uselessness of all lectures of the kind. Mr Whistler began his lecture with a very pretty
aria on prehistoric history, describing how in earlier times hunter
and warrior would go forth to chase and foray, while the artist sat at
home making cup and bowl for their service. Rude imitations of
nature they were first, like the gourd bottle, till the sense of beauty
and form developed, and, in all its exquisite proportions, the first
vase was fashioned. Then came a higher civilisation of architecture
and arm-chairs, and with exquisite design, and dainty diaper, the
useful things of life were made lovely; and the hunter and the warrior lay on the couch when they were tired, and, when they were
thirsty, drank from the bowl, and never cared to lose the exquisite
proportions of the one, or the delightful ornament of the other; and
this attitude of the primitive anthropophagous Philistine formed the
text of the lecture, and was the attitude which Mr Whistler entreated
his audience to adopt towards art. Remembering, no doubt, many
charming invitations to wonderful private views, this fashionable
assemblage seemed somewhat aghast, and not a little amused, at
being told that the slightest appearance among a civilised people of
any joy in beautiful things is a grave impertinence to all painters; but
Mr Whistler was relentless, and with charming ease, and much grace
of manner, explained to the public that the only thing they should
cultivate was ugliness, and that on their permanent stupidity rested
all the hopes of art in the future.

  The scene was in every way delightful; he stood there, a miniature
Mephistopheles, mocking the majority!* he was like a brilliant surgeon lecturing to a class composed of subjects destined ultimately for
dissection, and solemnly assuring them how valuable to science their
maladies were, and how absolutely uninteresting the slightest symp-
toms of health on their part would be. In fairness to the audience,
however, I must say that they seemed extremely gratified at being rid
of the dreadful responsibility of admiring anything, and nothing

[1] 21 February 1885. A review of James Abbott McNeill Whistler's lecture at Prince's
Hall, Piccadilly on 20 February 1885.

could have exceeded their enthusiasm when they were told by Mr Whistler that no matter how vulgar their dresses were, or how hideous their surroundings at home, still it was possible that a great painter, if there was such a thing, could, by contemplating them in the twilight, and half closing his eyes, see them under really picturesque conditions, and produce a picture which they were not to attempt to understand, much less dare to enjoy. Then there were some arrows, barbed and brilliant, shot off, with all the speed and splendour of fireworks, and the archæologists, who spend their lives in verifying the birthplaces of nobodies, and estimate the value of a work of art by its date or its decay, at the art critics who always treat a picture as if it were a novel, and try and find out the plot; at dilettanti in general, and amateurs in particular, and (*O mea culpa!*) at dress reformers most of all. 'Did not Velasquez* paint crinolines? What more do you want?'

Having thus made a holocaust of humanity, Mr Whistler turned to Nature, and in a few moments convicted her of the Crystal Palace,* Bank holidays, and a general overcrowding of detail, both in omnibuses and in landscapes; and then, in a passage of singular beauty, not unlike one that occurs in Carot's letters,* spoke of the artistic value of dim dawns and dusks, when the mean facts of life are lost in exquisite and evanescent effects, when common things are touched with mystery and transfigured with beauty; when the warehouses become as palaces, and the tall chimneys of the factory seem like campaniles in the silver air.

Finally, after making a strong protest against anybody but a painter judging of painting, and a pathetic appeal to the audience not to be lured by the æsthetic movement into having beautiful things about them, Mr Whistler concluded his lecture with a pretty passage about Fusiyama* on a fan, and made his bow to an audience which he had succeeded in completely fascinating by his wit, his brilliant paradoxes, and, at times, his real eloquence. Of course, with regard to the value of beautiful surroundings I differ entirely from Mr Whistler. An artist is not an isolated fact, he is the resultant of a certain milieu and a certain entourage, and can no more be born of a nation that is devoid of any sense of beauty than a fig can grow from a thorn or a rose blossom from a thistle. That an artist will find beauty in ugliness, *le beau dans l'horrible*, is now a commonplace of the schools, the argot of the atelier, but I strongly deny that charming people should be condemned to live with magenta ottomans and

Albert blue curtains in their rooms in order that some painter may observe the side lights on the one and the values of the other. Nor do I accept the dictum that only a painter is a judge of painting, I say that only an artist is a judge of art; there is a wide difference. As long as a painter is a painter merely, he should not be allowed to talk of anything but mediums and megilp, and on those subjects should be compelled to hold his tongue; it is only when he becomes an artist that the secret laws of artistic creation are revealed to him. For there are not many arts, but one art merely: poem, picture and Parthenon,* sonnet and statue—all are in their essence the same, and he who knows one, knows all. But the poet is the supreme artist, for he is the master of colour and of form, and the real musician besides, and is lord over all life and all arts; and so to the poet beyond all others are these mysteries known; to Edgar Allan Poe and to Baudelaire, not to Benjamin West and Paul Delaroche.* However, I would not enjoy anybody else's lectures unless in a few points I disagreed with them, and Mr Whistler's lecture last night was, like everything that he does, a masterpiece. Not merely for its clever satire and amusing jests will it be remembered, but for the pure and perfect beauty of many of its passages—passages delivered with an earnestness which seemed to amaze those who had looked on Mr Whistler as a master of persiflage merely, and had not known him as we do, as a master of painting also. For that he is indeed one of the very greatest masters of painting, is my opinion. And I may add that in this opinion Mr Whistler himself entirely concurs.

DINNERS AND DISHES[1]

A MAN can live for three days without bread, but no man can live for one day without poetry, was an aphorism of Baudelaire's:* you can live without pictures and music, but you can't live without eating, says the author of 'Dinners and Dishes:' and this latter view is no doubt the more popular. Who indeed, in these degenerate days, would hesitate between an ode and an omelette, a sonnet and a salmi?* Yet the position is not entirely Philistine; cookery is an art; are not its principles the subject of South Kensington lectures, and does not

---

[1] 7 March 1885. Wanderer, *Dinners and Dishes* (London, 1885).

the Royal Academy give a banquet once a year. Besides, as the coming democracy will no doubt insist on feeding us all on penny dinners, it is well that the laws of cookery should be explained: for were the national meal burned, or badly seasoned, or served up with the wrong sauce, a dreadful revolution might follow.

Under these circumstances we strongly recommend 'Dinners and Dishes' to every one: it is brief, and concise, and makes no attempts at eloquence, which is extremely fortunate. For even on ortolans* who could endure oratory? It also has the advantage of not being illustrated. The subject of a work of art has of course nothing to do with its beauty, but still there is always something depressing about the coloured lithograph of a leg of mutton.

As regards the author's particular views, we entirely agree with him on the important question of macaroni. 'Never,' he says, 'ask me to back a bill for a man who has given me a macaroni pudding.' Macaroni is essentially a savoury dish, and may be served with cheese, or tomatoes, but never with sugar and milk. There are also useful descriptions of how to cook risotto, a delightful dish too rarely seen in England, an excellent chapter on the different kinds of salads, which should be carefully studied by those many hostesses whose imaginations never pass beyond lettuce and beetroot, and actually a recipe for making Brussels sprouts eatable. The last is of course a masterpiece.

The real difficulty, however, that we all have to face in life, is not so much the science of cookery, as the stupidity of cooks. And in this little handbook to practical Epicureanism, the tyrant of the English kitchen is shown in her proper light. Her entire ignorance of herbs, her passion for extracts and essences, her total inability to make a soup which is anything more than a combination of pepper and gravy, her inveterate habit of sending up bread poultices with pheasants,—all these sins, and many others, are ruthlessly unmasked by the author. Ruthlessly and rightly. For the British cook is a foolish woman, who should be turned, for her iniquities, into a pillar of that salt* which she never knows how to use.

But our author is not local merely. He has been in many lands; he has eaten back-hendl at Vienna, and kulibatsch at St Petersburg; he has had the courage to face the buffalo veal of Roumania, and to dine with a German family at one o'clock; he has serious views on the right method of cooking those famous white truffles of Turin, of which Alexandre Dumas* was so fond, and, in the face of the Oriental Club, declares that Bombay curry is better than the curry of Bengal. In fact he seems to have had experience of almost every kind of meal, except the 'square meal' of the Americans. This he should study at once; there is a great field for the philosophic epicure in the United States. Boston beans may be dismissed at once as delusions, but soft-shell crabs, terrapin, canvas-back ducks, blue fish, and the pompono of New Orleans, are all wonderful delicacies, particularly when one gets them at Delmonico's.* Indeed, the two most remarkable bits of scenery in the States are undoubtedly Delmonico's and the Yosemité Valley,* and the former place has done more to promote a good feeling between England and America than anything else has in this century.

We hope that 'Wanderer' will go there soon, and add a chapter to 'Dinners and Dishes,' and that his book will have in England the influence it deserves. There are twenty ways of cooking a potato, and three hundred and sixty-five ways of cooking an egg, yet the British cook up to the present moment knows only three methods of sending up either one or the other.

A HANDBOOK TO MARRIAGE[1]*

IN spite of its somewhat alarming title, this book may be highly recommended to every one. As for the authorities he quotes, they are almost numberless, and range from Socrates down to Artemus Ward.* He tells us of the wicked bachelor who spoke of marriage as 'a very harmless amusement,' and advised a young friend of his to 'marry early and marry often;' of Dr Johnson, who proposed that marriage should be arranged by the Lord Chancellor* without the parties concerned having any choice in the matter; of the Sussex labourer who asked, 'Why should I give a woman half my victuals* for cooking the other half?' and of Lord Verulam,* who thought that unmarried men did the best public work. And, indeed, marriage is the one subject on which all women agree and all men disagree. Our author, however, is clearly of the same opinion as the Scotch lassie, who, on her father warning her what a solemn thing it was to get married, answered, 'I

[1] 18 November 1885. Revd Edward J. Hardy, *How to be Happy Though Married: Being a Handbook to Marriage* (London, 1885).

ken that, father, but it's a great deal solemner to be single.' He may be regarded as the champion of the married life. Indeed, he has a most interesting chapter on marriage-made men, and though he dissents, and we think rightly, from the view recently put forward by a lady or two on the women's rights platform, that Solomon owed all his wisdom to the number of his wives,* still he appeals to Bismarck, John Stuart Mill, Mahommed,* and Lord Beaconsfield* as instances of men whose success can be traced to the influence of the women they married. Archbishop Whately* once defined woman as 'a creature that doesn't reason and pokes the fire from the top,' but since his day the higher education of women has considerably altered their position. Women have always had an emotional sympathy with those they love; Girton and Nuneham* have rendered intellectual sympathy also possible. In our day it is best for a man to be married, and men must give up the tyranny in married life which was once so dear to them, and which, we are afraid, lingers still here and there. 'Do you wish to be my wife, Mabel?' said a little boy. 'Yes,' incautiously answered Mabel. 'Then pull off my boots.'

On marriage vows our author has two very sensible views, and very amusing stories. He tells of a nervous bridegroom who, confusing the baptismal and marriage ceremonies, replied, when asked if he consented to take the bride for his wife: 'I renounce them all': of a Hampshire rustic, who, when giving the ring, said solemnly to the bride, 'With my body I thee wash up, and with all my hurdle goods I thee and thou': of another who, when asked whether he would take his partner to be his wedded wife, replied with shameful indecision, 'Yes, I'm willin'; but I'd a sight rather have her sister': and of a Scotch lady who, on the occasion of her daughter's wedding, was asked by an old friend whether she might congratulate her on the event, and answered, 'Yes, yes, upon the whole it is very satisfactory: it is true Jeannie hates her goodman; but then there's always a something!' Indeed the good stories contained in this book are quite endless, and make it very pleasant reading, while the good advice is on all points admirable. Most young married people nowadays start in life with a dreadful collection of ormolu inkstands covered with sham onyxes,* or with a perfect museum of salt-cellars. We strongly recommend this book as one of the best of wedding presents. It is a complete handbook to an earthly Paradise, and its author may be regarded as the Murray of matrimony and the Baedeker of bliss.*

TO READ, OR NOT TO READ[1]*

BOOKS, I fancy, may be conveniently divided into three classes:—

1 Books to read, such as Cicero's Letters, Suetonius, Vasari's Lives of the Painters, the Autobiography of Benvenuto Cellini, Sir John Mandeville, Marco Polo, St Simon's Memoirs, Mommsen, and (till we get a better one,) Grote's History of Greece.*

2 Books to re-read, such as Plato and Keats.* In the sphere of poetry, the masters not the minstrels, in the sphere of philosophy, the seers not the *savants*.

3 Books not to read at all, such as Thomson's Seasons, Rogers' Italy, Paley's Evidences, all the Fathers except St Augustine, all John Stuart Mill, except the essay on Liberty, all Voltaire's plays without any exception, Butler's Analogy, Grant's Aristotle, Hume's England, Lewes' History of Philosophy,* all argumentative books, and all books that try to prove anything.

The third class is by far the most important. To tell people what to read is as a rule, either useless or harmful, for the true appreciation of literature is a question of temperament not of teaching, to Parnassus there is no primer, and nothing that one can learn is ever worth learning.* But to tell people what not to read is a very different matter, and I venture to recommend it as a mission to the University Extension Scheme.* Indeed, it is one that is eminently needed in this age of ours, an age which reads so much that it has no time to admire, and writes so much that it has no time to think. Whoever will select out of the chaos of our modern curricula 'The Worst Hundred Books,' and publish a list of them, will confer on the rising generation a real and lasting benefit.

After expressing these views I suppose I should not offer any suggestions at all with regard to 'The Best Hundred Books,' but I hope that you will allow me the pleasure of being inconsistent, as I am anxious to put in a claim for a book that has been strangely omitted by most of the excellent judges who have contributed to your columns. I mean the Greek Anthology.* The beautiful poems contained in this collection seem to me to hold the same position

---

[1] 8 February 1886. Wilde's letter to the editor appeared with reference to a series that the *Pall Mall Gazette* was running on 'The Best Hundred Books by The Best Hundred Judges'.

with regard to Greek Dramatic Literature, as do the delicate little figurines of Tanagra to the Pheidian marbles,* and to be quite as necessary for the complete understanding of the Greek Spirit.

I am also amazed to find that Edgar Allan Poe has been passed over. Surely this marvellous lord of rhythmic expression deserves a place? If in order to make room for him, it be necessary to elbow out some one else, I should elbow out Southey, and I think that Baudelaire might be most advantageously substituted for Keble.* No doubt, both in The Curse of Kehama and in the Christian Year* there are poetical qualities of a certain kind, but absolute catholicity of taste is not without its dangers. It is only an auctioneer who should admire all schools of art.

BALZAC IN ENGLISH[1]

MANY years ago, in a number of *All the Year Round*, Charles Dickens complained that Balzac* was very little read in England, and although since then the public have become more familiar with the great masterpieces of French fiction, still it may be doubted whether the 'Comédie Humaine'* is at all appreciated or understood by the general run of novel-readers. It is really the greatest monument that literature has produced in our century, and M Taine* hardly exaggerates when he says that, after Shakespeare, Balzac is our most important magazine of documents on human nature. Balzac's aim, in fact, was to do for humanity what Buffon* had done for the animal creation. As the naturalist studied lions and tigers, so the novelist studied men and women. Yet he was no mere reporter. Photography and procès-verbal were not the essentials of his method. Observation gave him the facts of life, but his genius converted facts into truths, and truths into truth. He was, in a word, a marvellous combination of the artistic temperament with the scientific spirit. The latter he bequeathed to his disciples; the former was entirely his own. The distinction between such a book as M Zola's 'L'Assommoir' and such a book as Balzac's 'Illusions Perdues' is the distinction between unimaginative realism and imaginative reality.* 'All Balzac's characters,' said Baudelaire, 'are gifted with the same ardour of life that

---

[1] 13 September 1886. Honoré de Balzac, *Balzac's Novels in English* (London, 1886).

animated himself. All his fictions are as deeply coloured as dreams. Every mind is a weapon loaded to the muzzle with will. The very scullions have genius.'* He was of course accused of being immoral. Few writers who deal directly with life escape that charge. His answer to the accusation was characteristic and conclusive. 'Whoever contributes his stone to the edifice of ideas,' he wrote, 'whoever proclaims an abuse, whoever sets his mark upon an evil to be abolished, always passes for immoral. If you are true in your portraits, if, by dint of daily and nightly toil, you succeed in writing the most difficult language in the world, the word immoral is thrown in your face.' The morals of the personages of the 'Comédie Humaine' are simply the morals of the world around us. They are part of the artist's subject-matter, they are not part of his method. If there be any need of censure it is to life not to literature that it should be given. Balzac, besides, is essentially universal. He sees life from every point of view. He has no preferences and no prejudices. He does not try to prove anything. He feels that the spectacle of life contains its own secret. 'Il crée un monde et se tait.'

And what a world it is! What a panorama of passions! What a pell-mell of men and women! It was said of Trollope* that he increased the number of our acquaintances without adding to our visiting lists; but after reading the 'Comédie Humaine' one begins to believe that the only real people are the people who have never existed. Lucien de Rubempré, le Père Goriot, Ursule Mirouët, Marguerite Claës, the Baron Hulot, Mdme Marneffe, le Cousin Pons, De Marsay*—all bring with them a kind of contagious illusion of life. They have a fierce vitality about them: their existence is fervent and fiery-coloured: we not merely feel for them, but we see them—they dominate our fancy and defy scepticism. A steady course of Balzac reduces our living friends to shadows, and our acquaintances to the shadows of shades. Who would care to go out to an evening party to meet Tomkins, the friend of one's boyhood, when one can sit at home with Lucien de Rubempré? It is pleasanter to have the entrée to Balzac's society than to receive cards from all the duchesses in Mayfair.

In spite of this there are many people who have declared the 'Comédie Humaine' to be indigestible. Perhaps it is, but then what about truffles? Balzac's publisher refused to be disturbed by any such criticism as that. 'Indigestible, is it?' he exclaimed with what, for a publisher, was rare good sense. 'Well, I should hope so; who ever

thinks of a dinner that isn't?' And our English publisher Mr
Routledge, clearly agrees with M Poulet-Malassis,* as he is occupied
in producing a complete translation of the 'Comédie Humaine.' The
two volumes that at present lie before us contain 'César Birotteau,'
that terrible tragedy of finance, and 'L'Illustre Gaudissart,' the
apotheosis of the commercial traveller, the 'Duchesse de Langeais,'
most marvellous of modern love stories, 'Le Chef d'Œuvre
Inconnu,' from which Mr Henry James took his 'Madonna of the
Future,'* and that extraordinary romance 'Une Passion dans le
Désert.' The choice of stories is quite excellent, but the translations
are very unequal,* and some of them are positively bad. 'L'Illustre
Gaudissart,' for instance, is full of the most grotesque mistakes,
mistakes that would disgrace a schoolboy. 'Bon conseil vaut un œil
dans la main,' is translated, 'Good advice is an egg in the hand!'
'Ecus rebelles' is rendered 'rebellious lucre,' and such common
expressions as 'faire la barbe,' 'attendre la vente,' 'n'entendre rien,'
'pâlir sur une affaire,' are all mistranslated. 'Des bois de quoi se faire
un cure-dent' is not 'a few trees to slice into toothpicks,' but 'as
much timber as would make a toothpick;' 'son horloge enfermée
dans une grande armoire oblongue,' is not 'a clock which he kept
shut up in a large oblong closet,' but simply a clock in a tall clock-
case; 'journal viager' is not 'an annuity,' 'garce' is not the same as
'farce,' and 'dessins des Indes' are not 'drawings of the Indies.' On
the whole, nothing can be worse than this translation, and if Mr
Routledge wishes the public to read his version of the 'Comédie
Humaine' he should engage translators who have some slight knowledge of French. 'César Birotteau' is better, though it is not by any
means free from mistakes. 'To suffer under the maximum' is an
absurd rendering of 'subir le maximum;' 'perse' is 'chintz,' not 'Persian chintz;' 'rendre le pain bénit' is not 'to take the wafer;' 'rivière'
is hardly a *fillet* of diamonds;' and to translate 'son cœur avait un
calus à l'endroit du loyer,' by 'His heart was a callus in the direction
of a lease,' is an insult to two languages. On the whole the best
version is that of the 'Duchesse de Langeais,' though even this leaves
much to be desired. Such a sentence as 'to imitate the rough logician
who marched before the Pyrrhonians *while denying his own movement*' entirely misses the point of Balzac's 'imiter le rude logicien qui
marchait devant les pyrrhoniens, qui niaient le mouvement.' We fear
Mr Routledge's edition will not do. It is well printed, and nicely

bound;* but his translators do not understand French. It is a great
pity, for 'La Comédie Humaine' is one of the masterpieces of the
age.

THE POET'S CORNER[1]

AMONG the social problems of the nineteenth century the tramp
has always held an important position, but his appearance among
the nineteenth-century poets is extremely remarkable. Not that the
tramp's mode of life is at all unsuited to the development of the
poetic faculty. Far from it! He if any one should possess that freedom of mood which is so essential to the artist, for he has no taxes to
pay, and no relations to worry him. The man who possesses a permanent address, and whose name is to be found in the Directory,
is necessarily limited and localized. Only the tramp has absolute
liberty of living. Was not Homer himself a vagrant, and did not
Thespis* go about in a caravan? It is then with feelings of intense
expectation that we open the little volume that lies before us. It is
entitled 'Low Down by Two Tramps,' and is marvellous even to
look at. It is clear that art has at last reached the criminal classes.
The cover is of brown paper, like the covers of Mr Whistler's bro-
chures. The printing exhibits every fantastic variation of type, and
the pages range in colour from blue to brown, from grey to sage
green, and from rose pink to chrome yellow. The Philistine may
sneer at this chromatic chaos, but we do not. As the painters are
always pilfering from the poets, why should not the poet annex the
domain of the painter, and use colour for the expression of his
moods and music, blue for sentiment, and red for passion, grey for
cultured melancholy, and green for descriptions? The book then is a
kind of miniature rainbow, and with all its varied sheets is as lovely
as an advertisement hoarding. As for the peripatetics—alas! they are
not nightingales. Their note is harsh and rugged, Mr G. R. Sims* is
the god of their idolatry, their style is the style of the Surrey
Theatre,* and we are sorry to see that that disregard of the rights
of property which always characterises the able-bodied vagrant
is extended by our tramps from the defensible pilfering from

---

[1] 27 September 1886. Two Tramps, *Low Down: Wayside Thoughts in Ballad and Other
Verse* (London, 1886); H. C. Irwin, *Rhymes and Renderings* (London, 1886).

hen roosts to the indefensible pilfering from poets. When we read such lines as—

> And builded him a pyramid, four square,
> Open to all the sky and every wind,

we feel that bad as poultry-snatching is, plagiarism is worse. 'Facilis descensus Averno!'* From highway robbery and crimes of violence one sinks gradually to literary petty larceny. However, there are coarsely effective poems in the volume, such as 'A Super's Philosophy,' 'Dick Hewlett,' a ballad of the Californian school, and 'Gentleman Bill,' and there is one rather pretty poem called 'The Return of Spring':—

> When robins hop on naked boughs,
>   And swell their throats with song,
> When lab'rours trudge behind their ploughs
>   And blithely whistle their teams along.
>
> When glints of summer sunshine chase
>   Park shadows on the distant hills
> And scented tufts of pansies grace
>   Moist grots that 'scape rude Borean chills.

The last line is very disappointing. No poet nowadays should write of 'rude Boreas,' he might just as well call the dawn 'Aurora,' or say that 'Flora decks the enamelled meads.' But there are some nice touches in the poem, and it is pleasant to find that tramps have their harmless moments. On the whole, the volume, if it is not quite worth reading, is at least worth looking at. The fool's motley in which it is arrayed is extremely curious, and extremely characteristic.

Mr Irwin's muse comes to us more simply clad, and more gracefully. She gains her colour-effect from the poet not from the publisher. No cockneyism or colloquialism mars the sweetness of her speech. She finds music for every mood, and form for every feeling. In art as in life the law of heredity holds good. *On est toujours fils de quelqu'un.** And so it is easy to see that Mr Irwin is a fervent admirer of Mr Matthew Arnold.* But he is in no sense of the word a plagiarist. He has succeeded in studying a fine poet without stealing from him, a very difficult thing to do, and though many of the reeds through which he blows have been touched by other lips, yet he is able to draw new music from them. Like most of our younger poets, Mr Irwin is at his best in his sonnets, and those entitled 'The Seeker the text.

after God' and 'The Pillar of the Empire' are really remarkable. All through this volume, however, one comes across good work, and the descriptions of Indian scenery are excellent. India in fact is the picturesque background to these poems, and her monstrous beasts, strange flowers and fantastic birds are used with much subtlety for the production of artistic effect. Perhaps there is a little too much about the pipal-tree, but when we have a proper sense of Imperial unity no doubt the pipal-tree will be as dear and as familiar to us as the oaks and elms of our own woodlands.

A NEW BOOK ON DICKENS[1]

MR MARZIALS'* 'Dickens' is a great improvement on the 'Longfellow' and 'Coleridge' of his predecessors. It is certainly a little sad to find our old friend the manager of the Theatre Royal, Portsmouth, appearing as 'Mr Vincent Crumules' (sic), but such misprints are not by any means uncommon in Mr Walter Scott's publications,* and on the whole this is a very pleasant book indeed. It is brightly and cleverly written, admirably constructed, and gives a most vivid and graphic picture of that strange modern drama, the drama of Dickens' life. The earlier chapters are quite excellent, and, though the story of the famous novelist's boyhood has been often told before, Mr Marzials shows that it can be told once again without losing any of the charm of its interest, while the account of Dickens in the plenitude of his glory is most appreciative and genial. We are really brought close to the man with his indomitable energy, his extraordinary capacity for work, his high spirits, his fascinating, tyrannous personality. The description of his method of reading is admirable, and the amazing stump-campaign in America* attains, in Mr Marzials' hands, to the dignity of a mock-heroic poem. One side of Dickens' character, however, is left almost entirely untouched, and yet it is one in every way deserving of close study. That Dickens should have felt bitterly towards his father and mother is quite explicable, but that, while feeling so bitterly, he should have caricatured them for the amusement of the public, with an evident delight in his own humour, has always seemed to us a most curious

[1] 31 March 1887. Frank T. Marzials, *Dickens* (London, 1887).

psychological problem. We are far from complaining that he did so. Good novelists are much rarer than good sons, and none of us would part readily with Micawber and Mrs Nickleby.* Still the fact remains that a man who was affectionate and loving to his children, generous and warm-hearted to his friends, and whose books are the very bacchanalia of benevolence, pilloried his parents to make the groundlings laugh, and this fact every biographer of Dickens should face, and if possible explain.

As for Mr Marzials' critical estimate of Dickens as a writer, he tells us quite frankly that he believes that Dickens at his best was 'one of the greatest masters of pathos who ever lived,' a remark that seems to us an excellent example of what novelists call 'the fine courage of despair.' Of course no biographer of Dickens could say anything else just at present. A popular series is bound to express popular views, and cheap criticisms may be excused in cheap books. Besides, it is always open to every one to accept G. H. Lewes' unfortunate maxim that any author who makes one cry possesses the gift of pathos, and, indeed there is something very flattering in being told that one's own emotions are the ultimate test of literature. When Mr Marzials discusses Dickens' power of drawing human nature we are upon somewhat safer ground, and we cannot but admire the cleverness with which he passes over his hero's innumerable failures. For in some respects Dickens might be likened to those old sculptors of our Gothic cathedrals who could give form to the most fantastic fancy, and crowd with grotesque monsters a curious world of dreams, but saw little of the grace and dignity of the men and women among whom they lived, and whose art lacking sanity was therefore incomplete. Yet they at least knew the limitations of their art, while Dickens never knew the limitations of his. When he tries to be serious, he succeeds only in being dull, when he aims at truth, he merely reaches platitude. Shakespeare could place Ferdinand and Miranda by the side of Caliban,* and Life recognizes them all as her own, but Dickens' Mirandas are the young ladies out of a fashion-book, and his Ferdinands the walking-gentlemen of an unsuccessful company of third-rate players. So little sanity indeed had Dickens' art, that he was never able even to satirise, he could only caricature; and so little does Mr Marzials realize where Dickens' true strength and weakness lie, that he actually complains that Cruikshank's illustrations* are too much exaggerated and that he

could never draw either a lady or a gentleman. The latter was hardly
a disqualification for illustrating Dickens as few such characters
occur in his books, unless we are to regard Lord Frederick Verisopht
and Sir Mulberry Hawk* as valuable studies of high life, and for our
own part we have always considered that the greatest injustice ever
done to Dickens has been done by those who have tried to illustrate
him seriously. In conclusion Mr Marzials expresses his belief that a
century hence Dickens will be read as much as we now read Scott,
and says rather prettily that as long as he is read 'there will be one
gentle and humanizing influence the more at work among men,'
which is always a useful tag to append to the life of any popular
author. Remembering that of all forms of error prophecy is the most
gratuitous, we will not take upon ourselves to decide the question of
Dickens' immortality. If our descendants do not read him they will
miss a great source of amusement, and if they do, we hope they will
not model their style upon his. Of this however there is but little
danger, for no age ever borrows the slang of its predecessor. As for
'the gentle and humanizing influence,' this is taking Dickens just a
little too seriously.

MR PATER'S *IMAGINARY PORTRAITS*[1]

To convey ideas through the medium of images has always been the
aim of those who are artists as well as thinkers in literature, and it is
to a desire to give a sensuous environment to intellectual concepts
that we owe Mr Pater's* last volume. For these Imaginary or, as we
should prefer to call them, Imaginative Portraits of his, form a series
of philosophic studies, in which the philosophy is tempered by personality, and the thought shown under varying conditions of mood
and manner, the very permanence of each principle gaining something through the change and colour of the life through which it
finds expression. The most fascinating of all these pictures is
undoubtedly that of Sebastian Van Storck.* The account of Watteau*
is perhaps a little too fanciful, and the description of him as one who
was 'always a seeker after something in the world that is there in no
satisfying measure, or not at all,' seems to us more applicable to him

---

[1] 11 June 1887. Walter Pater, *Imaginary Portraits* (London, 1887).

who saw Monna Lisa sitting among the rocks* than to the gay and debonair *peintre des fêtes galantes*.* But Sebastian, the grave young Dutch philosopher, is charmingly drawn. From the first glimpse we get of him, skating over the watermeadows with his plume of squirrel's tail and his fur muff, in all the modest pleasantness of boyhood, down to his strange death in the desolate house amid the sands of the Helder,* we seem to see him, to know him, almost to hear the low music of his voice. He is a dreamer, as the common phrase goes, and yet he is practical in this sense, that his theorems shape life for him, directly. Early in youth he is stirred by a fine saying of Spinoza,* and sets himself to realize the ideal of an intellectual disinterestedness, separating himself more and more from the transient world of sensation, accident, and even affection, till what is finite and relative becomes of no interest to him, and he feels that as Nature is but a thought of his, so he himself is but a passing thought of God. This conception, of the power of a mere metaphysical abstraction over the mind of one so fortunately endowed for the reception of the sensible world, is exceedingly delightful, and Mr Pater has never written a more subtle psychological study, the fact that Sebastian dies in an attempt to save the life of a little child giving to the whole story a touch of poignant pathos and sad irony.

'Denys l'Auxerrois' is suggested by a figure found, or said to be found, on some old tapestries in Auxerre, the figure of a 'flaxen and flowery creature, sometimes well-nigh naked among the vine-leaves, sometimes muffled in skins against the cold, sometimes in the dress of a monk,' but always with a strong impress of real character and incident from the veritable streets of the town itself. From this strange design Mr Pater has fashioned a curious mediæval myth of the return of Dionysus* among men, a myth steeped in colour and passion and old romance, full of wonder and full of worship, Denys himself being half animal and half god, making the world mad with a new ecstasy of living, stirring the artists simply by his visible presence, drawing the marvel of music from reed and pipe, and slain at last in a stage play by those who had loved him. In its rich affluence of imagery this story is like a picture by Mantegna,* and indeed Mantegna might have suggested the description of the pageant in which Denys rides upon a gaily-painted chariot, in soft silken raiment and, for headdress, a strange elephant scalp with gilded tusks.

If 'Denys l'Auxerrois' symbolizes the passion of the senses, and

'Sebastian Van Storck' the philosophic passion, as they certainly seem to do, though no mere formula or definition can adequately express the freedom and variety of the life that they portray, the passion for the imaginative world of art is the basis of the story of 'Duke Carl of Rosenmold'. Duke Carl is not unlike the late King of Bavaria,* in his love of France, his admiration for the *Grand Monarque* and his fantastic desire to amaze and to bewilder, but the resemblance is possibly only a chance one. In fact Mr Pater's young hero is the precursor of the *Aufklärung** of the last century, the German precursor of Herder, and Lessing, and Goethe* himself, and finds the forms of art ready to his hand without any national spirit to fill them, or make them vital and responsive. He too dies, trampled to death by the soldiers of the country he so much admired, on the night of his marriage with a peasant girl, the very failure of his life lending him a certain melancholy grace and dramatic interest.

On the whole, then, this is a singularly attractive book. Mr Pater is an intellectual impressionist. He does not weary us with any definite doctrine, or seek to suit life to any formal creed. He is always looking for exquisite moments, and, when he has found them, he analyzes them with delicate and delightful art, and then passes on, often to the opposite pole of thought or feeling, knowing that every mood has its own quality and charm, and is justified by its mere existence. He has taken the sensationalism of Greek philosophy and made it a new method of art criticism. As for his style, it is curiously ascetic. Now and then we come across phrases with a strange sensuousness of expression, as when he tells us how Denys l'Auxerrois, on his return from a long journey, 'ate flesh for the first time, tearing the hot, red morsels with his delicate fingers in a kind of wild greed,' but such passages are rare. Asceticism is the keynote of Mr Pater's prose; at times it is almost too severe in its self-control and makes us long for a little more freedom. For indeed, the danger of such prose as his is that it is apt to become somewhat laborious. Here and there one is tempted to say of Mr Pater that he is 'a seeker after something in language that is there in no satisfying measure, or not at all.' The continual preoccupation with phrase and epithet has its drawbacks as well as its virtues. And yet, when all is said, what wonderful prose it is, with its subtle preferences, its fastidious purity, its rejection of what is common or ordinary! Mr Pater has the true spirit of selection, the true tact of omission. If he be not among the greatest prose-writers of our literature he is at least our greatest artist in prose; and though it may be admitted that the best style is that which seems an unconscious result rather than a conscious aim, still in these latter days, when violent rhetoric does duty for eloquence, and vulgarity usurps the name of nature, we should be grateful for a style that deliberately aims at perfection of form, that seeks to produce its effect by artistic means, and that sets before itself an ideal of grave and chastened beauty.

MR MAHAFFY'S NEW BOOK[1]

MR MAHAFFY'S* new book will be a great disappointment to everybody except the Paper-Unionists and the members of the Primrose League.* His subject, the history of Greek life and thought from the age of Alexander* to the Roman conquest, is extremely interesting, but the manner in which the subject is treated is quite unworthy of a scholar, nor can there be anything more depressing than Mr Mahaffy's continual efforts to degrade history to the level of the ordinary political pamphlet of contemporary party warfare. There is, of course, no reason why Mr Mahaffy should be called upon to express any sympathy with the aspirations of the old Greek cities for freedom and autonomy. The personal preferences of modern historians on these points are matters of no import whatsoever. But in his attempts to treat the Hellenic world as 'Tipperary writ large', to use Alexander the Great as a means of whitewashing Mr Smith, and to finish the battle of Chaeronea on the plains of Mitchelstown,* Mr Mahaffy shows an amount of political bias and literary blindness that is quite extraordinary. He might have made his book a work of solid and enduring interest, but he has chosen to give it a merely ephemeral value, and to substitute for the scientific temper of the true historian the prejudice, the flippancy, and the violence of the platform partisan. For the flippancy parallels can no doubt be found in some of Mr Mahaffy's earlier books, but the prejudice and the violence are new, and their appearance is very much to be regretted. There is always something peculiarly impotent about the violence of a literary man. It seems to bear no reference to facts, for it is never kept in check by

[1] 9 November 1887. J. P. Mahaffy, *Greek Life and Thought: From the Age of Alexander to the Roman Conquest* (London, 1887).

action. It is simply a question of adjectives and rhetoric, of exaggeration and overemphasis. Mr Balfour is very anxious that Mr William O'Brien should wear prison clothes, sleep on a plank bed, and be subjected to other indignities, but Mr Mahaffy goes far beyond such mild measures as these, and begins his history by frankly expressing his regret that Demosthenes* was not summarily put to death for his attempts to keep the spirit of patriotism alive among the citizens of Athens! Indeed, he has no patience with what he calls 'the foolish and senseless opposition to Macedonia;' regards the revolt of the Spartans against 'Alexander's Lord Lieutenant for Greece' as an example of 'parochial politics;' indulges in Primrose League platitudes against a low franchise and the iniquity of allowing 'every pauper' to have a vote; and tells us that the 'demagogues' and 'pretended patriots' were so lost to shame that they actually preached to the parasitic mob of Athens the doctrine of Autonomy—'not now extinct,' Mr Mahaffy adds regretfully—and propounded, as a principle of political economy, the curious idea that people should be allowed to manage their own affairs! As for the personal character of the despots, Mr Mahaffy admits that if he had to judge by the accounts in the Greek historians, from Herodotus downwards, he 'would certainly have said that the ineffaceable passion for autonomy, which marks every epoch of Greek history, and every canton within its limits, must have arisen from the excesses committed by the officers of foreign potentates, or local tyrants,' but a careful study of the cartoons published in *United Ireland** has convinced him 'that a ruler may be the soberest, the most conscientious, the most considerate, and yet have terrible things said of him by mere political malcontents.' In fact, since Mr Balfour has been caricatured Greek history must be entirely rewritten! This is the pass to which the distinguished professor of a distinguished university has been brought. Nor can anything equal Mr Mahaffy's prejudice against the Greek patriots, unless it be his contempt for those few fine Romans who, sympathising with Hellenic civilization and culture, recognized the political value of autonomy and the intellectual importance of a healthy national life. He mocks at what he calls their 'vulgar mawkishness about Greek liberties,' their 'anxiety to redress historical wrongs', and congratulates his readers that this feeling was not intensified by the remorse that their own forefathers had been the oppressors. 'Luckily,' says Mr Mahaffy, 'the old Greeks had conquered Troy, and so the pangs of conscience which now so deeply affect a Gladstone and a Morley for the sins of their ancestors could hardly affect a Marcius or a Quinctius!'* It is quite unnecessary to comment on the silliness and bad taste of passage of this kind, but it is interesting to note that the facts of history are too strong even for Mr Mahaffy. In spite of his sneers at the provinciality of national feeling, and his vague panegyrics on cosmopolitan culture, he is compelled to admit (p. 403) that, 'however patriotism may be superseded in stray individuals by larger benevolence, bodies of men who abandon it will only replace it by meaner motives,' and cannot help expressing his regret that the better classes among the Greek communities were so entirely devoid of public spirit that they squandered 'as idle absentees, or still older residents, the time and means given them to benefit their country,' and failed to recognise their opportunity of founding a Hellenic Federal Empire. Even when he comes to deal with art, he cannot help admitting that the noblest sculpture of the time was that which expressed the spirit of the first great *national* struggle, the repulse of the Gallic hordes which overran Greece in 278 B.C., and that to the patriotic feeling evoked at this crisis we owe the Belvedere Apollo, the Artemis of the Vatican, the Dying Gaul, and the finest achievements of the Perganene school.* In literature, also, Mr Mahaffy is loud in his lamentations over what he considers to be the shallow society tendencies of the new comedy, and misses the fine freedom of Aristophanes,* with his intense patriotism, his vital interest in politics, his large issues, and his delight in vigorous national life. He confesses the decay of oratory under the blighting influences of imperialism, and the sterility of those pedantic disquisitions upon style which are the inevitable consequence of the lack of healthy subject-matter. Indeed on the last page of his history Mr Mahaffy makes a formal recantation of most of his political prejudices. He is still of opinion that Demosthenes should have been put to death for resisting the Macedonian invasion, but admits that the imperialism of Rome, which followed the imperialism of Alexander, produced incalculable mischief, beginning with intellectual decay, and ending with financial ruin. 'The touch of Rome,' he says, 'numbed Greece and Egypt, Syria and Asia Minor, and if there are great buildings attesting the splendour of the Empire, where are the signs of intellectual and moral vigour, if we except that stronghold of nationality, the little land of Palestine?'

This palinode is no doubt intended to give a plausible air of fairness to the book, but such a death-bed repentance comes too late, and makes the whole preceding history seem not fair, but foolish.

It is a relief to turn to the few chapters that deal directly with the social life and thought of the Greeks. Here Mr Mahaffy is very pleasant reading indeed. His account of the colleges at Athens and Alexandria, for instance, is extremely interesting, and so is his estimate of the schools of Zeno, of Epicurus, and of Pyrrho.* Excellent, too, in many points is the description of the literature and art of the period. We do not agree with Mr Mahaffy in his panegyric of the Laocoon,* and we are surprised to find a writer, who is very indignant at what he considers to be the modern indifference to Alexandrine poetry, gravely stating that no study is 'more wearisome and profitless' than that of the Greek Anthology. The criticism of the new comedy, also, seems to us somewhat pedantic. The aim of social comedy, in Menander no less than in Sheridan,* is to mirror the manners, not to reform the morals of its day, and the censure of the Puritan, whether real or affected, is always out of place in literary criticism, and shows a want of recognition of the essential distinction between art and life. After all, it is only the Philistine who thinks of blaming Jack Absolute for his deception, Bob Acres for his cowardice, and Charles Surface* for his extravagance, and there is very little use in airing one's moral sense at the expense of one's artistic appreciation. Valuable, also, though modernity of expression undoubtedly is, still it requires to be used with tact and judgment. There is no objection to Mr Mahaffy's describing Philopoenen as the Garibaldi, and Antigonus Doson as the Victor Emmanuel* of his age. Such comparisons have no doubt a certain cheap popular value. But, on the other hand, a phrase like 'Greek Pre-raphaelitism' is rather awkward; not much is gained by dragging in an allusion to Mr Shorthouse's 'John Inglesant' in a description of the Argonautics of Apollonius Rhodius; and when we are told that the superb Pavilion erected in Alexandria by Ptolemy Philadelphus was 'a sort of glorified Holborn Restaurant,' we must say that the elaborate description of the building given in Athenaeus* could have been summed up in a better and a more intelligible epigram.

On the whole, however, Mr Mahaffy's book may have the effect of drawing attention to a very important and interesting period in the history of Hellenism. We can only regret that, just as he has spoiled his account of Greek politics by a foolish partizan bias, so he should have marred the value of some of his remarks on literature by a bias that is quite as unmeaning. It is uncouth and harsh to say that 'the superannuated schoolboy who holds fellowships and masterships at English colleges' knows nothing of the period in question except what he reads in Theocritus, or that a man may be considered in England a distinguished Greek professor 'who does not know a single date in Greek history between the death of Alexander and the battle of Cynoscephalae,' and the statement that Lucian, Plutarch, and the Four Gospels* are excluded from English school and college studies in consequence of the pedantry of 'pure scholars, as they are pleased to call themselves,' is of course quite inaccurate. In fact, not merely does Mr Mahaffy miss the spirit of the true historian, but he often seems entirely devoid of the temper of the true man of letters. He is clever, and at times even brilliant, but he lacks reasonableness, moderation, style, and charm. He seems to have no sense of literary proportion, and as a rule spoils his case by overstating it. With all his passion for imperialism, there is something about Mr Mahaffy that is, if not parochial, at least provincial, and we cannot say that this last book of his will add anything to his reputation either as a historian, a critic, or a man of taste.

POETRY AND PRISON[1]

Mr Wilfrid Blunt's 'In Vinculis'

PRISON has had an admirable effect on Mr Wilfrid Blunt* as a poet. The 'Love Sonnets of Proteus,'* in spite of their clever Musset-like modernities,* and their swift brilliant wit, were but affected or fantastic at best. They were simply the records of passing moods and moments, of which some were sad, and others sweet, and not a few shameful. Their subject was not of high or serious import. They contained much that was wilful and weak. 'In Vinculis,'* upon the other hand, is a book that stirs one by its fine sincerity of purpose, its lofty and impassioned thought, its depth and ardour of intense feeling. 'Imprisonment,' says Mr Blunt in his preface, 'is a reality of discipline most useful to the modern soul, lapped as it is in physical

---

[1] 3 January 1889. Wilfrid Scawen Blunt, *In Vinculis* (London, 1889); Andrew Lang, *Grass of Parnassus* (London, 1888).

sloth and self-indulgence. Like a sickness or a spiritual retreat it purifies and ennobles; and the soul emerges from it stronger and more self-contained.' To him, certainly, it has been a mode of purification. The opening sonnets, composed in the bleak cell of Galway gaol, and written down on the fly-leaves of the prisoner's prayer-book, are full of things nobly conceived and nobly uttered, and show that though Mr Balfour* may enforce 'plain living' by his prison regulations, he cannot prevent 'high thinking,' or in any way limit or constrain the freedom of a man's soul. They are, of course, intensely personal in expression. They could not fail to be so. But the personality that they reveal has nothing petty or ignoble about it. The petulant cry of the shallow egoist, which was the chief characteristic of the 'Love Sonnets of Proteus,' is not to be found here. In its place we have wild grief and terrible scorn, fierce rage and flame-like passion. Such a sonnet as the following comes out of the very fire of heart and brain:—

> God knows, 'twas not with a forereasoned plan
>   I left the easeful dwellings of my peace,
> And sought this combat with ungodly man,
>   And ceaseless still through years that do not cease
>   Have warred with powers and principalities.
> My natural soul, ere yet these strifes began
>   Was as a sister diligent to please
> And loving all, and most the human clan.
>
> God knows it. And He knows how the world's tears
>   Touched me. And He is witness of my wrath,
> How it was kindled against murderers
>   Who slew for gold, and how upon their path
> I met them. Since which day the world in arms
> Strikes at my life with angers and alarms.

And this sonnet has all the strange strength of that despair which is but the prelude to a larger hope:—

> I thought to do a deed of chivalry,
>   An act of worth, which haply in her sight
> Who was my mistress should recorded be
>   And of the nations. And, when thus the fight
>   Faltered and men once bold with faces white
> Turned this and that way in excuse to flee,

I only stood, and by the foeman's might
Was overborne and mangled cruelly.

Then crawled I to her feet, in whose dear cause
    I made this venture, and 'Behold,' I said,
'How I am wounded for thee in these wars.'
    But she, 'Poor cripple, wouldst thou I should wed
A limbless trunk?' and laughing turned from me:
Yet she was fair, and her name 'Liberty.'

The sonnet beginning

> A prison is a convent without God—
>   Poverty, Chastity, Obedience
> Its precepts are:—

is very fine, and this, written just after entering the gaol, is powerful:—

Naked I came into the world of pleasure,
    And naked come I to this house of pain.
Here at the gate I lay down my life's treasure,
    My pride, my garments, and my name with men.
    The world and I henceforth shall be as twain,
No sound of me shall pierce for good or ill
    These walls of grief. Nor shall I hear the vain
Laughter and tears of those who love me still.

Within, what new life waits me? Little ease,
    Cold lying, hunger, nights of wakefulness,
Harsh orders given, no voice to soothe or please,
    Poor thieves for friends, for books rules meaningless;
This is the grave—nay, hell. Yet, Lord of Might
Still in Thy light my spirit shall see light.

But indeed all the sonnets are worth reading, and 'The Canon of
Aughrim,' the longest poem in the book, is a most masterly and
dramatic description of the tragic life of the Irish peasant. Literature
is not much indebted to Mr Balfour for his sophistical 'Defence of
Philosophic Doubt,'* which is one of the dullest books we know, but
it must be admitted that by sending Mr Blunt to gaol he has converted a clever rhymer into an earnest and deep-thinking poet. The
narrow confines of the prison-cell seem to suit the sonnet's 'scanty
plot of ground,' and an unjust imprisonment for a noble cause
strengthens as well as deepens the nature.

Mr Andrew Lang's 'Grass of Parnassus'

WHETHER or not Mr Andrew Lang should be sent to prison, is another matter. We are inclined to think that he should not, except as a punishment for writing sonnets to Mr Rider Haggard.* His gay pleasant Muse, with her dainty if somewhat facile graces, her exquisite triviality, and her winsome irresponsible manner, would probably gain very little from such a dreary exile. When Leigh Hunt was in gaol* he was allowed to console himself with a pretty wall-paper, but Mr Balfour permits nothing but white-washed walls, and we are quite sure that Mr Lang would find their monotony unbearable. Prison is for souls stronger than the soul revealed to us in the charming whisperings and musical echoes of the 'Grass of Parnassus;' which, however, is a very fascinating little volume, in its way, and possesses many delicately-carved 'ivories of speech,' to borrow one of Mr Pater's phrases.* The translation of Rémy Belleau's* well-known poem on April is excellent:—

April with thy gracious wiles,
    Like the smiles,
Smiles of Venus; and thy breath
Like her breath, the gods' delight,
    (From their height
They take the happy air beneath;)

It is thou that, of thy grace,
    From their place
In the far-off isles dost bring

Swallows over earth and sea,
    Glad to be
Messengers of thee and Spring.

Daffodil and eglantine,
    And woodbine,
Lily, violet, and rose
Plentiful in April fair,
    To the air,
Their pretty petals to unclose.

The assonance of 'their' in the last line with 'air' in the line preceding is not very pleasing, and indeed the word seems otiose, but the translation as a whole is admirably done. The version of poor Henri Murger's* 'Old Loves' is also very good. It is a little masterpiece of felicitous rendering, and the versions from the Greek anthology show the fine taste of a true scholar and man of letters. Where Mr Lang pipes on his own reed, we like him less, and his sonnets are deficient in any fine central motive, and really show him at his worst. But such poems as 'Colinette' and 'The Singing Rose' are certainly wonderfully pretty. Mr Lang has recently been christened 'the Divine Amateur,'* and the little book that lies before us is a good instance of how well he deserves that graceful compliment. However, this book should not have been brought out in winter. It is made for summer. On a lazy June evening no more delightful companion could be found than a poet who has the sweetest of voices and absolutely nothing to say.

THE NEW PRESIDENT[1]

IN a little book that he calls 'The Enchanted Island,' Mr Wyke Bayliss* the new President of the Royal Society of British Artists has just given his gospel of art to the world. His predecessor in office* had also a gospel of art, but it usually took the form of an autobiography. Mr Whistler always spelt art, and we believe still spells it, with a capital 'I.' However, he was never dull. His brilliant wit, his caustic satire, and his amusing epigrams, or perhaps we should say epitaphs on his contemporaries made his views on art as delightful as they were misleading, and as fascinating as they were unsound. Besides, he introduced American humour into art criticism, and for this if for no other reason he deserves to be affectionately remembered. Mr Wyke Bayliss, upon the other hand, is rather tedious. The last President never said much that was true, but the present President never says anything that is new, and if art be a fairy-haunted wood or an enchanted island, we must say that we prefer the old Puck to the fresh Prospero.* Water is an admirable thing—at least, the Greeks said it was—and Mr Ruskin* is an admirable writer; but a combination of both is a little depressing.

Still, it is only right to add that Mr Wyke Bayliss, at his best, writes very good English. Mr Whistler, for some reason or other, always adopted the phraseology of the minor prophets. Possibly it was in order to emphasize his well-known claims to verbal inspiration, or perhaps he thought with Voltaire that 'Habakkuk est capable de tout,'* and wished to shelter himself under the shield of a definitely irresponsible writer none of whose prophecies, according to the French philosopher, have ever been fulfilled. The idea was clever enough at the beginning, but ultimately the manner became monotonous. The spirit of the Hebrews is excellent, but their mode of writing is not to be imitated, and no amount of American jokes

[1] 26 January 1889. Wyke Bayliss, *The Enchanted Island* (London, 1888).

will give it that modernity which is so essential to a good literary style. Admirable as are Mr Whistler's fire-works on canvas, his fire-works in prose are abrupt, violent, and exaggerated. However, oracles, since the days of the Pythia,* have never been remarkable for style, and the modest Mr Wyke Bayliss is as much Mr Whistler's superior as a writer, as he is his inferior as a painter and an artist. Indeed, some of the passages in this book are so charmingly written, and with such dexterous felicity of phrase that we cannot help feeling that the President of the British Artists, like a still more Famous President of our day, can express himself far better through the medium of literature than he can through the medium of line and colour. This, however, only applies to Mr Wyke Bayliss's prose. His poetry is very bad, and the sonnets at the end of the book are almost as mediocre as the drawings that accompany them. As we read them we cannot but regret that in this point at any rate Mr Bayliss has not imitated the wise example of his predecessor, who with all his faults was never guilty of writing a line of poetry, and who is indeed quite incapable of doing anything of the kind.

As for the matter of Mr Bayliss's discourses, his views on art must be admitted to be very commonplace and old fashioned. What is the use of telling artists that they should try and paint Nature as she really is? What Nature really is, is a question for metaphysics not for art. Art deals with appearances, and the eye of the man who looks at Nature, the vision in fact of the artist, is far more important to us than what he looks at. There is more truth in Corot's aphorism,* that a landscape is simply the 'mood of a man's mind,' than there is in all Mr Bayliss's laborious disquisitions on naturalism. Again, why does Mr Bayliss waste a whole chapter in pointing out real or supposed resemblances between a book of his published twelve years ago and an article by Mr Palgrave* which appeared recently in the *Nineteenth Century*? Neither the book nor the article contains anything of real interest, and as for the hundred or more parallel passages which Mr Wyke Bayliss solemnly prints side by side, most of them are like parallel lines and never meet. The only original proposal that Mr Bayliss has to offer us is that the House of Commons should every year select some important event from national and contemporary history, and hand it over to the artists, who are to choose from among themselves a man to make a picture of it. In this way Mr Bayliss believes that we could have the historic art, and suggests as examples of what he means, a picture of Florence Nightingale in the hospital at Scutari, a picture of the opening of the first London Board school, and a picture of the Senate House at Cambridge with the girl-graduate receiving a degree 'that shall acknowledge her to be as wise as Merlin himself, and leave her still as beautiful as Vivien.'* This proposal is, of course, very well meant, but to say nothing of the danger of leaving historic art at the mercy of a majority in the House of Commons, who would naturally vote for their own view of things, Mr Bayliss does not seem to realise that a great event is not necessarily a pictorial event. 'The decisive events of the world,' as has been well said, 'take place in the intellect,' and as for Board schools academic ceremonies, hospital wards, and the like they may well be left to the artists of the illustrated papers, who do them admirably and quite as well as they need be done. Indeed, the pictures of contemporary events, Royal marriages naval reviews and things of this kind, that appear in the Academy every year, are always extremely bad, while the very same subjects treated in black and white in the *Graphic* or the *London News* are excellent. Besides if we want to understand the history of a nation through the medium of art it is to the imaginative and ideal arts that we have to go, and not to the arts that are definitely imitative. The visible aspect of life no longer contains for us the secret of life's spirit. Probably it never did contain it. And if Mr Barker's 'Waterloo Banquet,' and Mr Frith's 'Marriage of the Prince of Wales'* are examples of healthy historic art, the less we have of such art the better. However, Mr Bayliss is full of the most ardent faith and speaks quite gravely of genuine portraits of St John, St Peter and St Paul dating from the first century, and of the establishment by the Israelites of a school of art in the wilderness under the now little-appreciated Bezaleel.* He is a pleasant picturesque writer, but he should not speak about art. Art is a sealed book to him.

POETICAL SOCIALISTS[1]

MR STOPFORD BROOKE* said some time ago that Socialism and the Socialistic spirit would give our poets nobler and loftier themes for song, would widen their sympathies and enlarge the horizon of their

[1] 15 February 1889. *Chants of Labour: A Song-Book of the People*, ed. Edward Carpenter (London, 1888).

vision, and would touch with the fire and fervour of a new faith lips that had else been silent, hearts that but for this fresh gospel had been cold. What Art gains from contemporary events is always a fascinating problem, and a problem that is not easy to solve. It is, however, certain that Socialism starts well-equipped. She has her poets and her painters, her art lecturers and her cunning designers, her powerful orators and her clever writers. If she fails it will not be for lack of expression. If she succeeds, her triumph will not be a triumph of mere brute force. The first thing that strikes one, as one looks over the list of contributors to Mr Edward Carpenter's* 'Chants of Labour,' is the curious variety of their several occupations, the wide differences of social position that exist between them, and the strange medley of men whom a common passion has for the moment united. The editor is a 'science lecturer;' he is followed by a draper and a porter; then we have two late Eton masters, and then two bootmakers; and these are in their turn succeeded by an ex-Lord Mayor of Dublin, a bookbinder, a photographer, a steelworker and an authoress. On one page we have a journalist, a draughtsman, and a music-teacher, and on another a Civil servant, a machine-fitter, a medical student, a cabinet-maker and a minister of the Church of Scotland. Certainly, it is no ordinary movement that can bind together in close brotherhood men of such dissimilar pursuits; and when we mention that Mr William Morris is one of the singers and that Mr Walter Crane* has designed the cover and frontispiece of the book, we cannot but feel that, as we pointed out before, Socialism starts well-equipped.

As for the songs themselves, some of them, to quote from the editor's preface, are 'purely revolutionary; others are Christian in tone; there are some that might be called merely material in their tendency, while many are of a highly ideal and visionary character.' This is, on the whole, very promising. It shows that Socialism is not going to allow herself to be trammelled by any hard-and-fast creed or to be stereotyped into an iron formula. She welcomes many and multiform natures. She rejects none, and has room for all. She has the attraction of a wonderful personality, and touches the heart of one and the brain of another, and draws this man by his hatred of injustice, and his neighbour by his faith in the future, and a third, it may be, by his love of art, or by his wild worship of a lost and buried past. And all of this is well. For, to make men Socialists is nothing, but to make Socialism human is a great thing.

They are not of any very high literary value, these poems that have been so dexterously set to music. They are meant to be sung, not to be read. They are rough, direct, and vigorous, and the tunes are stirring and familiar. Indeed, almost any mob could warble them with ease. The transpositions that have been made are rather amusing. ' 'Twas in Trafalgar Square' is set to the tune of ' 'Twas in Trafalgar's Bay'; 'Up, Ye People!' a very revolutionary song by Mr John Gregory, bootmaker, with a refrain of

> Up, ye People! or down into your graves!
> Cowards ever will be slaves!

is to be sung to the tune of 'Rule, Britannia!' the old melody of 'The Vicar of Bray' is to accompany the new 'Ballade of Law and Order,' which, however, is not a ballade at all; and to the air of 'Here's to the Maiden of Bashful Fifteen' the democracy of the future is to thunder forth one of Mr T. D. Sullivan's* most powerful and pathetic lyrics. It is clear that the Socialists intend to carry on the musical education of the people simultaneously with their education in political science, and here as elsewhere they seem to be entirely free from any narrow bias or formal prejudice. Mendelssohn is followed by Moody and Sankey;* the 'Wacht am Rhein' stands side by side with the 'Marseillaise';* 'Lillibulero,' a chorus from 'Norma,' 'John Brown' and an air from Beethoven's Ninth Symphony* are all equally delightful to them. They sing the National Anthem in Shelley's version and chant William Morris's 'Voice of Toil' to the flowing numbers of 'Ye Banks and Braes of Bonny Doon.'* Victor Hugo* talks somewhere of the terrible cry of '*le tigre populaire*,' but it is evident from Mr Carpenter's book that should the Revolution ever break out in England we shall have no inarticulate roar, but rather pleasant glees and graceful part-songs. The change is certainly for the better. Nero fiddled while Rome was burning, at least inaccurate historians say he did, but it is for the building up of an eternal city that the Socialists of our day are making music, and they have complete confidence in the art instincts of the people.

> They say that the people are brutal
>   That their instincts of beauty are dead
> Were it so, shame on those who condemn them

> To the desperate struggle for bread.
> But they lie in their throats when they say it,
> For the people are tender at heart,
> And a well-spring of beauty lies hidden
> Beneath their life's fever and smart,

is a stanza from one of the poems in this volume, and the feeling expressed in these words is paramount everywhere. The Reformation gained much from the use of popular hymns and hymn-tunes,* and the Socialists seem determined to gain by similar means a similar hold upon the people. However, they must not be too sanguine about the result. The walls of Thebes rose up to the sound of music,* and Thebes was a very dull city indeed.

MR FROUDE'S BLUE BOOK[1]

BLUE BOOKS* are generally dull reading, but Blue Books on Ireland have always been interesting. They form the record of one of the great tragedies of modern Europe. In them England has written down her indictment against herself, and has given to the world the history of her shame. If in the last century she tried to govern Ireland with an insolence that was intensified by race-hatred and religious prejudice, she has sought to rule her in this century with a stupidity that is aggravated by good intentions. The last of these Blue Books, Mr Froude's heavy novel,* has appeared, however, somewhat too late. The society that he describes has long since passed away. An entirely new factor has appeared in the social development of the country, and this factor is the Irish-American, and his influence. To mature its powers, to concentrate its action, to learn the secret of its own strength and of England's weakness, the Celtic intellect has had to cross the Atlantic. At home it had but learned the pathetic weakness of nationality; in a strange land it realized what indomitable forces nationality possesses. What captivity was to the Jews, exile has been to the Irish. America and American influence has educated them. Their first practical leader is an Irish American.*

But while Mr Froude's book has no practical relation to modern Irish politics, and does not offer any solution of the present question,

---

[1] 13 April 1889. J. A. Froude, *The Two Chiefs of Dunboy* (London, 1889). This review was published under Wilde's initials, 'O. W.'.

it has a certain historical value. It is a vivid picture of Ireland in the latter half of the eighteenth century, a picture often false in its lights and exaggerated in its shadows, but a picture none the less. Mr Froude admits the martyrdom of Ireland, but regrets that the martyrdom was not completely carried out. His ground of complaint against the executioner is not his trade, but his bungling. It is the bluntness, not the cruelty, of the sword that he objects to. Resolute government, that shallow shibboleth of those who do not understand how complex a thing the art of government is, is his posthumous panacea for past evils. His hero, Colonel Goring, has the words Law and Order ever on his lips, meaning by the one the enforcement of unjust legislation, and implying by the other the suppression of every fine national aspiration. That the Government should enforce iniquity, and the governed submit to it, seems to Mr Froude, as it certainly is to many others, the true ideal of political science. Like most pen-men he overrates the power of the sword. Where England has had to struggle she has been wise. Where physical strength has been on her side, as in Ireland, she has been made unwieldy by that strength. Her own strong hands have blinded her. She has had force, but no direction.

There is, of course, a story in Mr Froude's novel. It is not simply a political disquisition. The interest of the tale, such as it is, centres round two men, Colonel Goring and Morty Sullivan, the Cromwellian and the Celt. These men are enemies by race, and creed, and feeling. The first represents Mr Froude's cure for Ireland. He is a resolute Englishman, with strong Nonconformist tendencies, who plants an industrial colony on the coast of Kerry, and has deep-rooted objections to that illicit trade with France, which in the last century was the sole method by which the Irish people were enabled to pay their rents to their absentee landlords. Colonel Goring bitterly regrets that the Penal Laws against Catholics are not vigorously carried out. He is a '*Police* at any price' man:—

And this, said Goring scornfully, is what you call governing Ireland, hanging up your law like a scarecrow in the garden till every sparrow has learnt to make a jest of it. Your Popery Acts! Well, you borrow them from France. The French Catholics did not choose to keep the Huguenots among them, and recalled the Edict of Nantes.* As they treated the Huguenots, so you said to all the world that you would treat the Papists. You borrowed from the French the very language of your Statute, but they are not afraid to stand by their law, and you are afraid to stand by yours. You let the people laugh at it, and in teaching them to despise one law you teach them to despise all laws—God's and man's alike. I cannot say how it will end; but I can tell you this, that you are training up a race with the education which you are giving them that will astonish mankind by and by.

Mr Froude's résumé of the History of Ireland is not without power, though it is far from being really accurate. The Irish, he tells us, had disowned the facts of life, and the facts of life had proved the strongest. The English, unable to tolerate anarchy so near their shores, consulted the Pope. The Pope gave them leave to interfere, and the Pope had the best of the bargain. For the English brought him in, and the Irish kept him there. England's first settlers were Norman nobles. They became more Irish than the Irish, and England found herself in this difficulty. To abandon Ireland would be discreditable, to rule it as a province would be contrary to English tradition. She then tried to rule by dividing, and failed. The Pope was too strong for her. At last she made her great political discovery. What Ireland wanted was evidently an entirely new population of the same race and the same religion as her own. The new policy was partly carried out:—

Elizabeth first, and then James, and then Cromwell replanted the island, introducing English, Scots, Huguenots, Flemings, Dutch, tens of thousands of families of vigorous and earnest Protestants who brought their industries along with them. Twice the Irish tried to drive out this new element. They failed. But England had no sooner accomplished her long task than she set herself to work to spoil it again. She destroyed the industries of her colonists by her trade laws. She set the Bishops to rob them of their religion. . . . As for the gentry, the purpose for which they had been introduced into Ireland was unfulfilled. They were but alien intruders, who did nothing, who were allowed to do nothing. The time would come when an exasperated population would demand that the land should be given back to them, and England would then, perhaps, throw the gentry to the wolves, in the hope of a momentary peace. But her own turn would follow. She would be face to face with the old problem, either to make a new conquest or to retire with disgrace.

Political disquisitions of this kind, and prophecies after the event, are found all through Mr Froude's book, and on almost every second page we come across aphorisms on the Irish character, on the teachings of Irish history and on the nature of England's mode of government. Some of these represent Mr Froude's own views, others are entirely dramatic, and introduced for the purpose of characterization. We append some specimens. As epigrams, they are not very felicitous, but they are interesting from some points of view.

Irish society grew up in happy recklessness. Insecurity added zest to enjoyment.

We Irish must either laugh or cry, and if we went in for crying, we should all hang ourselves.

Too close a union with the Irish had produced degeneracy both of character and creed in all the settlements of English.

We age quickly in Ireland with the whisky and the broken heads.

The Irish leaders cannot fight. They can make the country ungovernable, and keep an English army occupied in watching them.

No nation can ever achieve a liberty that will not be a curse to it, except by arms in the field.

The Irish are taught from their cradles that English rule is the cause of all their miseries. They were as ill off under their own chiefs; but they would bear from their natural leaders what they will not bear from us, and if we have not made their lot more wretched, we have not made it any better.

Patriotism? Yes! Patriotism of the Hibernian order. That the country has been badly treated, and is poor and miserable. This is the patriot's stock in trade. Does he want it mended? Not he. His own occupation would be gone.

Irish corruption is the twin-brother of Irish eloquence.

England will not let us break the heads of our scoundrels: she will not break them herself: we are a free country, and must take the consequences.

The functions of the Anglo-Irish Government were to do what ought not to be done, and to leave undone what ought to be done.

The Irish race have always been noisy, useless, and ineffectual. They have produced nothing, they have done nothing which it is possible to admire. What they are that they have always been, and the only hope for them is that their ridiculous Irish nationality should be buried and forgotten.

The Irish are the best actors in the world.

Order is an exotic in Ireland. It has been imported from England, but it will not grow. It suits neither soil nor climate. If the English wanted order in Ireland, they should have left none of us alive.

When ruling powers are unjust, nature reasserts her rights.

Even anarchy has its advantages.

Nature keeps an accurate account. The longer a bill is left unpaid, the heavier the accumulation of interest.

You cannot live in Ireland without breaking laws on one side or another. *Pecca fortiter*, therefore, as Luther says.*

The animal spirits of the Irish remained when all else was gone, and if there was no purpose in their lives they could at least enjoy themselves.

The Irish peasants can make the country hot for the Protestant gentleman, but that is all they are fit for.

As we said before, if Mr Froude intended his book to help the Tory Government to solve the Irish question he has entirely missed his aim. The Ireland of which he writes has disappeared. As a record, however, of the incapacity of a Teutonic to rule a Celtic people against their own wishes his book is not without value. It is dull, but dull books are very popular at present, and as people have grown a little tired of talking about 'Robert Elsmere,'* they will probably take to discussing 'The Two Chiefs of Dunboy.' There are some who will welcome with delight the idea of solving the Irish question by doing away with the Irish people. There are others who will remember that Ireland has extended her boundaries, and that we have now to reckon with her not merely in the Old World but also in the New.

MR SWINBURNE'S LAST VOLUME[1]

MR SWINBURNE* once set his age on fire by a volume of very perfect and very poisonous poetry. Then he became revolutionary, and pantheistic, and cried out against those who sit in high places both in heaven and on earth. Then he invented Marie Stuart and laid upon us the heavy burden of 'Bothwell.'* Then he retired to the nursery, and wrote poems about children of a somewhat over-subtle character. He is now extremely patriotic, and manages to combine with his patriotism a strong affection for the Tory party. He has always been a great poet. But he has his limitations, the chief of which is, curiously enough, an entire lack of any sense of limit. His song is nearly always too loud for his subject. His magnificent rhetoric, nowhere more magnificent than in the volume that now lies before

[1] 27 June 1889. Algernon Swinburne, *Poems and Ballads: Third Series* (London, 1889).

us, conceals rather than reveals. It has been said of him, and with truth, that he is a master of language, but with still greater truth it may be said that Language is his master. Words seem to dominate him. Alliteration tyrannizes over him. Mere sound often becomes his lord. He is so eloquent that whatever he touches becomes unreal.

Let us turn to the poem on the Armada:

> The wings of the south-west wind are widened; the breath of his fervent lips,
> More keen than a sword's edge, fiercer than fire, falls full on the plunging ships.
> The pilot is he of the northward flight, their stay and their steersman be;
> A helmsman clothed with the tempest, and girdled with strength to constrain the sea.
> And the host of them trembles and quails, caught fast in his hand as a bird in the toils;
> For the wrath and the joy that fulfil him are mightier than man's, whom he slays and spoils.
> And vainly, with heart divided in sunder, and labour of wavering will,
> The lord of their host takes counsel with hope if haply their star shine still.

Somehow, we seem to have heard all this before. Does it come from the fact that of all poets who ever lived Mr Swinburne is the one who is the most limited in imagery? It must be admitted that he is so. He has wearied us with his monotony. 'Fire' and the 'Sea' are the two words ever on his lips. We must confess also that this shrill singing—marvellous as it is—leaves us out of breath. Here is a passage from a poem called 'A Word with the Wind':

> Be the sunshine bared or veiled, the sky superb or shrouded,
>   Still the waters, lax and languid, chafed and foiled,
> Keen and thwarted, pale and patient, clothed with fire or clouded,
>   Vex their heart in vain, or sleep like serpents coiled.
> Thee they look for, blind and baffled, wan with wrath and weary
>   Blown for ever back by winds that rock the bird:
> Winds that seamews breast subdue the sea, and bid the dreary
>   Waves be weak as hearts made sick with hope deferred.
> Let the clarion sound from westward, let the south bear token
>   How the glories of thy godhead sound and shine:
> Bid the land rejoice to see the land-wind's broad wings broken,
>   Bid the sea take comfort, bid the world be thine.

Verse of this kind may be justly praised for the sustained strength and vigour of its metrical scheme. Its purely technical excellence is extraordinary. But is it more than an oratorical *tour-de-force*? Does it really convey much? Does it charm? Could we return to it again and again with renewed pleasure? We think not. It seems to us empty.

Of course, we must not look to these poems for any revelation of human life. To be at one with the elements seems to be Mr Swinburne's aim. He seeks to speak with the breath of wind and wave. The roar of the fire is ever in his ears. He puts his clarion to the lips of Spring and bids her blow, and the Earth wakes from her dreams and tells him her secret. He is the first lyric poet who has tried to make an absolute surrender of his own personality, and he has succeeded. We hear the song, but we never know the singer. We never even get near to him. Out of the thunder and splendour of words he himself says nothing. We have often had man's interpretation of Nature; now we have Nature's interpretation of man, and she has curiously little to say. Force and Freedom form her vague message. She deafens us with her clangours.*

But Mr Swinburne is not always riding the whirlwind, and calling out of the depths of the sea. Romantic ballads in Border dialect have not lost their fascination for him, and this last volume contains some very splendid examples of this curious artificial kind of poetry. The amount of pleasure one gets out of dialect is a matter entirely of temperament. To say 'mither' instead of 'mother' seems to many the acme of romance. There are others who are not quite so ready to believe in the pathos of provincialisms. There is, however, no doubt of Mr Swinburne's mastery over the form, whether the form be quite legitimate or not. 'The Weary Wedding' has the concentration and colour of a great drama, and the quaintness of its style lends it something of the power of a grotesque. The ballad of 'The Witch-Mother,' a mediæval Medea* who slays her children because her lord is faithless, is worth reading on account of its horrible simplicity. 'The Bride's Tragedy' with its strange refrain of

> In, in, out and in,
> Blaws the wind and whirls the whin:

The 'Jacobite's Exile,'

> O lordly flow the Loire and Seine,
> And loud the dark Durance:

> But bonnier shine the braes of Tyne
>   Than a' the fields of France;
> And the waves of Till that speak sae still
>   Gleam goodlier where they glance:

'The Tyneside Widow,' and 'A Reiver's Neck-verse' are all poems of fine imaginative power, and some of them are terrible in their fierce intensity of passion. There is no danger of English poetry narrowing itself to a form so limited as the romantic ballad in dialect. It is of too vital a growth for that. So we may welcome Mr Swinburne's masterly experiments with the hope that things which are inimitable will not be imitated. The collection is completed by a few poems on children, some sonnets, a threnody on John William Inchbold,* and a lovely lyric entitled 'The Interpreters.'

> In human thought have all things habitation;
>   Our days
> Laugh, lower, and lighten past, and find no station
>   That stays.
>
> But thought and faith are mightier things than time
>   Can wrong,
> Made splendid once by speech, or made sublime
>   By song.
>
> Remembrance, though the tide of change that rolls
>   Wax hoary,
> Gives earth and heaven, for song's sake and the soul's,
>   Their glory.

Certainly, 'for song's sake' we should love Mr Swinburne's work, cannot indeed help loving it, so marvellous a music-maker is he. But what of the soul? For the soul we must go elsewhere.

THE DRAMATIC REVIEW

SHAKESPEARE ON SCENERY[1]*

I HAVE often heard people wonder what Shakespeare would say, could he see Mr Irving's production of his *Much Ado About Nothing*, or Mr Wilson Barrett's setting of his *Hamlet*.* Would he take pleasure in the glory of the scenery, and the marvel of the colour? Would he be interested in the Cathedral of Messina, and the battlements of Elsinore?* Or would he be indifferent, and say the play, and the play only, is the thing?*

Speculations like these are always pleasurable, and in the present case happen to be profitable also. For it is not difficult to see what Shakespeare's attitude would be; not difficult, that is to say, if one reads Shakespeare himself, instead of reading merely what is written about him.

Speaking, for instance, directly, as the manager of a London theatre, through the lips of the chorus in *Henry V*, he complains of the smallness of the stage* on which he has to produce the pageant of a big historical play, and of the want of scenery which obliges him to cut out many of its most picturesque incidents, apologises for the scanty number of supers who have to play the soldiers, and for the shabbiness of the properties, and, finally, expresses his regret at being unable to bring on real horses. In the *Midsummer Night's Dream*, again, he gives us a most amusing picture of the straits to which theatrical managers of his day were reduced by the want of proper scenery. In fact, it is impossible to read him without seeing that he is constantly protesting against the two special limitations of the Elizabethan stage, the lack of suitable scenery, and the fashion of men playing women's parts. Just as he protests against other difficulties with which managers of theatres have still to contend, such as actors who don't understand their words; actors who miss their cues; actors who overact their parts; actors who mouth; actors who gag; actors who play to the gallery; and amateur actors.

And, indeed, a great dramatist, like he was, could not but have felt

[1] 14 March 1885.

very much hampered at being obliged continually to interrupt the progress of a play, in order to send on some one to explain to the audience that the scene was to be changed to a particular place, on the entrance of a particular character, and after his exit to somewhere else; that the stage was to represent the deck of a ship in a storm, or the interior of a Greek temple, or the streets of a certain town, to all of which inartistic devices Shakespeare is reduced, and for which he always amply apologises. Besides this clumsy method, Shakespeare had two other substitutes for scenery—the hanging out of a placard, and his descriptions. The first of these could hardly have satisfied his passion for picturesqueness and his feeling for beauty, and certainly did not satisfy the dramatic critics of his day. But as regards the descriptions, to those of us who look on Shakespeare not merely as a play-wright, but as a poet, and who enjoy reading him at home just as much as we enjoy seeing him acted, it may be a matter of congratulation that he had not at his command such skilled machinists as are in use now at the Princess's and at the Lyceum.* For had Cleopatra's barge,* for instance, been a structure of canvas and Dutch metal, it would probably have been painted over or broken up after the withdrawal of the piece, and, even had it survived to our own day, would, I am afraid, have become extremely shabby by this time. Whereas now the beaten gold of its poop is still bright, and the purple of its sails still beautiful; its silver oars are not tired of keeping time to the music of the flutes they follow, nor the Nereid's* flower-soft hands of touching its silken tackle; the mermaid still lies at its helm, and still on its deck stand the boys with their coloured fans. Yet lovely as all Shakespeare's descriptive passages are, a description is in its essence undramatic. Theatrical audiences are far more impressed by what they look at than by what they listen to; and the modern dramatist, in having the surroundings of his play visibly presented to the audience when the curtain rises, enjoys an advantage for which Shakespeare often expresses his desire. It is true that Shakespeare's descriptions are not what descriptions are in modern plays—accounts of what the audience can observe for themselves; they are the imaginative method by which he creates in the mind of the spectators the image of that which he desires them to see. Still the quality of the drama is action. It is always dangerous to pause for picturesqueness. And the introduction of self-explanatory scenery enables the modern method to be far more direct, while the loveliness of form and colour which it gives us, seems to me often to create an artistic temperament in the audience, and to produce that joy in beauty for beauty's sake,* without which the great master-pieces of art can never be understood, to which, and to which only, are they ever revealed.

To talk of the passion of a play being hidden by the paint, and of sentiment being killed by scenery, is mere emptiness and folly of words. A noble play, nobly mounted, gives us double artistic pleas-ure. The eye as well as the ear is gratified, and the whole nature is made exquisitely receptive of the influence of imaginative work. And as regards a bad play, have we not all seen large audiences lured by the loveliness of scenic effect into listening to rhetoric posing as poetry, and to vulgarity doing duty for realism? Whether this be good or evil for the public I will not here discuss, but it is evident that the playwright, at any rate, never suffers.

Indeed, the artist who really has suffered through the modern mounting of plays is not the dramatist at all, but the scene painter proper. He is rapidly being displaced by the stage-carpenter. Now and then at Drury Lane I have seen beautiful old front cloths let down, as perfect as pictures some of them, and pure painter's work, and there are many which we all remember at other theatres, in front of which some dialogue was reduced to graceful dumb show through the hammer and tin-tacks behind. But as a rule the stage is over-crowded with enormous properties, which are not merely far more expensive and cumbersome than scene-paintings, but far less beauti-ful, and far less true. Properties kill perspective. A painted door is more like a real door than a real door is itself,* for the proper condi-tions of light and shade can be given to it; and the excessive use of built up structures always makes the stage too glaring, for as they have to be lit from behind, as well as from the front, the gas-jets become the absolute light of the scene, instead of the means merely by which we perceive the conditions of light and shadow which the painter has desired to show us.

So, instead of bemoaning the position of the play-wright, it were better for the critics to exert whatever influence they may possess towards restoring the scene-painter to his proper position as an art-ist, and not allowing him to be built over by the property man, or hammered to death by the carpenter. I have never seen any reason myself why such artists as Mr Beverley, Mr Walter Hann, and Mr

Telbin should not be entitled to become Academicians.* They have
certainly as good a claim as have many of those R.A.'s whose total
inability to paint we can see every May for a shilling.*

And lastly, let those critics who hold up for our admiration the
simplicity of the Elizabethan stage, remember that they are lauding a
condition of things against which Shakespeare himself, in the spirit
of a true artist, always strongly protested.

HAMLET AT THE LYCEUM[1]

IT sometimes happens that at a *première* in London, the least enjoy-
able part of the performance is the play. I have seen many audiences
more interesting than the actors, and have often heard better dialogue in the *foyer* than I have on the stage. At the Lyceum, however,
this is rarely the case, and when the play is a play of Shakespeare's,
and among its exponents are Mr Irving and Miss Ellen Terry,* we
turn from the gods in the gallery and from the goddesses in the stalls,
to enjoy the charm of the production, and to take delight in the art.
The lions are behind the footlights and not in front of them when
we have a noble tragedy nobly acted. And I have rarely witnessed
such enthusiasm as that which greeted on last Saturday night the
two artists I have mentioned. I would like, in fact, to use the word
ovation, but a pedantic professor has recently informed us, with the
Batavian buoyancy of misapplied learning, that this expression is not
to be employed except when a sheep has been sacrificed.* At the
Lyceum last week I need hardly say nothing so dreadful occurred.
The only inartistic incident of the evening was the hurling of a
bouquet from a box at Mr Irving while he was engaged in portraying
the agony of Hamlet's death, and the pathos of his parting with
Horatio. The Dramatic College might take up the education of spectators as well as that of players, and teach people that there is a
proper moment for the throwing of flowers, as well as a proper
method.

As regards Mr Irving's own performance, it has been already so
elaborately criticised and described, from his business with the supposed pictures in the closet scene down to his use of 'peacock' for

[1] 9 May 1885. A review of Shakespeare's *Hamlet*, produced by Henry Irving at the
Lyceum Theatre, London.

'paddock,' that little remains to be said; nor indeed does a Lyceum audience require the interposition of the dramatic critic in order to understand or to appreciate the Hamlet of this great actor. I call him a great actor because he brings to the interpretation of a work of art the two qualities which we in this century so much desire, the qualities of personality and of perfection. A few years ago it seemed to many, and perhaps rightly, that the personality overshadowed the art. No such criticism would be fair now. The somewhat harsh angularity of movement and faulty pronunciation have been replaced by exquisite grace of gesture and by clear precision of word, where such precision is necessary. For delightful as good elocution is, few things are so depressing as to hear a passionate passage recited instead of being acted. The quality of a fine performance is its life more than its learning, and every word in a play has a musical as well as an intellectual value, and must be made expressive of a certain emotion. So it does not seem to me that in all parts of a play perfect pronunciation is necessarily, dramatic. When the words are 'wild and whirling,' the expression of them must be wild and whirling also. Mr Irving, I think, manages his voice with singular art, it was impossible to discern a false note or wrong intonation in his dialogue or his soliloquies, and his strong dramatic power, his realistic power as an actor, is as effective as ever. A great critic at the beginning of this century said that Hamlet is the most difficult part to personate on the stage, that it is like the attempt to 'embody a shadow.' I cannot say that I agree with this idea. Hamlet seems to me essentially a good acting part, and in Mr Irving's performance of it there is that combination of poetic grace with absolute reality which is so eternally delightful. Indeed, if the words easy and difficult have any meaning at all in matters of art, I would be inclined to say that Ophelia is the more difficult part. She has, I mean, less material by which to produce her effects. She is the occasion of the tragedy, but she is neither its heroine nor its chief victim. She is swept away by circumstances, and gives the opportunity for situations of which she is not herself the climax, and which she does not herself command. And of all the parts which Miss Terry has acted in her brilliant career, there is none in which her infinite powers of pathos and her imaginative and creative faculty are more shown than in her Ophelia. Miss Terry is one of those rare artists who needs for her dramatic effect no elaborate dialogue, and for whom the simplest words are sufficient. 'I loved you not,' says Hamlet, and all that Ophelia answers is, 'I was the more deceived.' These are not very grand words to read, but as Miss Terry gave them in acting they seemed to be the highest possible expression of Ophelia's character. Beautiful too was the quick remorse she conveyed by her face and gesture the moment she had lied to Hamlet and told him her father was at home. This I thought a masterpiece of good acting, and her mad scene was wonderful beyond all description. The secrets of Melpomene are known to Miss Terry as well as the secrets of Thalia.* As regards the rest of the company there is always a high standard at the Lyceum, but some particular mention should be made of Mr Alexander's* brilliant performance of Laertes. Mr Alexander has a most effective presence, a charming voice, and a capacity for wearing lovely costumes with ease and elegance. Indeed in the latter respect his only rival was Mr Norman Forbes,* who played either Guildenstern or Rosencrantz very gracefully. I believe one of our budding Hazlitts* is preparing a volume to be entitled 'Great Guildensterns and Remarkable Rosencrantzes,' but I have never been able myself to discern any difference between these two characters. They are I think the only characters Shakespeare has not cared to individualise. Whichever of the two however Mr Forbes acted, he acted it well. Only one point in Mr Alexander's performance seemed to me open to question, that was his kneeling during the whole of Polonius' speech. For this I see no necessity at all, and it makes the scene look less natural than it should, gives it, I mean, too formal an air. However, the performance was most spirited, and gave great pleasure to every one. Mr Alexander is an artist from whom much will be expected, and who I have no doubt will give us much that is fine and noble. He seems to have all the qualifications for a good actor.

There is just one other character I should like to notice. The first player seemed to me to act far too well. He should act very badly. The first player, besides his position in the dramatic evolution of the tragedy, is Shakespeare's caricature of the ranting actors of his day, just as the passage he recites is Shakespeare's own parody on the dull plays of some of his rivals. The whole point of Hamlet's advice to the players seems to me to be lost unless the player himself has been guilty of the faults which Hamlet reprehends, unless he has sawn the air with his hand, mouthed his lines, torn his passion to tatters, and out-Heroded Herod.* The very sensibility which Hamlet notices in the actor, such as his real tears and the like, is not the quality of a good artist. The part should be played after the manner of a provincial tragedian. It is meant to be a satire, and to play it well is to play it badly. The scenery and costumes were excellent with the exception of the King's dress, which was coarse in colour and tawdry in effect. And the Player Queen should have come in boy's attire* to Elsinore.

However, last Saturday night was not a night for criticism. The theatre was filled with those who desired to welcome Mr Irving back to his own theatre, and we were all delighted at his re-appearance among us. I hope that some time will elapse before he and Miss Terry cross again that disappointing Atlantic Ocean.*

HENRY THE FOURTH AT OXFORD[1]

I HAVE been told that the ambition of every Dramatic Club is to act *Henry IV*.* I am not surprised. The spirit of comedy is as fervent in this play as is the spirit of chivalry; it is an heroic pageant as well as an heroic poem, and like most of Shakespeare's historical dramas it contains an extraordinary number of thoroughly good acting parts, each of which is absolutely individual in character, and each of which contributes to the evolution of the plot.

Rumour, from time to time, has brought in tidings of a proposed production by the banks of the Cam, but it seems at the last moment *Box and Cox** has always had to be substituted in the bill. To Oxford belongs the honour of having been the first to present on the stage this noble play, and the production which I saw last week was in every way worthy of that lovely town, that mother of sweetness and of light. For in spite of the roaring of the young lions at the Union, and the screaming of the rabbits in the home of the vivisector, in spite of Keble College, and the tramways, and the sporting prints, Oxford still remains the most beautiful thing in England, and nowhere else are life and art so exquisitely blended, so perfectly made one. Indeed, in most other towns art has often to present herself in the form of a reaction against the sordid ugliness of ignoble lives, but at Oxford she comes to us as an exquisite flower born of the beauty of life and expressive of life's joy. She finds her

[1] 23 May 1885. A review of Shakespeare's *Henry IV*, produced by the Oxford University Dramatic Society at the Town Hall, Oxford.

home by the Isis as once she did by the Ilyssus; the Magdalen walks and the Magdalen cloisters are as dear to her as were ever the silver olives of Colonos and the golden gateway of the house of Pallas: she covers with fan-like tracery the vaulted entrance to Christ Church Hall, and looks out from the windows of Merton; her feet have stirred the Cumnor cowslips,* and she gathers fritillaries in the river-fields. To her the clamour of the schools and the dullness of the lecture-room are a weariness and a vexation of spirit; she seeks not to define virtue, and cares little for the categories; she smiles on the swift athlete whose plastic grace has pleased her, and rejoices in the young Barbarians at their games; she watches the rowers from the reedy bank and gives measured music to the pulse of their oars; she gives myrtle to her lovers, and laurel to her poets, and rue to those who talk wisely in the street; she makes the earth lovely to all who dream with Keats; she opens high heaven to all who soar with Shelley; and turning away her head from pedant, proctor, and Philistine, she has welcomed to her shrine a band of youthful actors, knowing that they have sought with much ardour for the stern secret of Melpomene, and caught with much gladness the sweet laughter of Thalia. And to me this ardour and this gladness were the two most fascinating qualities of the Oxford performance as indeed they are qualities which are necessary to any fine dramatic production. For without a quick and imaginative observation of life the most beautiful play becomes dull in presentation, and what is not conceived with delight by the actor can give no delight at all to others.

I know that there are many who consider that Shakespeare is more for the study than for the stage. With this view I do not for a moment agree. Shakespeare wrote his plays to be acted, and we have no right to alter the form which he himself selected for the full expression of his work. Indeed many of the beauties of that work can only be adequately conveyed to us through the actor's art. As I sat in the Town Hall of Oxford the other night, the majesty of the mighty lines of the play seemed to me to gain new music from the clear young voices that uttered them, and the ideal grandeur of the heroism to be made more real to the spectators by the chivalrous bearing, the noble gestures and the fine passion of its exponents. Even the dresses had their dramatic value. Their archaeological accuracy* gave us, immediately on the rise of the curtain, a perfect picture of the time. As the knights and nobles moved across the stage in the flowing robes of peace and in the burnished steel of battle, we needed no dreary chorus to tell us in what age or land the play's action was passing, for the fifteenth century in all the dignity and grace of its apparel was living actually before us, and the delicate harmonies of colour struck from the first a dominant note of beauty which added to the intellectual realism of archæology the sensuous charm of art.

As for individual actors, Mr Mackinnon's* Prince Hal was a most gay and graceful performance, lit here and there with charming touches of princely dignity and of noble feeling. Mr Coleridge's* Falstaff was full of delightful humour, though perhaps at times he did not take us sufficiently into his confidence. An audience looks at a tragedian, but a comedian looks at his audience. However, he gave much pleasure to everyone, and Mr Bourchier's* Hotspur was really most remarkable. Mr Bourchier has a fine stage presence, a beautiful voice, and produces his effects by a method as dramatically impressive as it is artistically right. Once or twice he seemed to me to spoil his last line by walking through it. The part of Harry Percy is one full of climaxes which must not be let slip. But still there was always a freedom and spirit in his style which was very pleasing, and his delivery of the colloquial passages I thought excellent, notably of that in the first act:

> 'What d'ye call the place?
> A plague upon 't—it is in Gloucestershire;—
> 'Twas where the madcap duke his uncle kept,
> His uncle York;'

lines by the way in which Kemble* made a great effect. Mr Bourchier has the opportunity of a fine career on the English stage, and I hope he will take advantage of it. Among the minor parts in the play, Glendower, Mortimer and Sir Richard Vernon, were capitally acted, Worcester was a performance of some subtlety, Mrs Woods was a charming Lady Percy, and Lady Edward Spencer Churchill, as Mortimer's wife, made us all believe that we understood Welsh.* Her dialogue and her song were most pleasing bits of artistic realism which fully accounted for the Celtic chair at Oxford.

But though I have mentioned particular actors, the real value of the whole representation was to be found in its absolute unity, in its delicate sense of proportion, and in that breadth of effect which is to be got only by the most careful elaboration of detail. I have rarely seen a production better stage-managed. Indeed I hope that the University will take some official notice of this delightful work of art. Why should not degrees be granted for good acting? Are they not given to those who misunderstand Plato and who mistranslate Aristotle? And should the artist be passed over? No. To Prince Hal, Hotspur, and Falstaff, D.C.L.'s* should be gracefully offered. I feel sure they would be gracefully accepted. To the rest of the company the crimson or the sheep-skin hood* might be assigned *honoris causâ*, to the eternal confusion of the Philistine, and the rage of the industrious and the dull. Thus would Oxford confer honour on herself, and the artist be placed in his proper position. However, whether or not convocation recognises the claims of culture, I hope that the Oxford Dramatic Society will produce every summer for us some noble play like *Henry IV*. For in plays of this kind, plays which deal with bygone times, there is always this peculiar charm, that they combine in one exquisite presentation the passions that are living with the picturesqueness that is dead. And when we have the modern spirit given to us in an antique form, the very remoteness of that form can be made a method of increased realism. This was Shakespeare's own attitude towards the ancient world, this is the attitude we in this century should adopt towards his plays, and with a feeling akin to this it seemed to me that these brilliant young Oxonians were working. If it was so, their aim is the right one. For while we look to the dramatist to give romance to realism, we ask of the actor to give realism to romance.

OLIVIA AT THE LYCEUM[1]

WHETHER or not it is an advantage for a novel to be produced in a dramatic form, is, I think, open to question. The psychological analysis of such work as that of Mr George Meredith, for instance, would probably lose by being transmuted into the passionate action of the stage, nor does M Zola's '*formule scientifique*'* gain anything at all by theatric presentation. With Goldsmith* it is somewhat different. In 'The Vicar of Wakefield'* he seeks simply to please his readers, and desires not to prove a theory; he looks on life rather as a picture

---

[1] 30 May 1885. A review of W. G. Wills's *Olivia*, produced by Henry Irving at the Lyceum Theatre.

to be painted than as a problem to be solved; his aim is to create men and women more than to vivisect them; his dialogue is essentially dramatic, and his novel seems to pass naturally into the dramatic form. And to me there is something very pleasurable in seeing and studying the same subject under different conditions of art. For life remains eternally unchanged; it is art which, by presenting it to us under various forms, enables us to realise its many-sided mysteries, and to catch the quality of its most fiery-coloured moments. The originality, I mean, which we ask from the artist, is originality of treatment, not of subject. It is only the unimaginative who ever invent. The true artist is known by the use he makes of what he annexes, and he annexes everything.*

Looking in this light at Mr Wills's *Olivia*,* it seems to me a very exquisite work of art. Indeed, I know no other dramatist who could have retold this beautiful English tale with such tenderness and such power, neither losing the charm of the old story nor forgetting the conditions of the new form. The sentiment of the poet and the science of the playwright are exquisitely balanced in it. For though in prose it is a poem, and while a poem it is also a play.

But fortunate as Mr Wills has been in the selection of his subject and in his treatment of it, he is no less fortunate in the actors who interpret his work. To whatever character Miss Terry plays she brings the infinite charm of her beauty, and the marvellous grace of her movements and gestures. It is impossible to escape from the sweet tyranny of her personality. She dominates her audience by the secret of Cleopatra. In her Olivia, however, it is not merely her personality that fascinates us but her power also, her power over pathos, and her command of situation. The scene in which she bade good-bye to her family was touching beyond any scene I remember in any modern play, yet no harsh or violent note was sounded: and when in the succeeding act she struck in natural and noble indignation the libertine who had betrayed her, there was, I think, no one in the theatre who did not recognise that in Miss Terry our stage possesses a really great artist, who can thrill an audience without harrowing it, and by means that seem simple and easy can produce the finest dramatic effects. Mr Irving, as Dr Primrose, intensified the beautiful and blind idolatry of the old pastor for his daughter till his own tragedy seemed almost greater than hers; the scene in the third act, where he breaks down in his attempt to reprove the lamb that has strayed from the fold, was a masterpiece of fine acting; and the whole performance, while carefully elaborate in detail, was full of breadth and dignity. I acknowledge that I liked him least at the close of the second act. It seems to me that here we should be made to feel not merely the passionate rage of the father, but the powerlessness of the old man. The taking down of the pistols, and the attempt to follow the young duellist, are pathetic because they are useless, and I hardly think that Mr Irving conveyed this idea. As regards the rest of the characters, Mr Terriss'* Squire Thornhill was an admirable picture of a fascinating young rake. Indeed it was so fascinating that the moral equilibrium of the audience was quite disturbed, and nobody seemed to care very much for the virtuous Mr Burchell. I was not sorry to see this triumph of the artistic over the ethical sympathy. Perfect heroes are the monsters of melodramas, and have no place in dramatic art. Life possibly contains them, but Parnassus often rejects what Peckham may welcome. I look forward to a reaction in favour of the cultured criminal. Mr Norman Forbes was a very pleasing Moses, and gave his Latin quotations charmingly, Miss Emery's* Sophy was most winning, and indeed every part seemed to me well acted except that of the virtuous Mr Burchell. This fact, however, rather pleased me than otherwise, as it increased the charm of his attractive nephew.

The scenery and costumes were excellent, as indeed they always are at the Lyceum when the piece is produced under Mr Irving's direction. The first scene was really very beautiful, and quite as good as the famous cherry orchard of the Théâtre-Français.* A critic who posed as an authority on field sports assured me that no one ever went out hunting when roses were in full bloom. Personally, that is exactly the season I would select for the chase, but then I know more about flowers than I do about foxes, and like them much better. If the critic was right, either the roses must wither, or Squire Thornhill must change his coat. A more serious objection may be brought against the division of the last act into three scenes. There I think there was a distinct dramatic loss. The room to which Olivia returns should have been exactly the same room she had left. As a picture of the eighteenth century, however, the whole production was admirable, and the details, both of acting and of *mise-en-scène*, wonderfully perfect. I wish Olivia would take off her pretty mittens when her fortune is being told. Chiromancy* is a science which deals almost entirely with the lines on the palm of the hand, and mittens would seriously interfere with its mysticism.

Still, when all is said, how easily does this lovely play, this artistic presentation, survive criticisms founded on chiromancy and cub-hunting! The Lyceum under Mr Irving's management has become a centre of art. We are all of us in his debt. I trust that we may see some more plays by living dramatists produced at his theatre, for *Olivia* has been exquisitely mounted and exquisitely played.

AS YOU LIKE IT AT COOMBE HOUSE[1]

IN Théophile Gautier's first novel,* that golden book of spirit and sense, that holy writ of beauty, there is a most fascinating account of an amateur performance of *As You Like It* in the large orangery of a French country house. Yet, lovely as Gautier's description is, the real presentation of the play last week at Coombe* seemed to me lovelier still, for not merely were there present in it all those elements of poetry and picturesqueness which *le maître impeccable* so desired, but to them was added also the exquisite charm of the open woodland and the delightful freedom of the open air. Nor indeed could the Pastoral Players have made a more fortunate selection of a play. A tragedy under the same conditions would have been impossible. For tragedy is the exaggeration of the individual, and nature thinks nothing of dwarfing a hero by a holly bush, and reducing a heroine to a mere effect of colour. The subtleties also of facial expression are in the open air almost entirely lost, and while this would be a serious defect in the presentation of a play which deals immediately with psychology, in the case of a comedy, where the situations predominate over the characters, we do not feel it nearly so much; and Shakespeare himself seems to have clearly recognised this difference, for while he had *Hamlet* and *Macbeth* always played by artificial light he acted *As You Like It* and the rest of his comedies *en plein jour*.

The condition then under which this comedy was produced by Lady Archiebald Campbell* and Mr Godwin did not place any great limitations on the actor's art, and increased tenfold the value of the play as a picture. Through an alley of white hawthorn and gold

---

[1] 6 June 1885. A review of Shakespeare's *As You Like It*, produced by Lady Archibald Campbell and E. W. Godwin at Coombe House.

laburnum we passed into the green pavilion that served as the theatre, the air sweet with odour of the lilac and with the blackbird's song; and when the curtain fell into its trench of flowers, and the play commenced, we saw before us a real forest, and we knew it to be Arden. For with whoop and shout, up through the rustling fern came the foresters trooping, the banished Duke took his seat beneath the tall elm, and as his lords lay around him on the grass, the rich melody of Shakespeare's blank verse began to reach our ears. And all through the performance this delightful sense of joyous woodland life was sustained, and even when the scene was left empty for the shepherd to drive his flock across the sward, or for Rosalind to school Orlando in love-making, far away we could hear the shrill halloo of the hunter, and catch now and then the faint music of some distant horn. One distinct dramatic advantage was gained by the *mise-en-scène*. The abrupt exits and entrances, which are necessitated on the real stage by the inevitable limitations of space, were in many cases done away with, and we saw the characters coming gradually towards us through brake and underwood, or passing away down the slope till they were lost in some deep recess of the forest; the effect of distance thus gained being largely increased by the faint wreaths of blue mist that floated at times across the background. Indeed I never saw an illustration at once so perfect and so practical of the æsthetic value of smoke.

As for the players themselves the pleasing naturalness of their method harmonised delightfully with their natural surroundings. Those of them who were amateurs were too artistic to be stagy, and those who were actors too experienced to be artificial. The humorous sadness of Jaques, that philosopher in search of sensations, found a perfect exponent in Mr Hermann Vezin.* Touchstone has been so often acted as a low comedy part that Mr Elliott's rendering of the swift sententious fool was a welcome change, and a more graceful and winning Phœbe than Mrs Plowden,* a more tender Celia than Miss Schletter, a more realistic Audrey than Miss Fulton, I have never seen. Rosalind suffered a good deal through the omission of the first act; we saw, I mean, more of the saucy boy than we did of the noble girl; and though the *persiflage* always told, the poetry was often lost; still Miss Calhoun* gave much pleasure; and Lady Archiebald Campbell's Orlando was a really remarkable performance. Too melancholy some seemed to think it. Yet is not Orlando love-sick? Too

dreamy, I heard it said. Yet Orlando is a poet. And even admitting
that the vigour of the lad who tripped up the Duke's wrestler was
hardly sufficiently emphasised, still in the low music of Lady Archiebald Campbell's voice, and in the strange beauty of her movements
and gestures, there was a wonderful fascination, and the visible presence of romance quite consoled me for the possible absence of
robustness. Among the other characters should be mentioned Mr
Claude Ponsonby's First Lord, Mr De Cordova's Corin, a bit of
excellent acting, and the Silvius of Mr Webster.

As regards the costumes the colour-scheme was very perfect.
Brown and green were the dominant notes, and yellow was most
artistically used. There were however two distinct discords. Touchstone's motley was far too glaring, and the crude white of Rosalind's
bridal raiment in the last act was absolutely displeasing. A contrast
may be striking but should never be harsh. And lovely in colour as
Mrs Plowden's dress was, a sort of panegyric on a pansy, I am afraid
that in Shakespeare's Arden there were no Chelsea China Shepherdesses,* and I am sure that the romance of Phœbe does not need to be
intensified by any reminiscences of porcelain. Still, *As You Like It*
has probably never been so well mounted, nor costumes worn with
more ease and simplicity. Not the least charming part of the whole
production was the music, which was under the direction of the
Rev. Arthur Batson.* The boys' voices were quite exquisite, and Mr
Walsham* sang with much spirit.

On the whole the Pastoral Players are to be warmly congratulated
on the success of their representation, and to the artistic sympathies
of Lady Archiebald Campbell, and the artistic knowledge of Mr
Godwin, I am indebted for a most delightful afternoon. Few things
are so pleasurable as to be able by an hour's drive to exchange
Piccadilly for Parnassus.*

TWELFTH NIGHT AT OXFORD[1]

ON Saturday last the new theatre at Oxford* was opened by the
University Dramatic Society. The play selected was Shakespeare's
delightful comedy of *Twelfth Night*, a play eminently suitable for

[1] 20 February 1886. A review of Shakespeare's *Twelfth Night*, produced by the
Oxford University Dramatic Society at the New Theatre, Oxford.

performance by a club, as it contains so many good acting parts. Shakespeare's tragedies may be made for a single star, but his comedies are made for a galaxy of constellations. In the first he deals with the pathos of the individual, in the second he gives us a picture of life. The Oxford undergraduates, then, are to be congratulated on the selection of the play, and the result fully justified their choice. Mr Bourchier as Feste the clown was easy, graceful, and joyous, as fanciful as his dress and as funny as his bauble. The beautiful songs which Shakespeare has assigned to this character were rendered by him as charmingly as they were dramatically. To act singing is quite as great an art as to sing. Mr Letchmere Stuart was a delightful Sir Andrew, and gave much pleasure to the audience. One may hate the villains of Shakespeare, but one cannot help loving his fools. Mr Macpherson was perhaps hardly equal to such an immortal part as that of Sir Toby Belch, though there was much that was clever in his performance. Mr Lindsay threw new and unexpected light on the character of Fabian, and Mr Clark's Malvolio was a most remarkable piece of acting. What a difficult part Malvolio is! Shakespeare undoubtedly meant us to laugh all through at the pompous steward, and to join in the practical joke upon him, and yet how impossible not to feel a good deal of sympathy with him! Perhaps in this century we are too altruistic to be really artistic. Hazlitt says somewhere* that poetical justice is done him in the uneasiness which Olivia suffers on account of her mistaken attachment to Cesario, as her insensibility to the violence of the Duke's passion is atoned for by the discovery of Viola's concealed love for him; but it is difficult not to feel Malvolio's treatment is unnecessarily harsh. Mr Clark, however, gave a very clever rendering, full of subtle touches. If I ventured on a bit of advice, which I feel most reluctant to do, it would be to the effect that while one should always study the method of a great artist, one should never imitate his manner. The manner of an artist is essentially individual, the method of an artist is absolutely universal. The first is personality, which no one should copy; the second is perfection, which all should aim at. Miss Arnold was a most sprightly Maria, and Miss Farmer a dignified Olivia; but as Viola Mrs Bewicke was hardly successful. Her manner was too boisterous and her method too modern. Where there is violence there is no Viola, where there is no illusion there is no Illyria, where there is no style there is no Shakespeare. Mr Higgins looked the part of Sebastian to perfection, and some of the minor characters were excellently played by Mr Adderley, Mr King-Harman, Mr Coningsby Disraeli,* and Lord Albert Osborne. On the whole, the performance reflected much credit on the Dramatic Society; indeed, its excellence was such that I am led to hope that the University will some day have a theatre of its own, and that proficiency in scene-painting will be regarded as a necessary qualification for the Slade Professorship.* On the stage, literature returns to life and archæology becomes art. A fine theatre is a temple where all the muses may meet, a second Parnassus, and the dramatic spirit, though she has long tarried at Cambridge, seems now to be migrating to Oxford.

> 'Thebes did her green unknowing youth engage;
> She chooses Athens in her riper age.'*

THE CENCI[1]

THE production of the *Cenci** last week at the Grand Theatre, Islington, may be said to have been an era in the literary history of this century, and the Shelley Society deserves the highest praise and warmest thanks of all for having given us an opportunity of seeing Shelley's play under the conditions he himself desired for it. For the *Cenci* was written absolutely with a view to theatric presentation, and had Shelley's own wishes been carried out it would have been produced during his lifetime at Covent Garden, with Edmund Kean and Miss O'Neill* in the principal parts. In working out his conception, Shelley had studied very carefully the æsthetics of dramatic art. He saw that the essence of the drama is disinterested presentation, and that the characters must not be merely mouthpieces for splendid poetry but must be living subjects for terror and for pity. 'I have endeavoured,' he says, 'as nearly as possible to represent the characters as they probably were, and have sought to avoid the error of making them actuated by my own conception of right or wrong, false or true, thus, under a thin veil, converting names and actions of the sixteenth century into cold impersonations of my own mind. I have avoided with great care the introduction of what is commonly called

[1] 15 May 1886. A review of Percy Bysshe Shelley's *The Cenci*, produced by the Shelley Society and E. W. Godwin at the Grand Theatre, Islington.

mere poetry, and I imagine there will scarcely be found a detached simile or a single isolated description, unless Beatrice's description of the chasm appointed for her father's murder should be judged to be of that nature.' He recognised that a dramatist must be allowed far greater freedom of expression than what is conceded to a poet. 'In a dramatic composition,' to use his own words, 'the imagery and the passion should interpenetrate one another, the former being reserved simply for the full development and illustration of the latter. Imagination is as the immortal God, which should assume flesh for the redemption of mortal passion. It is thus that the most remote and the most familiar imagery may alike be fit for dramatic purposes when employed in the illustration of strong feeling, which raises what is low, and levels to the apprehension that which is lofty, casting over all the shadow of its own greatness. In other respects I have written more carelessly, that is, without an over-fastidious and learned choice of words. In this respect I entirely agree with those modern critics, who assert that in order to move men to true sympathy we must use the familiar language of men.' He knew that if the dramatist is to teach at all it must be by example, not by precept. 'The highest moral purpose,' he remarks, 'aimed at in the highest species of the drama, is the teaching the human heart, through its sympathies and antipathies, the knowledge of itself; in proportion to the possession of which knowledge every human being is wise, just, sincere, tolerant, and kind. If dogmas can do more it is well, but a drama is no fit place for the enforcement of them.' He fully realised that it is by a conflict between our artistic sympathies and our moral judgment that the greatest dramatic effects are produced. 'It is in the restless and anatomising casuistry with which men seek the justification of Beatrice, yet feel that she has done what needs justification; it is in the superstitious horror with which they contemplate alike her wrongs and their revenge, that the dramatic character of what she did and suffered consists.'* In fact no one has more clearly understood than Shelley the mission of the dramatist and the meaning of the drama.

And yet I hardly think that the production of the *Cenci*, its absolute presentation on the stage, can be said to have added anything to its beauty, its pathos, or even its realism. Not that the principal actors were at all unworthy of the work of art they interpreted; Mr Hermann Vezin's Cenci was a noble and magnificent performance; Miss

Alma Murray stands now in the very first rank of our English actresses as a mistress of power and pathos; and Mr Leonard Outram's* Orsino was most subtle and artistic; but that the *Cenci* needs for the production of its perfect effect no interpretation at all. It is, as we read it, a complete work of art—capable, indeed, of being acted, but not dependent on theatric presentation; and the impression produced by its exhibition on the stage seemed to me to be merely one of pleasure at the gratification of an intellectual curiosity of seeing how far Melpomene could survive the wagon of Thespis.

In producing the play, however, the members of the Shelley Society were merely carrying out the poet's own wishes, and they are to be congratulated on the success of their experiment—a success due not to any gorgeous scenery or splendid pageant, but to the excellence of the actors who aided them.

HELENA IN TROAS[1]

ONE might have thought that to have produced *As You Like It* in an English forest would have satisfied the most ambitious spirit; but Mr Godwin has not contented himself with his sylvan triumphs. From Shakespeare he has passed to Sophokles, and has given us the most perfect exhibition of a Greek dramatic performance that has as yet been seen in this country. For beautiful as were the productions of the *Agamemnon* at Oxford and the *Eumenides** at Cambridge, their effects were marred in no small or unimportant degree by the want of a proper orchestra for the chorus with its dance and song, a want that was fully supplied in Mr Godwin's presentation by the use of the arena of a circus.*

In the centre of this circle, which was paved with the semblance of tesselated marble, stood the altar of Dionysos, and beyond it rose the long, shallow stage, faced with casts from the temple of Bassae, and bearing the huge portal of the house of Paris and the gleaming battlements of Troy.* Over the portal hung a great curtain, painted with crimson lions, which, when drawn aside, disclosed two massive gates of bronze; in front of the house was placed a golden image of Aphrodite, and across the ramparts on either hand could be seen a stretch

[1] 22 May 1886. A review of John Todhunter's *Helena in Troas*, produced by E. W. Godwin at Hengler's Circus, London.

of blue waters and faint purple hills. The scene was lovely, not merely in the harmony of its colour but in the exquisite delicacy of its architectural proportions. No nation has ever felt the pure beauty of mere construction so strongly as the Greeks, and in this respect Mr Godwin has fully caught the Greek feeling.

The play opened by the entrance of the chorus, white-vestured and gold-filleted, under the leadership of Miss Kinnaird,* whose fine gestures and rhythmic movements were quite admirable. In answer to their appeal, the stage curtains slowly divided, and from the house of Paris came forth Helen herself, in a robe woven with all the wonder of war, and broidered with the pageant of battle. With her were her two handmaidens—one in white and yellow, and one in green; Hecuba followed in sombre grey of mourning, and Priam in kingly garb of gold and purple, and Paris in Phrygian cap* and light archer's dress; and when at sunset the lover of Helen was borne back wounded from the field, down from the oaks of Ida stole Œnone in the flowing drapery of the daughter of a river-god, every fold of her garments rippling like dim water as she moved.

As regards the acting, the two things the Greeks valued most in actors were grace of gesture and music of voice. Indeed, to gain these virtues their actors used to subject themselves to a regular course of gymnastics and a particular *régime* of diet, health being to the Greeks not merely a quality of art, but a condition of its production. Whether or not our English actors hold the same view may be doubted; but Mr Vezin certainly has always recognised the importance of a physical as well as of an intellectual training for the stage, and his performance of King Priam was distinguished by stately dignity and most musical enunciation. With Mr Vezin, grace of gesture is an unconscious result—not a conscious effort. It has become nature, because it was once art. Mr Beerbohm-Tree* also is deserving of very high praise for his Paris. Ease and elegance characterised every movement he made, and his voice was extremely effective. Mr Tree is the perfect Proteus of actors. He can wear the dress of any century and the appearance of any age, and has a marvellous capacity of absorbing his personality into the character he is creating. To have method without mannerism is only given to a few, but among the few is Mr Tree. Miss Alma Murray does not possess the physique requisite for our conception of Helen, but the beauty of her movements and the extremely sympathetic quality of her voice gave an indefinable charm to her performance. Mrs Jopling* looked like a poem from the Parthenon, and, indeed, the *personae mutae* were not the least effective figures in the play. Hecuba was hardly a success. In acting, the impression of sincerity is conveyed by tone, not by mere volume of voice, and whatever influence emotion has on utterance it is certainly not in the direction of false emphasis. Mrs Beerbohm-Tree's* Œnone was much better, and had some fine moments of passion; but the harsh realistic shriek with which the nymph flung herself from the battlements, however effective it might have been in a comedy of Sardou, or in one of Mr Burnand's* farces, was quite out of place in the representation of a Greek tragedy. The classical drama is an imaginative, poetic art, which requires the grand style for its interpretation, and produces its effects by the most ideal means. It is in the operas of Wagner, not in popular melodrama, that any approximation to the Greek method can be found. Better to wear mask and buskin than to mar by any modernity of expression the calm majesty of Melpomene.

As an artistic whole, however, the performance was undoubtedly a great success. It has been much praised for its archæology, but Mr Godwin is something more than a mere antiquarian. He takes the facts of archæology, but he converts them into artistic and dramatic effects, and the historical accuracy, that underlies the visible shapes of beauty that he presents to us, is not by any means the distinguishing quality of the completed work of art. This quality is the absolute unity and harmony of the entire presentation, the presence of one mind controlling the most minute details, and revealing itself only in that true perfection which hides personality. On more than one occasion it seemed to me that the stage was kept a little too dark, and that a purely picturesque effect of light and shade was substituted for the plastic clearness of outline that the Greeks so desired; some objection, too, might be made to the late character of the statue of Aphrodite, which was decidedly post-Periklean; these, however, are unimportant points. The performance was not intended to be an absolute reproduction of the Greek stage in the fifth century before Christ: it was simply the presentation in Greek form of a poem conceived in the Greek spirit; and the secret of its beauty was the perfect correspondence of form and matter, the delicate equilibrium of spirit and sense.

As for the play, it had of course to throw away many sweet

superfluous graces of expression before it could adapt itself to the conditions of theatrical presentation, but much that is good was retained; and the choruses, which really possess some pure notes of lyric loveliness, were sung in their entirety. Here and there, it is true, occur such lines as—

> What wilt thou do? What can the handful still
> Left—

lines that owe their blank-verse character more to the courtesy of the printer than to the genius of the poet, for without rhythm and melody there is no verse at all; and the attempt to fit Greek forms of construction to our English language often gives the work the air of an awkward translation; however, there is a great deal that is pleasing in *Helena in Troas*,* and on the whole the play was worthy of its pageant, and the poem deserved the peplums.

It is much to be regretted that Mr Godwin's beautiful theatre cannot be made a permanent institution. Even looked at from the low standpoint of educational value, such a performance as that given last Monday might be of the greatest service to modern culture; and who knows but a series of these productions might civilise South Kensington and give tone to Brompton? Still, it is something to have shown our artists 'a dream of form in days of thought,' and to have allowed the Philistines to peer into Paradise. And this is what Mr Godwin has done.

THE COURT AND SOCIETY REVIEW

THE AMERICAN INVASION[1]

A TERRIBLE danger is hanging over the Americans in London. Their future, and their reputation this season, depend entirely on the success of Buffalo Bill and Mrs Brown-Potter.* The former is certain to draw; for English people are far more interested in American barbarism than they are in American civilisation. When they sight Sandy Hook, they look to their rifles and ammunition; and after dining once at Delmonico's,* start off for Colorado or California, for Montana or the Yellow Stone Park. Rocky Mountains charm them more than riotous millionaires; they have been known to prefer buffaloes to Boston. Why should they not? The cities of America are inexpressibly tedious. The Bostonians take their learning too sadly; culture with them is an accomplishment rather than an atmosphere; their 'Hub,' as they call it, is the paradise of prigs. Chicago is a sort of monster-shop, full of bustle and bores. Political life at Washington is like political life in a suburban vestry. Baltimore is amusing for a week, but Philadelphia is dreadfully provincial; and though one can dine in New York, one could not dwell there. Better the Far West, with its grizzly bears and untamed cowboys, its free, open-air life and its free, open-air manners, its boundless prairie and its boundless mendacity! This is what Buffalo Bill is going to bring to London; and we have no doubt that London will fully appreciate his show.

With regard to Mrs Brown-Potter, as acting is no longer considered absolutely essential for success on the English stage, there is really no reason why the pretty, bright-eyed lady, who charmed us all last June by her merry laugh and her *nonchalant* ways, should not, to borrow an expression from her native language, make a big boom, and paint the town red. We sincerely hope she will; for, on the whole, the American invasion has done English society a great deal of good. American women are bright, clever, and wonderfully cosmopolitan. Their patriotic feelings are limited to an admiration for Niagara, and

[1] 23 March 1887.

a regret for the Elevated Railway, and, unlike the men, they never bore us with Bunker's Hill.* They take their dresses from Paris, and their manners from Piccadilly, and wear both charmingly. They have a quaint pertness, a delightful conceit, a naïve self-assertion. They insist on being paid compliments, and have almost succeeded in making Englishmen eloquent. For our aristocracy they have an ardent admiration; they adore titles, and are a permanent blow to Republican principles. In the art of amusing men they are adepts, both by nature and education, and can actually tell a story without forgetting the point—an accomplishment that is extremely rare among the women of other countries. It is true that they lack repose, and that their voices are somewhat harsh and strident when they land first at Liverpool; but after a time one gets to love these pretty whirlwinds in petticoats, that sweep so recklessly through society, and are so agitating to all duchesses who have daughters. There is something fascinating in their funny, exaggerated gestures, and their petulant way of tossing the head. Their eyes have no magic nor mystery in them, but they challenge us for combat; and when we engage, we are always worsted. Their lips seem made for laughter, and yet they never grimace. As for their voices, they soon get them into tune. Some of them have been known to acquire a fashionable drawl in two seasons; and after they have been presented to Royalty they roll their R's as vigorously as a young equerry or an old lady-in-waiting. Still, they never really lose their accent, it keeps peeping out here and there, and when they chatter together they are like a bevy of peacocks. Nothing is more amusing than to watch two American girls greeting each other in a drawing room or in the Row. They are like children, with their shrill *staccato* cries of wonder, their odd little exclamations. Their conversation sounds like a series of exploding crackers; they are exquisitely incoherent, and use a sort of primitive, emotional language. After five minutes, they are left beautifully breathless, and look at each other, half in amusement and half in affection. If a stolid young Englishman is fortunate enough to be introduced to them, he is amazed at their extraordinary vivacity; their electric quickness of repartee; their inexhaustible store of curious catchwords. He never really understands them, for their thoughts flutter about with a sweet irresponsibility of butterflies; but he is pleased and amused, and feels as if he were in an aviary. On the whole, American girls have a wonderful charm, and, perhaps, the chief secret of their charm is that they never talk seriously, except to their dressmaker, and never think seriously, except about amusements.*

They have, however, one grave fault—their mothers.

Dreary as were those old Pilgrim Fathers, who left our shores more than two centuries ago to found a New England beyond seas, the Pilgrim Mothers, who have returned to us in the nineteenth century, are drearier still. Here and there, of course, there are exceptions, but as a class they are either dull, dowdy, or dyspeptic. It is only fair to the rising generation of America to state that they are not to blame for this. Indeed, they spare no pains at all to bring up their parents properly, and to give them a suitable, if somewhat late, education. From its earliest years, every American child spends most of its time correcting the faults of its father and mother; and no one who has had the opportunity of watching an American family on the deck of an Atlantic steamer, or in the refined seclusion of a New York boarding-house, can fail to have been struck by this characteristic of their civilisation. In America, the young are always ready to give to those who are older than themselves the full benefits of their inexperience.* A boy of only eleven or twelve years of age will firmly, but kindly, point out to his father his defects of manner or temper; will never weary of warning him against extravagance, idleness, late hours, unpunctuality, and the other temptations to which the aged are so particularly exposed; and sometimes, should he fancy that he is monopolising too much of the conversation at dinner, will remind him, across the table, of the new child's adage, 'Parents should be seen, not heard.' Nor does any mistaken idea of kindness prevent the little American girl from censuring her mother whenever it is necessary. Often, indeed, feeling that a rebuke conveyed in the presence of others is more truly efficacious than one merely whispered in the quiet of the nursery, she will call the attention of perfect strangers to her mother's general untidiness, her want of intellectual Boston conversation, immoderate love of iced-water and green corn, stinginess in the matter of candy, ignorance of the usages of the best Baltimore society, bodily ailments, and the like. In fact, it may truly be said that no American child is ever blind to the deficiencies of its parents, no matter how much it may love them.

Yet, somehow, this educational system has not been so successful as it deserved. In many cases, no doubt, the material with which the

children had to deal was crude and incapable of real development;
but the fact remains that the American mother is a tedious person.
The American father is better, for he is never seen in London. He
passes his life entirely in Wall Street, and communicates with his
family once a month by means of a telegram in cipher. The mother,
however, is always with us, and, lacking the quick imaginative faculty
of the younger generation, remains uninteresting and provincial to
the last. In spite of her, however, the American girl is always welcome. She brightens our dull dinner parties for us, and makes life go
pleasantly by for a season. In the race for coronets she often carries
off the prize; but once that she has gained the victory, she is generous, and forgives her English rivals everything, even their beauty.
Warned by the examples of her mother that American women do not
grow old gracefully, she tries not to grow old at all, and often succeeds. She has exquisite feet and hands, is always *bien chausée et bien
gantée*,* and can talk brilliantly upon any subject, provided she knows
nothing about it. Her sense of humour keeps her from the tragedy of
a *grande passion*, and, as there is neither romance nor humility in her
love, she makes an excellent wife. What her ultimate influence on
English life will be, it is difficult to estimate at present; but there can
be no doubt that of all the factors that have contributed to the social
revolution of London, there are few more important, and none more
delightful, than the American invasion.

THE AMERICAN MAN[1]

ONE of our prettiest Duchesses enquired the other day of a distinguished traveller whether there was really such a thing as an
American man, explaining, as the reason for her question, that,
though she knew many fascinating American women, she had never
come across any fathers, grandfathers, uncles, brothers, husbands,
cousins, or, indeed, male relatives of any kind whatsoever.

The exact answer the Duchess received is not worth recording, as
it took the depressing form of useful and accurate information; but
there can be no doubt that the subject is an extremely interesting
one, pointing, as it does, to the curious fact that, as far as society is

[1] 13 April 1887.

concerned, the American invasion has been purely female in character. With the exception of the United States Minister, always a welcome personage wherever he goes, and an occasional lion from Boston* or the Far West, no American man has any social existence in London. His women-folk, with their wonderful dresses, and still more wonderful dialogue, shine in our *salons*, and delight our dinner-parties; our guardsmen are taken captive by their brilliant complexions, and our beauties made jealous by their clever wit; but the poor American man remains permanently in the background, and never rises beyond the level of the tourist. Now and then he makes an appearance in the Row,* looking a somewhat strange figure in his long frock-coat of glossy black cloth, and his sensible soft-felt hat; but his favourite haunt is the Strand, and the American Exchange his idea of Heaven. When he is not lounging in a rocking-chair with a cigar, he is loafing through the streets with a carpet bag, gravely taking stock of our products, and trying to understand Europe through the medium of the shop window. He is M Renan's *l'homme sensuel moyen*, Mr Arnold's middle-class Philistine.* The telephone is his test of civilisation, and his wildest dreams of Utopia do not rise above elevated railways and electric bells. His chief pleasure is to get hold of some unsuspecting stranger, or some sympathetic countryman, and then to indulge in the national game of 'matching.' With a *naivete* and a nonchalance that are absolutely charming, he will gravely compare St James' Palace to the grand central depot at Chicago, or Westminster Abbey to the Falls of Niagara. Bulk is his canon of beauty, and size his standard of excellence. To him the greatness of a country consists in the number of square miles that it contains; and he is never tired of telling the waiters at his hotel that the State of Texas is larger than France and Germany put together.

Yet, on the whole, he is happier in London than anywhere else in Europe. Here he can always make a few acquaintances, and, as a rule, can speak the language. Abroad, he is terribly at sea. He knows no one, and understands nothing, and wanders about in a melancholy manner, treating the Old World as if it were a Broadway store, and each city a counter for the sampling of shoddy goods. For him Art has no marvel, and Beauty no meaning, and the Past no message. He thinks that civilisation began with the introduction of steam, and looks with contempt upon all centuries that had no hot-water apparatuses in their houses. The ruin and decay of Time has no pathos in his eyes. He turns away from Ravenna, because the grass grows in her streets, and can see no loveliness in Verona,* because there is rust on her balconies. His one desire is to get the whole of Europe into thorough repair. He is severe on the modern Romans for not covering the Colosseum with a glass roof, and utilising the building as a warehouse for dry goods. In a word, he is the Don Quixote of common sense,* for he is so utilitarian that he is absolutely unpractical. As a *compagnon de voyage* he is not desirable, for he always looks *deplacé*,* and feels depressed. Indeed, he would die of weariness if he were not in constant telegraphic communication with Wall Street; and the only thing that can console him for having wasted a day in a picture-gallery is a copy of the New York Herald or the Boston Times. Finally, having looked at everything, and seen nothing, he returns to his native land.

There he is delightful. For the strange thing about American civilisation is, that the women are most charming when they are away from their own country, the men most charming when they are at home.

At home, the American man is the best of companions, as he is the most hospitable of hosts. The young men are especially pleasant, with their bright, handsome eyes, their unwearying energy, their amusing shrewdness. They seem to get a hold on life much earlier than we do. At an age when we are still boys at Eton, or lads at Oxford,* they are practising some important profession, making money in some intricate business. Real experience comes to them so much sooner than it does to us, that they are never awkward, never shy, and never say foolish things, except when they ask one how the Hudson River compares with the Rhine, or whether Brooklyn Bridge is not really more impressive than the dome of St Paul's. Their education is quite different from ours. They know men much better than they know books, and life interests them more than literature. They have no time to study anything but the stock markets, no leisure to read anything but newspapers. Indeed, it is only the women in America who have any leisure at all; and, as a necessary result of this curious state of things, there is no doubt but that, within a century from now, the whole culture of the New World will be in petticoats. Yet, though these cute young speculators may not have culture, in the sense in which we use it, as the knowledge of the best that has been thought and said in the world, they are by no means dull. There is no such thing as a stupid American. Many Americans are horrid, vulgar, intrusive, and impertinent, just as many English people are also; but stupidity is not one of the national vices. Indeed, in America there is no opening for a fool. They expect brains even from a boot-black,* and get them.

As for marriage, it is one of their most popular institutions. The American man marries early, and the American woman marries often; and they get on extremely well together. From childhood, the husband has been brought up on the most elaborate fetch-and-carry system, and his reverence for the sex has a touch of compulsory chivalry about it; while the wife exercises an absolute despotism, based upon female assertion, and tempered by womanly charm. On the whole, the great success of marriage in the States is due partly to the fact that no American man is ever idle, and partly to the fact that no American wife is considered responsible for the quality of her husband's dinners. In America, the horrors of domesticity are almost entirely unknown. There are no scenes over the soup, nor quarrels over the *entrées*, and as, by a clause inserted into every marriage settlement, the husband solemnly binds himself to use studs and not buttons for his shirts, one of the chief sources of disagreement in ordinary middle-class life is absolutely removed. The habit also of residing in hotels and boarding-houses does away with any necessity for those tedious *tête-à-têtes* that are the dream of engaged couples, and the despair of married men. Vulgarising though a *table-d'hôte* may be, it is at least better than that eternal duologue about bills and babies to which Benedict and Beatrice* so often sink, when one has lost his wit, and the other her beauty. Even the American freedom of divorce, questionable though it undoubtedly is on many grounds, has at least the merit of bringing into marriage a new element of romantic uncertainty. When people are tied together for life they too often regard manners as a mere superfluity, and courtesy as a thing of no moment; but where the bond can be easily broken, its very fragility makes its strength, and reminds the husband that he should always try to please, and the wife that she should never cease to be charming.

As a consequence of this liberty of action, or, it may be, in spite of it, scandals are extremely rare in America, and should one occur, so paramount in society is female influence, that it is the man who is never forgiven. America is the only country in the world where Don

Juan is not appreciated, and where there is sympathy for Georges Dandin.*

On the whole, then, the American man at home is a very worthy person. There is just one point in which he is disappointing. American humour is a mere travellers' tale. It has no real existence. Indeed, so far from being humorous, the male American is the most abnormally serious creature who ever existed. He talks of Europe as being old; but it is he himself who has never been young. He knows nothing of the irresponsible light-heartedness of boyhood, of the graceful *insouciance* of animal spirits. He has always been prudent, always practical, and pays a heavy penalty for having committed no mistakes. It is only fair to admit that he can exaggerate; but even his exaggeration has a rational basis. It is not founded on wit or fancy; it does not spring from any poetic imagination; it is simply an earnest attempt on the part of language to keep pace with the enormous size of the country. It is evident that where it takes one twenty-four hours to go across a single parish, and seven days' steady railway travelling* to keep a dinner engagement in another State, the ordinary resources of human speech are quite inadequate to the strain put on them, and new linguistic forms have to be invented, new methods of description resorted to. But this is nothing more than the fatal influence of geography upon adjectives; for naturally humorous the American man certainly is not. It is true that when we meet him in Europe his conversation keeps us in fits of laughter; but this is merely because his ideas are so absolutely incongruous with European surroundings. Place him in his own environment, in the midst of the civilisation that he has made for himself, and the life that is the work of his own hands, and the very same observations will fail even to excite a smile. They have sunk to the level of the commonplace truism, or the sensible remark; and what seemed a paradox when we listened to it in London, becomes a platitude when we hear it in Milwaukee.

America has never quite forgiven Europe for having been discovered somewhat earlier in history than itself. Yet how immense are its obligations to us! How enormous its debt! To gain a reputation for humour, its men have to come to London; to be famous for their *toilettes*, its women have to shop in Paris.

Yet, though the American man may not be humorous, he is certainly humane. He is keenly conscious of the fact that there is a great deal of human nature in man, and tries to be pleasant to every stranger who lands on his shores. He has a healthy freedom from all antiquated prejudices, regards introductions as a foolish relic of mediæval etiquette, and makes every chance visitor feel that he is the favoured guest of a great nation. If the English girl ever met him, she would marry him; and if she married him, she would be happy. For, though he may be rough in manner, and deficient in the picturesque insincerity of romance, yet he is invariably kind and thoughtful, and has succeeded in making his own country the Paradise of Women.

This, however, is perhaps the reason why, like Eve,* the women are always so anxious to get out of it.

THE BUTTERFLY'S BOSWELL[1]*

EVERY great man nowadays has his disciples, and it is usually Judas who writes the biography.* Mr Whistler, however, is more fortunate than most of his *confrères*, as he has found in Mr Walter Dowdeswell* the most ardent of admirers, indeed we might almost say that most sympathetic of secretaries.

In the current number of the *Art Journal*, Mr Walter Dowdeswell publishes a very valuable account of Mr Whistler's life and work, and gives us an extremely graphic picture of this remarkable artist, from his tall hat and wand, of which an illustration is duly given, down to the sly smile that we have all heard echoing through the Suffolk Street Gallery on the occasion of a private view, and that used, in old days, to deafen the Royal Academicians at their annual *soirée*.

From Mr Dowdeswell's interesting monograph we learn that Mr Whistler is of most ancient English lineage. Indeed his family tree seems to go back perilously near to those old mediæval days that he himself has often so charmingly satirized, and always so cleverly misunderstood. The particular branch, however, from which the President of the British Artists is immediately descended is partly Irish and American, a fact that explains a great deal of the peculiar quality of his wonderful wit, just as to his early residence in Russia, where his father was a distinguished engineer, we may attribute the origin of that winning and fascinating manner that makes the

---

[1] 20 April 1887. Walter Dowdeswell, 'Mr Whistler', *Art Journal* (April 1887), 97–103.

disciples murmur to each other after each exhibition, '*Grattez le maître, et vous trouverez le Tartare!*'*

On his father's death, Mr Whistler seems to have returned to America, where in a short time we find him a cadet at West Point. Nature, however, seeing that he was destined to be a Velasquez, not a *Vilainton*, brought his military career to a premature and inglorious end, and we next come across him at Paris, in the *atelier* of Gleyre.* His Paris successes are well-known; but like all true Americans, he gravitated towards England, and having thrilled France with the strange beauty of his 'White Girl', a picture exhibited at the *Salon des Refusés*,* he crossed over to London, where, according to Mr Dowdeswell, he discovered the Thames.

From this point on, the article becomes extremely interesting, and Mr Dowdeswell displays a really remarkable power, not merely of writing, but of writing from dictation, especially in his very generous and appreciative estimate of Mr Whistler's genius. We are glad, too, to notice Mr Dowdeswell's distinct recognition of the complete absence from Mr Whistler's work of any alien quality, and of the great service he has rendered to Art by his absolute separation of painting from literature. Before the fortunate arrival of Mr Whistler on these benighted but expectant shores, our English painters, with but few exceptions, had spent their wicked and wasted lives in poaching upon the domain of the poets, marring their motives by clumsy treatment, and striving to render, by visible form and colour, the marvel of what is invisible, the splendour of what is not seen. Now that the *cénacle* is well established in Suffolk Street,* and the style of the master has produced the school of mediocrity, we have every reason to hope that the old state of things has passed away. For the domain of the painter is widely different from the domain of the poet. To the latter belongs Life in its full and absolute entirety; not only the world that men look at, but the world that men listen to also; not merely the momentary grace of form, or the transient gladness of colour, but the whole sphere of feeling, the perfect cycle of thought, the growth and progress of passion, the spiritual development of the soul. The painter is so far limited, that it is only through the mask of the body that he can show us the mystery of the soul; only through images that he can handle ideas; only through its physical equivalents that he can deal with psychology. And how inadequately does he do it then, asking us to accept a blackamoor with a frown for the noble rage of Othello, and an old gentleman in a storm for the wild madness of Lear.*

Yet, in emphasising the painter's limitation of subject matter, Mr Whistler has not, by any means, limited the painter's vision. It would be more just to say that he has pointed out possibilities of beauty hitherto undreamt of, and that by his keen critical faculty, no less than by the dominance of his assertive personality, he has given to Art itself a new creative impulse. Indeed, when the true history of Art comes to be written, a task that Mr Whistler is eminently capable of doing himself, at least in the form of an autobiography, there can be no doubt but that his name will stand high among the highest on its record, for he has opened the eyes of the blind, and given great encouragement to the short-sighted.

The best answer, however, to those who would censure him for suffering the poet to sing in peace, and mock at him for leaving to literature its proper province, is the rare and exquisite wonder of his own work; and not its wonder merely, but its width also, its mastery over all chords, its possession of all secrets. There is nothing of the specialist in Mr Whistler. As he can deal with every medium, so he can appeal to every mood. Some of his arrangements in colour, such as the 'Little Grey Note,' or the 'Note in Blue and Opal,' have all the delicate loveliness of lyrics. The silver silences of his nocturnes seem at times almost passing into music. He has done etchings with the brilliancy of epigrams, and pastels with the charm of paradoxes, and many of his portraits are pure works of fiction.*

On the whole, then, the biography in the *Art Journal*, is well worth reading. It is not, of course, complete, and some of the most distinguishing characteristics of Mr Whistler's nature are hardly alluded to at all. Still, as Mr Whistler once himself remarked, no man alive is life-size; and it would be ungracious to criticize with too much severity an article that shows such memory on the part of the writer, and such journalistic ability on the part of the subject. For one thing, however, we hope that Mr Dowdeswell is not responsible. Previous to this article's publication, there appeared in the daily newspapers an extremely vulgar and blatant advertisement, which ultimately found its way into the pages of some of the catalogues at the Suffolk Street Private View. It would be sad to think that a disciple so devoted as Mr Dowdeswell has shown himself to be could have thus desecrated the dignity of his master; for, while it is all very well to be the Butterfly's Boswell, to be the Butterfly's Barnum* is immodest, and unnecessary.

THE CHILD PHILOSOPHER[1]

THOUGH the Oracles are dumb, and the Prophets have taken to the turf, and the Sibyls are reduced to telling fortunes at bazaars,* the ancient power of divination has not yet left the world. Mr Mark Twain's* fascinating article, in the current number of the Century Magazine, on 'English as She is Taught' in his native country, throws an entirely new light on that *enfant terrible* of a commercial civilisation, the American child, and reminds us that we may all learn wisdom from the lips of babes and sucklings.* For the mistakes made by the interesting pupils of the American Board-Schools are not mistakes springing from ignorance of life or dulness of perception; they are, on the contrary, full of the richest suggestion and pregnant with the very highest philosophy. No wonder that the American child educates its father and mother,* when it can give us such luminous definitions as the following:—

> *Republican*, a sinner mentioned in the Bible.
> *Demagogue*, a vessel containing beer and other liquids.
> *The Constitution of the United States*, that part of the book at the end that nobody reads.
> *Plagiarist*, a writer of plays.
> *Equestrian*, one who asks questions.
> *Tenacious*, ten acres of land.
> *Quaternions*, a bird, with a flat beak and no bill, dwelling in New Zealand.
> *Franchise*, anything belonging to the French.

The last definition points very clearly to the fact that the fallacy of an extended Franchise is based on the French theory of equality, to which the child-philosopher seems also to allude when he says that—

> Things which are equal to each other are unequal to anything else.*

[1] 20 April 1887. Mark Twain, 'English as She is Taught', *The Century Magazine* (April 1887), 932–6.

while the description of the Plagiarist is the most brilliant thing that has been said on modern literature for some time.

How true, also, in their directness and simplicity of phrase are such aphorisms as:—

> Some of the best fossils are found in theological cabinets.
>
> There are a good many donkeys in theological gardens.
>
> We should endeavour to avoid extremes—like those of wasps and bees.
>
> Congress is divided into civilised, half civilised, and savage.
>
> Climate lasts all the time, and weather only a few days.
>
> The Constitution of the United States was established to ensure domestic hostility.
>
> The body is mostly composed of water, and about one half is avaricious tissue.

How excellent are these views on History:—

> The Puritans founded an insane asylum in the wilds of America.
>
> The middle ages come in between antiquity and posterity.
>
> Henry the Eight was famous for being a great widower having lost several wives.
>
> Julius Caesar was really a very great man. He was a very great soldier and wrote a book for beginners in Latin.
>
> The Stamp Act* was to make everybody stamp all materials, so they should be null and void.
>
> The only form of Government in Greece was a limited monkey.

How delightful these literary criticisms:—

> Bulwell is considered a good write.
>
> Gibbon wrote a history of his travels in Italy. This was original.
>
> Wm. Wordsworth wrote the Barefoot Boy and Imitations on Immortality.
>
> A sort of sadness kind of shone in Bryant's poem.
>
> Chaucer was the father of English pottery.
>
> Holmes is a very profligate and amusing writer.
>
> Sir Walter Scott, Charles Bronté, Alfred the Great, and Johnson were the first great novelists.
>
> Chaucer was succeeded by H. Wads. Longfellow, an American writer. His writings were chiefly prose, and nearly one hundred years elapsed.*

How valuable these results of a scientific education! How clearly they exemplify the importance of physiology as the basis of culture!

Physillogigy is to study about your bones, stummick, and vertebry.

The gastric juice keeps the bones from creaking.

The olfactory nerve* enters the cavity of the orbit, and is developed into the special sense of hearing.

Nor should the influence of mathematics in developing a logical habit be overlooked. How well it is shown in the following:—

A circle is a round straight line with a hole in the middle.

To find the number of square feet in a room, you multiply the room by the number of the feet. The product is the result.

The weight of the earth is found by comparing a mass of known lead with that of a mass of unknown lead.

Inertia is the negative quality of passiveness, either in recoverable latency or incipient latescence.

The metaphysical subtlety of the last statement shows that the child-philosopher is perfectly qualified to become a member of the psychical and hermetic societies, and that with a little more study, he might develop into the most esoteric of all the Brompton Buddhists.* Indeed, we sincerely hope that when the next bevy of beauties land on our shores from America, they will bring with them one specimen at least of the native school boy. For many of his utterances are obviously mystical, and possess that quality of absolute unintelligibility that is the peculiar privilege of the verbally inspired. In the case of such aphorisms, as—

The leopard is watching his sheep.

They had a strawberry vestibule.

The coercion of some things is remarkable; as bread and molasses.

The supercilious girl acted with vicissitude when the perennial time came.

You should take caution, and be precarious.

We must clearly, like Mr Posket in 'The Magistrate,'* read between the lines, and recognise that what to the uninitiated seems nonsense or platitude, to the humble transcendentalist is pure revelation. What a *trouvaille*, also for Parliamentary speakers of the school of Mr Conybeare and Mr Bradlaugh* is the child-philosopher's list of word definitions! If mendacious only means 'what can be mended,' mercenary 'one who feels for another,' and parasite 'a kind of umbrella,' it is evident that latent, in the very lowliest citizen of our community, lie capacities for platform oratory hitherto unsuspected. Even women, most complex of all modern problems, are analysed with a knowledge that in Europe is confined to poets and dandies. 'They make fun of boys,' says the child-philosopher, 'and then turn round and love them.'

Mr Mark Twain deserves our warmest thanks for bringing to light the true American genius. American patriots are tedious, American millionaires go bankrupt, and American beauties don't last, but the school-boy seems to be eternally delightful; and when the world has grown weary of the Boston novelists, and tired of the civilisation of the telephone, the utterances of the child-philosopher will be treasured by the scientific historian as the best criticism upon modern education, the best epigram upon modern life.

THE WOMAN'S WORLD

LITERARY AND OTHER NOTES I[1]

THE Princess Christian's translation of 'The Memoirs of Wilhelmine, Margravine of Bayreuth'* (David Stott), is a most fascinating and delightful book. The Margravine and her brother, Frederick the Great,* were, as the Princess herself points out in an admirably written introduction, 'among the first of those questioning minds that strove after spiritual freedom' in the last century. 'They had studied,' says the Princess, 'the English philosophers, Newton, Locke and Shaftesbury, and were roused to enthusiasm by the writings of Voltaire and Rousseau.* Their whole lives bore the impress of the influence of French thought on the burning questions of the day. In the eighteenth century began that great struggle of philosophy against tyranny and worn-out abuses which culminated in the French Revolution. The noblest minds were engaged in the struggle, and, like most reformers, they pushed their conclusions to extremes, and too often lost sight of the need of a due proportion in things. The Margravine's influence on the intellectual development of her country is untold. She formed at Bayreuth a centre of culture and learning which had before been undreamt of in Germany.'

The historical value of these 'Memoirs' is, of course, well known. Carlyle* speaks of them as being 'by far the best authority' on the early life of Frederick the Great. But considered merely as the autobiography of a clever and charming woman, they are no less interesting, and even those who care nothing for eighteenth-century politics, and look upon history itself as an unattractive form of fiction, cannot fail to be fascinated by the Margravine's wit, vivacity and humour, by her keen powers of observation, and by her brilliant and assertive egotism. Not that her life was by any means a happy one. Her father,* to quote the Princess Christian, 'ruled his family with the same harsh despotism with which he ruled his country, taking pleasure in

[1] November 1887. *Memoirs of Wilhelmine, Margravine of Bayreuth*, trans. and ed. by Her Royal Highness Princess Christian of Schleswig-Holstein, Princess of Great Britain and Ireland (London, 1887); *Women's Voices*, ed. Mrs William Sharp (London, 1887); Margaret L. Woods, *A Village Tragedy* (London, 1887).

making his power felt by all in the most galling manner,' and the Margravine and her brother 'had much to suffer, not only from his ungovernable temper, but also from the real privations to which they were subjected.' Indeed, the picture the Margravine gives of the King is quite extraordinary. 'He despised all learning,' she writes, 'and wished me to occupy myself with nothing but needlework and household duties or details. Had he found me writing or reading, he would probably have whipped me. He considered music a capital offence, and maintained that every one should devote himself to one object: men to the military service, and women to their household duties. Science and the arts he counted among the seven deadly sins.' Sometimes he took to religion, 'and then,' says the Margravine, 'we lived like Trappists, to the great grief of my brother and myself. Every afternoon the King preached a sermon, to which we had to listen as attentively as if it proceeded from an Apostle. My brother and I were often seized with such an intense sense of the ridiculous, that we burst out laughing, upon which an apostolic curse was poured out on our heads, which we had to accept with a show of humility and penitence.' Economy and soldiers were his only topics of conversation, his chief social amusement was to make his guests intoxicated, and as for his temper, the accounts the Margravine gives of it would be almost incredible if they were not amply corroborated from other sources. Suetonius has written of the strange madness that comes on kings, but even in his melodramatic chronicles there is hardly anything that rivals what the Margravine has to tell us. Here is one of her pictures of family life at a Royal Court in the last century, and it is not by any means the worst scene she describes:—

'On one occasion, when his temper was more than usually bad, he told the Queen that he had received letters from Anspach,* in which the Margrave announced his arrival at Berlin for the beginning of May. He was coming there for the purpose of marrying my sister,* and one of his Ministers would arrive previously with the betrothal ring. My father asked my sister whether she were pleased at this prospect, and how she would arrange her household. Now my sister had always made a point of telling him what-ever came into her head, even the greatest home-truths, and he had never taken her outspokenness amiss. On this occasion, therefore, relying on former experience, she answered him as follows:—"When I have a house of my own I shall take care to have a well-appointed dinner-table, better than yours is; and if I have children of my own, I shall not plague them as

you do yours, and force them to eat things they thoroughly dislike."—
"What is amiss with my dinner-table?" the King inquired, getting very red
in the face.—"You ask what is the matter with it," my sister replied; "there
is not enough on it for us to eat, and what there is, is cabbage and carrots,
which we detest." Her first answer had already angered my father, but now
he gave vent to his fury. But instead of punishing my sister he poured it all
on my mother, my brother, and myself. To begin with, he threw a plate at
my brother's head, who would have been struck, had he not got out of the
way; a second one he threw at me, which I also happily escaped; then
torrents of abuse followed these first signs of hostility. He reproached the
Queen with having brought up her children so badly. "You will curse your
mother," he said to my brother, "for having made you such a good-for-
nothing creature." . . . As my brother and I passed near him to leave the
room, he hit out at us with his crutch. Happily we escaped the blow, for it
would certainly have struck us down, and we at last escaped without
harm.'

Yet, as the Princess Christian remarks, 'despite the almost cruel
treatment Wilhelmine received from her father, it is noticeable that
throughout her "Memoirs" she speaks of him with the greatest
affection. She makes constant reference to his "good heart," and that
his faults "were more those of temper than of nature." ' Nor could
all the misery and wretchedness of her home life dull the brightness
of her intellect. What would have made others morbid, made her
satirical. Instead of weeping over her own personal tragedies, she
laughs at the general comedy of life. Here, for instance, is her
description of Peter the Great and his wife,* who arrived at Berlin in
1718:—

'The Czarina was small, broad, and brown-looking, without the slightest
dignity or appearance. You had only to look at her to detect her low origin.
She might have passed for a German actress, she had decked herself out in
such a manner. Her dress had been bought second-hand, and was
trimmed with some dirty-looking silver embroidery; the bodice was
trimmed with precious stones, arranged in such a manner as to represent
the double eagle. She wore a dozen Orders; and round the bottom of her
dress hung quantities of relics and pictures of saints, which rattled when
she walked, and reminded one of a smartly-harnessed mule. The Orders,
too, made a great noise, knocking against each other.

'The Czar, on the other hand, was tall and well-grown, with a handsome face, but his expression was coarse, and impressed one with fear. He
wore a simple sailor's dress. His wife, who spoke German very badly,

called her Court jester to her aid, and spoke Russian with her. This poor creature was a Princess Gallizin, who had been obliged to undertake this sorry office to save her life, as she had been mixed up in a conspiracy against the Czar, and had twice been flogged with the knout!

'The following day the Czar visited all the sights of Berlin, amongst others the very curious collection of coins and antiques. Amongst these last-named was a statue, representing a heathen god. It was anything but attractive, but was the most valuable in the collection. The Czar admired it very much, and insisted on the Czarina kissing it. On her refusing, he said to her, in bad German, that she should lose her head if she did not at once obey him. Being terrified at the Czar's anger she immediately complied with his orders without the least hesitation. The Czar asked the King to give him this and other statues, a request which he could not refuse. The same thing happened about a cupboard, inlaid with amber. It was the only one of its kind, and had cost King Frederick I an enormous sum, and the consternation was general on its having to be sent to Petersburg.

'This barbarous Court happily left after two days. The Queen rushed at once to Monbijou,* which she found in a state resembling that of the fall of Jerusalem. I never saw such a sight. Everything was destroyed, so that the Queen was obliged to rebuild the whole house.'

Nor are the Margravine's descriptions of her reception as a bride in the principality of Bayreuth less amusing. Hof was the first town she came to, and a deputation of nobles was waiting there to welcome her. This is her account of them:

'Their faces would have frightened little children, and, to add to their beauty, they had arranged their hair to resemble the wigs that were then in fashion. Their dresses clearly denoted the antiquity of their families, as they were composed of heirlooms, and were cut accordingly, so that most of them did not fit. In spite of their costumes being the "Court Dresses," the gold and silver trimmings were so black that you had a difficulty in making out of what they were made. The manners of these nobles suited their faces and their clothes. They might have passed for peasants. I could scarcely restrain my laughter when I first beheld these strange figures. I spoke to each in turn, but none of them understood what I said, and their replies sounded to me like Hebrew, because the dialect of the Empire is quite different from that spoken in Brandenburg.

'The clergy also presented themselves. These were totally different creatures. Round their necks they wore great ruffs, which resembled washing-baskets. They spoke very slowly, so that I might be able to under-stand them better. They said the most foolish things, and it was only with much difficulty that I was able to prevent myself from laughing. At last I got rid of all these people, and we sat down to dinner. I tried my best to converse with those at table, but it was useless. At last I touched on agricultural topics, and then they began to thaw. I was at once informed of all their different farmsteads and herds of cattle. An almost interesting discussion took place as to whether the oxen in the upper part of the country were fatter than those in the lowlands.

'I was told that as the next day was Sunday, I must spend it at Hof, and listen to a sermon. Never before had I heard such a sermon! The clergyman began by giving us an account of all the marriages that had taken place from Adam's time to that of Noah. We were spared no detail, so that the gentlemen all laughed and the poor ladies blushed. The dinner went off as on the previous day. In the afternoon all the ladies came to pay me their respects. Gracious heavens! What ladies, too! They were all as ugly as the gentlemen, and their head-dresses were so curious that swallows might have built their nests in them.'

As for Bayreuth itself, and its petty Court, the picture she gives of it is exceedingly curious. Her father-in-law, the reigning Margrave, was a narrow-minded mediocrity, whose conversation 'resembled that of a sermon read aloud for the purpose of sending the listener to sleep,' and he had only two topics, 'Telemachus, and Amelot de la Houssaye's "Roman History." '* The Ministers, from Baron von Stein, who always said 'yes' to everything, to Baron von Voit, who always said 'no,' were not by any means an intellectual set of men. 'Their chief amusement,' says the Margravine, 'was drinking from morning till night, and horses and cattle were all they talked about.' The palace itself was shabby, decayed, and dirty. 'I was like a lamb among wolves,' cries the poor Margravine; 'I was settled in a strange country, at a Court which more resembled a peasant's farm, surrounded by coarse, bad, dangerous, and tiresome people.'

Yet her *esprit* never deserted her. She is always clever, witty, and entertaining. Her stories about the endless squabbles over precedence are extremely amusing. The society of her day cared very little for good manners, knew indeed very little about them, but all questions of etiquette were of vital importance, and the Margravine herself, though she saw the shallowness of the whole system, was far too proud not to assert her rights when circumstances demanded it, as the description she gives of her visit to the Empress of Germany* shows very clearly. When this meeting was first proposed, the Margravine declined positively to entertain the idea. 'There was no precedent,' she writes, 'of a King's daughter and an Empress having met, and I did not know to what rights I ought to lay claim.' Finally, however, she is induced to consent, but she lays down three conditions for her reception:—

'I desired first of all that the Empress' Court should receive me at the foot of the stairs; secondly, that she should meet me at the door of her bedroom; and, thirdly, that she should offer me an arm-chair to sit on.

'They disputed all day over the conditions I had made. The two first were granted me, but all that could be obtained with respect to the third was that the Empress would use quite a small arm-chair, whilst she gave me a chair.

'Next day I saw this Royal personage. I own that had I been in her place I would have made all the rules of etiquette and ceremony the excuse for not being obliged to appear. The Empress was small and stout, round as a ball, very ugly, and without dignity or manner. Her mind corresponded to her body. She was terribly bigoted, and spent her whole day praying. The old and ugly are generally the Almighty's portion. She received me trembling all over, and was so upset that she could not say a word.

'After some silence I began the conversation in French. She answered me in her Austrian dialect that she could not speak in that language, and begged I would speak in German. The conversation did not last long, for the Austrian and low Saxon tongues are so different from each other that to those acquainted with only one the other is unintelligible. This is what happened to us. A third person would have laughed at our misunderstandings, for we caught only a word here and there, and had to guess the rest. The poor Empress was such a slave to etiquette that she would have thought it high treason had she spoken to me in a foreign language, though she understood French quite well.'

Many other extracts might be given from this delightful book, but from the few that have been selected some idea can be formed of the vivacity and picturesqueness of the Margravine's style. As for her character, it is very well summed up by the Princess Christian, who while admitting that she often appears almost heartless and inconsiderate, yet claims that, 'taken as a whole, she stands out in marked prominence among the most gifted women of the eighteenth century, not only by her mental powers, but by her goodness of heart, her self-sacrificing devotion, and true friendship.' An interesting sequel to her 'Memoirs' would be her correspondence with Voltaire, and it is to be hoped that we may shortly see a translation of these letters from the same accomplished pen to which we owe the present volume.

'Women's Voices' (Walter Scott) is an anthology of the most characteristic poems by English, Scotch and Irish women, selected and arranged by Mrs William Sharp.* 'The idea of making this anthology,' says Mrs Sharp, in her preface, 'arose primarily from the conviction that our women-poets had never been collectively represented with anything like adequate justice; that the works of many are not so widely known as they deserve to be; and that at least some fine fugitive poetry could be thus rescued from oblivion;' and Mrs Sharp proceeds to claim that 'the selections will further emphasise the value of women's work in poetry for those who are already well acquainted with English literature, and that they will convince many it is as possible to form an anthology of "pure poetry" from the writings of women as from those of men.' It is somewhat difficult to define what 'pure poetry' really is, but the collection is certainly extremely interesting, extending, as it does, over nearly three centuries of our literature. It opens with 'Revenge,' a poem by 'the learned, virtuous, and truly noble Ladie,' Elizabeth Carew, who published a 'Tragedie of Mariam the Faire Queene of Jewry,'* in 1613, from which 'Revenge' is taken. Then come some very pretty verses by Margaret, Duchess of Newcastle,* who produced a volume of poems in 1673. They are supposed to be sung by a sea-goddess, and their fantastic charm and the graceful wilfulness of their fancy are well worthy of note, as these first stanzas show:—

> 'My cabinets are oyster-shells
> In which I keep my Orient pearls;
> And modest coral I do wear
> Which blushes when it touches air.
>
> 'On silvery waves I sit and sing,
> And then the fish lie listening:
> Then resting on a rocky stone,
> I comb my hair with fishes' bone;
>
> 'The whilst Apollo with his beams
> Doth dry my hair from soaking streams:
> His light doth glaze the water's face,
> And make the sea my looking-glass.'

Then follow 'Friendship's Mystery,' by 'The Matchless Orinda,'
Mrs Katherine Philips; a 'Song,' by Mrs Aphra Behn, the first
English woman who adopted literature as a profession; and the
Countess of Winchelsea's 'Nocturnal Reverie.'* Wordsworth once
said that, with the exception of this poem and Pope's 'Windsor
Forest,' the 'poetry of the period intervening between "Paradise
Lost" and "The Seasons" does not contain a single new image of
external Nature,' and though the statement is hardly accurate, as it
leaves Gay* entirely out of account, it must be admitted that the
simple naturalism of Lady Winchelsea's description is extremely
remarkable. Passing on through Mrs Sharp's collection, we come
across poems by Lady Grisell Baillie; by Jean Adams, a poor serving-
maid in a Scotch manse, who died in the Greenock Workhouse; by
Isobel Pagan, an Ayrshire 'lucky,' who kept an alehouse, sold whisky
without a license, and sang her own songs as a means of subsistence;
by Mrs Thrale, Dr Johnson's friend; by Mrs Hunter, the wife of the
great anatomist; by the worthy Mrs Barbauld, and by the excellent
Mrs Hannah More.* Here is Miss Anna Seward, called by her
admirers 'the Swan of Lichfield,' who was so angry with Dr Darwin
for plagiarising some of her verses; Lady Anne Barnard, whose
'Auld Robin Gray' was described by Sir Walter Scott as 'worth all
the dialogues Corydon and Phyllis have together spoken from the
days of Theocritus downwards;' Jean Glover, a Scottish weaver's
daughter, who married a strolling player, and became the best singer
and actor of his troop; Joanna Baillie, whose tedious dramas thrilled
our grandfathers; Mrs Tighe, whose 'Psyche' was very much
admired by Keats in his youthful days; Frances Kemble, Mrs
Siddons' niece; poor L. E. L., whom Disraeli described as 'the per-
sonification of Brompton, pink satin dress, white satin shoes, red
cheeks, snub nose, and her hair à la Sappho;' the two beautiful
sisters, Lady Dufferin and Mrs Norton; Emily Brontë, whose poems
are instinct with tragic power, and quite terrible in their bitter intensity of passion, the fierce fire of feeling seeming almost to consume
the raiment of form; Eliza Cook, a kindly, vulgar writer; George
Eliot, whose poetry is too abstract, and lacks all rhythmical life; Mrs
Carlyle, who wrote much better poetry than her husband, though
this is hardly high praise; and Mrs Browning,* the first really great
poetess in our literature. Nor are contemporary writers forgotten.
Christina Rossetti, some of whose poems are quite priceless in their

beauty; Mrs Augusta Webster, Mrs Hamilton King, Miss Mary Robinson, Mrs Craik; Jean Ingelow, whose sonnet on 'A Chess-King' is like an exquisitely carved gem; Mrs Pfeiffer; Miss May Probyn, a poetess with the true lyrical impulse of song, whose work is as delicate as it is delightful; Mrs Nesbit, a very pure and perfect artist; Miss Rosa Mulholland, Miss Katharine Tynan, Lady Charlotte Elliot,* and many other well-known writers, are duly and adequately represented. On the whole, Mrs Sharp's collection is very pleasant reading indeed, and the extracts given from the works of living poetesses are extremely remarkable, not merely for their absolute artistic excellence, but also for the light they throw upon the spirit of modern culture.

It is not, however, by any means a complete anthology. Dame Juliana Berners is possibly too antiquated in style to be suitable to a modern audience, but where is Anne Askew, who wrote a ballad in Newgate, and where is Queen Elizabeth, whose 'most sweet and sententious ditty' on Mary Stuart is so highly praised by Puttenham* as an example of 'Exargasia,' or The Gorgeous in Literature? Why is the Countess of Pembroke* excluded? Sidney's* sister should surely have a place in any anthology of English verse. Where is Sidney's niece, Lady Mary Wroth, to whom Ben Jonson dedicated the 'Alchemist'?* Where is 'the noble ladie Diana Primrose,' who wrote 'A Chain of Pearl, or a memorial of the peerless graces and heroic virtue of Queen Elizabeth, of glorious memory'?* Where is Mary Morpeth, the friend and admirer of Drummond of Hawthornden?* Where is the Princess Elizabeth, daughter of James I, and where is Anne Killigrew, maid of honour to the Duchess of York?* The Marchioness of Wharton, whose poems were praised by Waller; Lady Chudleigh, whose lines beginning—

> 'Wife and servant are the same,
> But only differ in the name;'

are very curious and interesting; Rachel Lady Russell, Constantia Grierson, Mary Barber, Lætitia Pilkington; Eliza Haywood, whom Pope honoured by a place in the 'Dunciad'; Lady Luxborough, Lord Bolingbroke's half-sister; Lady Mary Wortley Montagu; Lady Temple, whose poems were printed by Horace Walpole; Perdita, whose lines on the snowdrop are very pathetic; the beautiful Duchess of Devonshire, of whom Gibbon said that 'she was made for something better than a Duchess;' Mrs Ratcliffe, Mrs Chapone, and Amelia Opie,* all deserve a place on historical, if not on artistic grounds. In fact, the space given by Mrs Sharp to modern and living poetesses is somewhat disproportionate, and I am sure that those on whose brows the laurels are still green would not grudge a little room to those the green of whose laurels is withered and the music of whose lyres is mute.

One of the most powerful and pathetic novels that has recently appeared is 'A Village Tragedy' (Bentley and Son) by Margaret L. Woods. To find any parallel to this lurid little story one must go to Dostoieffski, or to Guy de Maupassant.* Not that Mrs Woods can be said to have taken either of these two great masters of fiction as her model, but there is something in her work that recalls their method; she has not a little of their fierce intensity, their terrible concentration, their passionless yet poignant objectivity; like them, she seems to allow life to suggest its own mode of presentation; and, like them, she recognises that a frank acceptance of the facts of life is the true basis of all modern imitative art. The scene of Mrs Woods's story lies in one of the villages near Oxford; the characters are very few in number, and the plot is extremely simple. It is a romance of modern Arcadia—a tale of the love of a farm-labourer for a girl who, though slightly above him in social station and education, is yet herself also a servant on a farm. True Arcadians they are, both of them, and their ignorance and isolation serve only to intensify the tragedy that gives the story its title. It is the fashion now-a-days to label literature, so no doubt Mrs Woods's novel will be spoken of as 'realistic.' Its realism, however, is the realism of the artist, not of the reporter; its tact of treatment, subtlety of perception, and fine distinction of style, make it rather a poem than a *procès-verbal*; and though it lays bare to us the mere misery of life, it suggests something of life's mystery also. Very delicate, too, is the handling of external Nature. There are no formal guide-book descriptions of scenery, nor anything of what Byron petulantly called 'twaddling about trees,'* but we seem to breathe the atmosphere of the country, to catch the exquisite scent of the beanfields, so familiar to all who have ever wandered through the Oxfordshire lanes in June, to hear the birds singing in the thicket, and the sheep-bells tinkling from the hill. Characterisation, that enemy of literary form, is such an essential part of the method of the modern writer of fiction, that Nature has almost become to the novelist what light and shade are to the painter—the one permanent element of style; and if the power of 'A Village Tragedy' be due to its portrayal of human life, no small portion of its charm comes from its Theocritean setting.

It is, however, not merely in fiction and in poetry that the women of this century are making their mark. Their appearance amongst the prominent speakers at the Church Congress some weeks ago, was in itself a very remarkable proof of the growing influence of women's opinions on all matters connected with the elevation of our national life, and the amelioration of our social conditions. When the Bishops left the platform to their wives, it may be said that a new era began, and the change will no doubt be productive of much good. The Apostolic dictum, that women should not be suffered to teach, is no longer applicable to a society such as ours, with its solidarity of interests, its recognition of natural rights, and its universal education, however suitable it may have been to the Greek cities under Roman rule. Nothing in the United States struck me more than the fact that the remarkable intellectual progress of that country is very largely due to the efforts of American women, who edit many of the most powerful magazines and newspapers, take part in the discussion of every question of public interest, and exercise an important influence upon the growth and tendencies of literature and art.* Indeed, the women of America are the one class in the community that enjoys that leisure which is so necessary for culture. The men are, as a rule, so absorbed in business, that the task of bringing some element of form into the chaos of daily life is left almost entirely to the opposite sex, and an eminent Bostonian once assured me that in the twentieth century the whole culture of his country would be in petticoats. By that time, however, it is probable that the dress of the two sexes will be assimilated, as similarity of costume always follows similarity of pursuits.

In a recent article in *La France*, M Sarcey* puts this point very well. The further we advance, he says, the more apparent does it become that women are to take their share as bread-winners in the world. The task is no longer monopolised by men, and will, perhaps, be equally shared by the sexes in another hundred years. It will be necessary, however, for women to invent a suitable costume, as their present style of dress is quite inappropriate to any kind of mechanical labour, and must be radically changed before they can compete with men upon their own ground. As to the question of desirability, M Sarcey refuses to speak. 'I shall not see the end of this revolution,' he remarks, 'and I am glad of it.' But, as is pointed out in a very sensible article in the *Daily News*, there is no doubt that M Sarcey has reason and common sense on his side with regard to the absolute unsuitability of ordinary feminine attire to any sort of handicraft, or even to any occupation which necessitates a daily walk to business and back again in all kinds of weather. Women's dress can easily be modified and adapted to any exigencies of the kind; but most women refuse to modify or adapt it. They must follow the fashion, whether it be convenient or the reverse. And, after all, what is a fashion? From the artistic point of view, it is usually a form of ugliness so intolerable that we have to alter it every six months. From the point of view of science, it not unfrequently violates every law of health, every principle of hygiene. While from the point of view of simple ease and comfort it is not too much to say that, with the exception of M Félix's* charming tea-gowns, and a few English tailor-made costumes, there is not a single form of really fashionable dress that can be worn without a certain amount of absolute misery to the wearer. The contortion of the feet of the Chinese beauty, said Dr Naftel at the last International Medical Congress, held at Washington, is no more barbarous or unnatural than the panoply of the *femme du monde*.

And yet how sensible is the dress of the London milk woman, of the Irish or Scotch fishwife, of the North Country factory-girl! An attempt was made recently to prevent the pit-women from working, on the ground that their costume was unsuited to their sex, but it is really only the idle classes who dress badly. Wherever physical labour of any kind is required, the costume used is, as a rule, absolutely right, for labour necessitates freedom, and without freedom there is no such thing as beauty in dress at all. In fact, the beauty of dress depends on the beauty of the human figure, and whatever limits, constrains, and mutilates is essentially ugly, though the eyes of many are so blinded by custom that they do not notice the ugliness till it has become unfashionable.

What women's dress will be in the future it is difficult to say. The writer of the *Daily News* article is of opinion that skirts will always be worn as distinctive of the sex, and it is obvious that men's dress, in its present condition, is not by any means an example of a perfectly rational costume. It is more than probable, however, that the dress of the twentieth century will emphasise distinctions of occupation, not distinctions of sex.

It is hardly too much to say that, by the death of the author of 'John Halifax, Gentleman,'* our literature has sustained a heavy loss. Mrs Craik was one of the finest of our women-writers, and though her art had always what Keats called 'a palpable intention upon one,'* still its imaginative qualities were of no mean order. There is hardly one of her books that has not some distinction of style; there is certainly not one of them that does not show an ardent love of all that is beautiful and good in life. The good she perhaps loved somewhat more than the beautiful, but her heart had room for both. Her first novel appeared in 1849, the year of the publication of Charlotte Brontë's 'Jane Eyre,' and Mrs Gaskell's 'Ruth,'* and her last work was done for the magazine which I have the honour to edit. She was very much interested in the scheme for the foundation of THE WOMAN'S WORLD, suggested its title, and promised to be one of its warmest supporters. One article from her pen is already in proof, and will appear next month, and in a letter I received from her, a few days before she died, she told me that she had almost finished a second, to be called 'Between Schooldays and Marriage.' Few women have enjoyed a greater popularity than Mrs Craik, or have better deserved it. It is sometimes said that John Halifax is not a real man, but only a woman's ideal of a man. Well, let us be grateful for such ideals. No one can read the story of which John Halifax is the hero without being the better for it. Mrs Craik will live long in the affectionate memory of all who knew her, and one of her novels, at any rate, will always have a high and honourable place in English fiction. Indeed, for simple narrative power some of the chapters of 'John Halifax, Gentleman' are almost unequalled in our prose literature.

The news of the death of Lady Brassey* has been also received by the English people with every expression of sorrow and sympathy. Though her books were not remarkable for any perfection of literary style, they had the charm of brightness, vivacity, and unconventionality. They revealed a fascinating personality, and their touches of domesticity made them classics in many an English household. In all modern movements Lady Brassey took a keen interest. She gained a first-class certificate in the South Kensington School of Cookery, scullery department and all; was one of the most energetic members of the St John's Ambulance Association, many branches of which she succeeded in founding; and, whether at Normanhurst or in Park Lane, always managed to devote some portion of her day to useful and practical work. It is sad to have to chronicle in the first number of THE WOMAN'S WORLD the death of two of the most remarkable Englishwomen of our day.

LITERARY AND OTHER NOTES II[1]

LADY BELLAIRS'S* 'Gossips with Girls and Maidens' (William Blackwood and Sons) contains some very interesting essays, and a quite extraordinary amount of useful information on all matters connected with the mental and physical training of women. It is very difficult to give good advice without being irritating, and almost impossible to be at once didactic and delightful; but Lady Bellairs manages very cleverly to steer a middle course between the Charybdis of dulness and the Scylla* of flippancy. There is a pleasing *intimité* about her style, and almost everything that she says has both good sense and good humour to recommend it. Nor does she confine herself to those broad generalisations on morals, which are so easy to make, so difficult to apply. Indeed, she seems to have a wholesome contempt for the cheap severity of abstract ethics, enters into the most minute details for the guidance of conduct, and draws out elaborate lists of what girls should avoid, and what they should cultivate.

[1] December 1887. Lady Bellairs, *Gossips with Girls and Maidens* (Edinburgh and London, 1887); Constance Naden, *A Modern Apostle and Other Poems* (London, 1887); Phyllis Browne, *Mrs Somerville and Mary Carpenter* (London, 1887); May Hartley, *Ismay's Children* (London, 1887).

Here are some specimens of 'What to Avoid':—

'A loud, weak, affected, whining, harsh, or shrill tone of voice.

'Extravagances in conversation—such phrases as "Awfully this," "Beastly that," "Loads of time," "Don't you know," "hate" for "dislike," &c.

'Sudden exclamations of annoyance, surprise, or joy—often danger-ously approaching to "female swearing"—as "Bother!" "Gracious!" "How jolly!"

'Yawning when listening to any one.

'Talking on family matters, even to your bosom friends.

'Attempting any vocal or instrumental piece of music that you cannot execute with ease.

'Crossing your letters.

'Making a short, sharp nod with the head, intended to do duty for a bow.

'All nonsense in the shape of belief in dreams, omens, presentiments, ghosts, spiritualism, palmistry, &c.

'Entertaining wild flights of the imagination, or empty idealistic aspirations.'

I am afraid that I have a good deal of sympathy with what are called 'empty idealistic aspirations;' and 'wild flights of the imagin-ation' are so extremly rare in the nineteenth century, that they seem to me deserving rather of praise than of censure. The exclamation 'Bother,' also, though certainly lacking in beauty, might, I think, be permitted under circumstances of extreme aggravation, such as, for instance, the rejection of a manuscript by the editor of a magazine; but in all other respects the list seems to be quite excellent. As for 'What to Cultivate,' nothing could be better than the following:—

'An unaffected, low, distinct, silver-toned voice.

'The art of pleasing those around you, and seeming pleased with them, and all they may do for you.

'The charm of making little sacrifices quite naturally, as if of no account to yourself.

'The habit of making allowances for the opinions, feelings, or prejudices of others.

'An erect carriage—that is, a sound body.

'A good memory for faces, and facts connected with them—thus avoid-ing giving offence through not recognising or bowing to people, or saying to them what had best been left unsaid.

'The art of listening without impatience to prosy talkers, and smiling at the twice-told tale or joke.'

I cannot help thinking that the last aphorism aims at too high a standard. There is always a certain amount of danger in any attempt to cultivate impossible virtues. However, it is only fair to add that Lady Bellairs recognises the importance of self-development quite as much as the importance of self-denial; and there is a great deal of sound sense in everything that she says about the gradual growth and formation of character. Indeed, those who have not read Aristotle upon this point might with advantage read Lady Bellairs.

Miss Constance Naden's* little volume, 'A Modern Apostle, and Other Poems' (Kegan Paul, Trench, and Company), shows both culture and courage—culture in its use of language, courage in its selection of subject-matter. The modern apostle of whom Miss Naden sings is a young clergyman who preaches Pantheistic Socialism in the Free Church of some provincial manufacturing town, converts everybody except the woman whom he loves, and is killed in a street riot. The story is exceedingly powerful, but seems more suitable for prose than for verse. It is right that a poet should be full of the spirit of his age, but the external forms of modern life are hardly, as yet, expressive of that spirit. They are truths of fact, not truths of the imagination, and though they may give the poet an opportunity for realism, they often rob the poem of the reality that is so essential to it. Art, however, is a matter of result, not of theory, and if the fruit is pleasant, we should not quarrel about the tree. Miss Naden's work is distinguished by rich imagery, fine colour, and sweet music, and these are things for which we should be grateful wherever we find them. In point of mere technical skill her longer poems are the best, but some of the shorter poems are very fascinating. This, for instance, is pretty:—

> 'The copyist group was gathered round
> A time-worn fresco, world-renowned,
> Whose central glory once had been
> The face of Christ, the Nazarene.
>
> 'And every copyist of the crowd
> With his own soul that face endowed,
> Gentle, severe, majestic, mean;
> But which was Christ, the Nazarene?

> 'Then one who watched them made complaint,
> And marvelled, saying, "Wherefore paint
> Till ye be sure your eyes have seen
> The face of Christ, the Nazarene?" '

And this sonnet is full of suggestion:—

> 'The wine-flushed monarch slept, but in his ear
> An angel breathed—"Repent, or choose the flame
> Quenchless." In dread he woke, but not in shame,
> Deep musing—"Sin I love, yet hell I fear."
>
> 'Wherefore he left his feasts and minions dear,
> And justly ruled, and died a saint in name.
> But when his hasting spirit heavenward came,
> A stern voice cried—"O Soul! what dost thou here?"
>
> ' "Love I forswore, and wine, and kept my vow
> To live a just and joyless life, and now
> I crave reward." The voice came like a knell—
> "Fool! dost thou hope to find again thy mirth,
> And those foul joys thou didst renounce on earth?
> Yea, enter in! My heaven shall be thy hell." '

Miss Constance Naden deserves a high place among our living poetesses, and this, as Mrs Sharp has shown lately in her volume, entitled 'Women's Voices,' is no mean distinction.

Phyllis Browne's 'Life of Mrs Somerville' (Cassell and Co.) forms part of a very interesting little series, called 'The World's Workers'—a collection of short biographies catholic enough to include personalities so widely different as Turner and Richard Cobden, Handel and Sir Titus Salt, Robert Stephenson* and Florence Nightingale, and yet possessing a certain definite aim. As a mathematician and a scientist, the translator and populariser of Laplace's *La Mécanique Céleste*,* and the author of an important book on physical geography, Mrs Somerville is, of course, well known. The scientific bodies of Europe covered her with honours; her bust stands in the hall of the Royal Society, and one of the Women's Colleges at Oxford bears her name. Yet, considered simply in the light of a wife and a mother, she is no less admirable; and those who consider that stupidity is the proper basis for the domestic virtues, and that intellectual women must of necessity be helpless with their hands, cannot do better than read Phyllis Browne's pleasant little book, in which they will find that the greatest woman-mathematician of any age was a clever needle-woman, a good housekeeper, and a most skilful cook. Indeed, Mrs Somerville seems to have been quite renowned for her cookery. The discoverers of the North-west Passage christened an island 'Somerville,' not as a tribute to the distinguished mathematician, but as a recognition of the excellence of some orange marmalade which the distinguished mathematician had prepared with her own hands and presented to the ships before they left England; and to the fact that she was able to make currant jelly at a very critical moment she owed the affection of some of her husband's relatives, who up to that time had been rather prejudiced against her on the ground that she was merely an unpractical Blue-stocking.

Nor did her scientific knowledge ever warp or dull the tenderness and humanity of her nature. For birds and animals she had always a great love. We hear of her as a little girl watching with eager eyes the swallows as they built their nests in summer or prepared for their flight in the autumn; and when snow was on the ground she used to open the windows to let the robins hop in and pick crumbs on the breakfast-table. On one occasion she went with her father on a tour in the Highlands, and found on her return that a pet goldfinch, which had been left in the charge of the servants, had been neglected by them and had died of starvation. She was almost heart-broken at the event, and in writing her 'Recollections'* seventy years after, she mentioned it, and said that, as she wrote, she felt deep pain. Her chief pet in her old age was a mountain sparrow, which used to perch on her arm and go to sleep there while she was writing. One day the sparrow fell into the water-jug and was drowned, to the great grief of its mistress, who could hardly be consoled for its loss, though later on we hear of a beautiful paroquet taking the place of *le moineau d'Uranie*, and becoming Mrs Somerville's constant companion. She was also very energetic, Phyllis Browne tells us, in trying to get a law passed in the Italian Parliament for the protection of animals, and said once with reference to this subject, 'We English cannot boast of humanity so long as our sportsmen find pleasure in shooting down tame pigeons as they fly terrified out of a cage'—a remark with which I entirely agree. Mr Herbert's Bill for the protection of land birds gave her immense pleasure, though, to quote her own words, she was 'grieved to find that "the lark, which at heaven's gate sings," is thought unworthy of man's protection;' and she took a great fancy to a gentleman who, on being told of the number of singing birds that are eaten in Italy—nightingales, goldfinches, and robins—exclaimed in horror, 'What! robins!—our household birds! I would as soon eat a child!' Indeed, she believed to some extent in the immortality of animals, on the ground that if animals have no future it would seem as if some were created for uncompensated misery—an idea which does not seem to me to be either extravagant or fantastic, though it must be admitted that the optimism on which it is based receives absolutely no support from science.

On the whole, Phyllis Browne's book is very pleasant reading. Its only fault is that it is far too short, and this is a fault so rare in modern literature that it almost amounts to a distinction. However, Phyllis Browne has managed to crowd into the narrow limits at her disposal a great many interesting anecdotes. The picture she gives of Mrs Somerville working away at her translation of Laplace in the same room with her children, is very charming, and reminds one of what is told of George Sand; there is an amusing account of Mrs Somerville's visit to the widow of the young Pretender, the Countess of Albany,* who after talking with her for some time exclaimed, 'So you don't speak Italian! You must have had a very bad education!' And this story about the Waverley Novels may possibly be new to some of my readers:—

'A very amusing circumstance in connection with Mrs Somerville's acquaintance with Sir Walter arose out of the childish inquisitiveness of Woronzow Greig, Mrs Somerville's little boy.

'During the time Mrs Somerville was visiting Abbotsford, the Waverley Novels were appearing, and were creating a great sensation; yet even Scott's intimate friends did not know that he was the author; he enjoyed keeping the affair a mystery. But little Woronzow discovered what he was about. One day when Mrs Somerville was talking about a novel that had just been published, Woronzow said, "I knew all these stories long ago, for Mr Scott writes on the dinner-table; when he has finished he puts the green cloth with the papers in a corner of the dining-room, and when he goes out Charlie Scott and I read the stories." '

Phyllis Browne remarks that this incident shows 'that persons who want to keep a secret ought to be very careful when children are about;' but the story seems to me to be far too charming to require any moral of the kind.

Bound up in the same volume is a life of Miss Mary Carpenter,* also written by Phyllis Browne. Miss Carpenter does not seem to me to have the charm and fascination of Mrs Somerville. There is always something about her that is formal, limited, and precise. When she was about two years old she insisted on being called 'Doctor Carpenter' in the nursery; at the age of twelve she is described by a friend as a sedate little girl, who always spoke like a book; and before she entered on her educational schemes she wrote down a solemn dedication of herself to the service of humanity. However, she was one of the practical, hard-working saints of the nineteenth century, and it is no doubt quite right that the saints should take themselves very seriously. It is only fair, also, to remember that her work of rescue and reformation was carried on under great difficulties. Here, for instance, is the picture Miss Cobbe gives us of one of the Bristol night-schools:—

'It was a wonderful spectacle to see Mary Carpenter sitting patiently before the large school gallery in St Janes' Back, teaching, singing, and praying with the wild street-boys, in spite of endless interruptions caused by such proceedings as shooting marbles at any object behind her, whistling, stamping, fighting, shrieking out "Amen" in the middle of a prayer, and sometimes rising *en masse* and tearing, like a troop of bisons in hob-nailed shoes, down from the gallery, round the great school-room, and down the stairs, and into the street. These irrepressible outbreaks she bore with infinite good-humour.'

Her own account is somewhat pleasanter, and shows that 'the troop of bisons in hob-nailed shoes' was not always so barbarous.

'I had taken to my class on the preceding week some specimens of ferns neatly gummed on white paper. . . . This time I took a piece of coal-shale, with impressions of ferns, to show them. I told each to examine the specimen and tell me what he thought it was. W—— gave so bright a smile that I saw he knew; none of the others could tell; he said they were ferns, like what I showed them last week, but he thought they were chiselled on the stone. Their surprise and pleasure were great when I explained the matter to them.

'The history of Joseph. They all found a difficulty in realising that this had actually occurred. One asked if Egypt existed now, and if people lived in it. When I told them that buildings now stood which had been erected about the time of Joseph, one said that it was impossible, as they must have fallen down ere this. I showed them the form of a pyramid, and they were satisfied. *One asked if all books were true.*

'The story of Macbeth* impressed them very much. They knew the name of Shakespeare, having seen his name over a public-house.

'A boy defined conscience as "a thing a gentleman hasn't got who, when a boy finds his purse and gives it back to him, doesn't give the boy sixpence."

'Another boy was asked, after a Sunday evening lecture on "Thankful-ness," what pleasure he enjoyed most in the course of a year. He replied candidly, "Cock-fightin' ma'am: there's a pit up by the 'Black Boy' as is worth anythink in Brissel." '

There is something a little pathetic in the attempt to civilise the rough street-boy by means of the refining influence of ferns and fossils, and it is difficult to help feeling that Miss Carpenter rather over-estimated the value of elementary education. The poor are not to be fed upon facts. Even Shakespeare and the Pyramids are not sufficient; nor is there much use in giving them the results of culture, unless we also give them those conditions under which culture can be realised. In these cold, crowded cities of the North, the proper basis for morals, using the word in its wide Hellenic signification, is to be found in architecture, not in books.

Still it would be ungenerous not to recognise that Mary Carpenter gave to the children of the poor, not merely her learning, but her love. In early life, her biographer tells us, she had longed for the happiness of being a wife and a mother; but later she became content that her affection could be freely given to all who needed it, and the verse in the prophecies, 'I have given thee children whom thou hast not borne,' seemed to her to indicate what was to be her true mis-sion. Indeed, she rather inclined to Bacon's opinion,* that unmarried people do the best public work. 'It is quite striking,' she says in one of her letters, 'to observe how much the useful power and influence of woman has developed of later years. Unattached ladies, such as widows and unmarried women, have quite ample work to do in the world for the good of others to absorb all their powers. Wives and mothers have a very noble work given them by God, and want no more.' The whole passage is extremely interesting, and the phrase 'unattached ladies' is quite delightful, and reminds one of Charles Lamb.*

'Ismay's Children' (Macmillan and Co.) is by the clever authoress of that wonderful little story 'Flitters, Tatters, and the Counsellor,'* a story which delighted the realists by its truth, fascinated Mr Ruskin by its beauty, and remains to the present day the most perfect picture of street-Arab life in all English prose fiction. The scene of the novel is laid in the south of Ireland, and the plot is extremely dramatic and ingenious. Godfrey Mauleverer, a reckless young Irishman, runs away with Ismay Darcy, a pretty, penniless governess, and is privately married to her in Scotland. Some time after the birth of her third child, Ismay died, and her husband, who had never made his marriage public, nor taken any pains to establish the legitimacy of his children, is drowned while yachting off the coast of France. The care of Ismay's children then devolves on an old aunt, Miss Juliet Darcy, who brings them back to Ireland to claim their inheritance for them. But a sudden stroke of paralysis deprives her of her memory, and she forgets the name of the little Scotch village in which Ismay's informal marriage took place. So Tighe O'Malley holds Barrettstown, and Ismay's children live in an old mill close to the great park of which they are the rightful heirs. The boy, who is called Godfrey after his father, is a fascinating study, with his swarthy foreign beauty, his fierce moods of love and hate, his passionate pride, and his passionate tenderness. The account of his midnight ride to warn his enemy of an impending attack of Moonlighters is most powerful and spirited; and it is pleasant to meet in modern fiction a character that has all the fine inconsistencies of life, and, is neither too fantastic an exception to be true, not too ordinary a type to be common. Excellent also, in its direct simplicity of rendering, is the picture of Miss Juliet Darcy; and the scene in which, at the moment of her death, the old woman's memory returns to her is quite admirable, both in conception and in treatment. To me, however, the chief interest of the book lies in the little life-like sketches of Irish character with which it abounds. Modern realistic art has not yet produced a Hamlet, but at least it may claim to have studied Guildenstern and Rosencrantz very closely; and, for pure fidelity and truth to nature, nothing could be better than the minor characters in 'Ismay's Children.' Here we have the kindly old priest who arranges all the marriages in his parish, and has a strong objection to people who insist on making long confessions; the important young curate fresh from Maynooth, who gives himself more airs than a bishop, and has to be kept in order; the professional beggars, with their devout faith, their grotesque humour, and their incorrigible laziness; the shrewd shopkeeper, who imports arms in flour-barrels for the use of the Moonlighters, and, as soon as he has got rid of them, gives information of their whereabouts to the police; the young men who go out at night to be drilled by an Irish-American; the farmers with their wild land-hunger, bidding secretly against each other for every vacant field; the dispensary doctor who is always regretting that he has not got a Trinity College degree; the plain girls, who want to go into convents; the pretty girls, who want to get married; and the shopkeepers' daughters, who want to be thought young ladies. There is a whole pell-mell of men and women, a complete panorama of provincial life, an absolutely faithful picture of the peasant in his own home. This note of realism in dealing with national types of character has always been a distinguishing characteristic of Irish fiction, from the days of Miss Edgeworth down to our own days, and it is not difficult to see in 'Ismay's Children' some traces of the influence of 'Castle Rack-rent.'* I fear, however, that few people read Miss Edgeworth nowadays, though both Scott and Tourgénieff* acknowledged their indebtedness to her novels, and her style is always admirable in its clearness and precision.

Miss Leffler-Arnim's statement, in a lecture delivered recently at St Saviour's Hospital, that 'she had heard of instances where ladies were so determined not to exceed the fashionable measurement that they had actually held on to a cross-bar while their maids fastened the fifteen-inch corset,' has excited a good deal of incredulity, but there is nothing really improbable in it. From the sixteenth century to our own day there is hardly any form of torture that has not been inflicted on girls, and endured by women, in obedience to the dictates of an unreasonable and monstrous Fashion. 'In order to obtain a real Spanish figure,' says Montaigne, 'what a Gehenna of suffering will not women endure, drawn in and compressed by great *coches* entering the flesh; nay, sometimes they even die thereof!'* 'A few days after my arrival at school,' Mrs Somerville tells us in her memoirs, 'although perfectly straight and well made, I was enclosed in stiff stays, with a steel busk in front; while above my frock, bands drew my shoulders back till the shoulder-blades met. Then a steel rod with a semicircle, which went under my chin, was clasped to the steel busk in my stays. In this constrained state I and most of the younger girls had to prepare our lessons;' and in the life of Miss Edgeworth we read that, being sent to a certain fashionable establishment, 'she underwent all the usual tortures of back-boards, iron collars and dumbs, and also (because she was a very tiny person) the unusual one of being hung by the neck to draw out the muscles and increase the growth,' a signal failure in her case. Indeed, instances of absolute mutilation and misery are so common in the past that it is unnecessary to multiply them; but it is really sad to think that in our own day a civilised woman can hang on to a cross-bar while her maid laces her waist into a fifteen-inch circle. To begin with, the waist is not a circle at all, but an oval; nor can there be any greater error than to imagine that an unnaturally small waist gives an air of grace, or even of slightness to the whole figure. Its effect, as a rule, is to simply exaggerate the width of the shoulders and the hips; and those whose figures possess that stateliness, which is called stoutness by the vulgar, convert what is a quality into a defect by yielding to the silly edicts of Fashion on the subject of tight-lacing. The fashionable English waist, also, is not merely far too small, and consequently quite out of proportion to the rest of the figure, but it is worn far too low down. I use the expression 'worn' advisedly, for a waist nowadays seems to be regarded as an article of apparel to be put on when and where one likes. A long waist always implies shortness of the lower limbs, and from the artistic point of view has the effect of diminishing the height; and I am glad to see that many of the most charming women in Paris are returning to the idea of the Directoire style of dress. This style is not by any means perfect, but at least it has the merit of indicating the proper position of the waist. I feel quite sure that all English women of culture and position will set their faces against such stupid and dangerous practices as are related by Miss Leffler-Arnim. Fashion's motto is, *Il faut souffrir pour être belle*; but the motto of art and of common-sense is, *Il faut être bête pour souffrir*.*

Talking of Fashion, a critic in the *Pall Mall Gazette* expresses his surprise that I should have allowed an illustration of a hat, covered with 'the bodies of dead birds,' to appear in the first number of THE WOMAN'S WORLD; and as I have received many letters on the subject, it is only right that I should state my exact position in the matter. Fashion is such an essential part of the *mundus muliebris* of our day that it seems to me absolutely necessary that its growth, development, and phases should be duly chronicled; and the historical and practical value of such a record depends entirely upon its perfect fidelity to fact. Besides, it is quite easy for the children of light to adapt almost any fashionable form of dress to the requirements of utility and the demands of good taste. The Sarah Bernhardt tea-gown, for instance, figured in the present issue, has many good points about it, and the gigantic dress-improver does not appear to me to be really essential to the mode; and though the Postillion costume* of the fancy dress ball is absolutely detestable in its silliness and vulgarity, the so-called Late Georgian costume in the same plate is rather pleasing. I must, however, protest against the idea that to chronicle the development of Fashion implies any approval of the particular forms that Fashion may adopt.

Mrs Craik's article on the condition of the English stage will, I feel sure, be read with great interest by all who are watching the development of dramatic art in this country. It was the last thing written by the author of 'John Halifax, Gentleman,' and reached me only a few days before her lamented death. That the state of things is such as Mrs Craik describes, few will be inclined to deny; though, for my own part, I must acknowledge that I see more vulgarity than vice in the tendencies of the modern stage; nor do I think it possible to elevate dramatic art by limiting its subject-matter. *On tue une littérature quand on lui interdit la vérité humaine.** As far as the serious presentation of life is concerned, what we require is more imaginative treatment, greater freedom from theatric language and theatric convention. It may be questioned, also, whether the consistent reward of virtue and punishment of wickedness be really the healthiest ideal for an art that claims to mirror nature. However, it is impossible not to recognise the fine feeling that actuates every line of Mrs Craik's article; and though one may venture to disagree with the proposed method, one cannot but sympathise with the purity and delicacy of the thought, and the high nobility of the aim.

The French Minister of Education, M Spuller, has paid Racine* a very graceful and appropriate compliment, in naming after him the second college that has been opened in Paris for the higher education of girls. Racine was one of the privileged few who was allowed to read the celebrated *Traité de l'Education des Filles* before it appeared in print: he was charged, along with Boileau, with the task of revising the text of the constitution and rules of Madame de Maintenon's great college; it was for the Demoiselles de St Cyr that he composed *Athalie*;* and he devoted a great deal of his time to the education of his own children. The Lycée Racine will no doubt become as important an institution as the Lycée Fénelon, and the speech delivered by M Spuller on the occasion of its opening was full of the happiest augury for the future. M Spuller dwelt at great length on the value of Goethe's aphorism,* that the test of a good wife is her capacity to take her husband's place, and to become a father to his children, and mentioned that the thing that struck him most in America was the wonderful Brooklyn Bridge, a superb titanic structure, which was completed under the direction of the engineer's wife, the engineer himself having died while the building of the bridge was in progress. '*Il me semble*,' said M Spuller, '*que la femme de l'ingénieur du pont de Brooklyn a réalisé la pensée de Goethe, et que non seulement elle est devenue un père pour ses enfants, mais un autre père pour l'œuvre admirable, vraiment unique, qui a immortalisé le nom qu'elle portait avec son mari.*'* M Spuller also laid great stress on the necessity of a thoroughly practical education, and was extremely severe on the 'Blue-stockings' of literature. '*Il ne s'agit pas de former ici des "femmes savantes." Les "femmes savantes" ont été marquées pour jamais par un des plus grands génies de notre race d'une légère teinte de ridicule. Non, ce n'est pas des femmes savantes que nous voulons: ce sont tout simplement des femmes: des femmes dignes de ce pays de France, qui est la patrie du bons sens, de la mesure, et de la grâce; des femmes ayant la notion juste et le sens exquis du rôle qui doit leur appartenir dans la société moderne.*'* There is, no doubt, a great deal of truth in M Spuller's observations, but we must not mistake a caricature for the reality. After all, Les Précieuses Ridicules* contrasted very favourably with the ordinary type of womanhood of their day, not merely in France, but also in England; and an uncritical love of sonnets is preferable, on the whole, to coarseness, vulgarity, and ignorance.

I am glad to see that Miss Ramsay's* brilliant success at Cambridge is not destined to remain an isolated instance of what women can do in intellectual competitions with men. At the Royal University in Ireland, the Literature Scholarship of £100 a year for five years has been won by Miss Story, the daughter of a North of Ireland clergyman. It is pleasant to be able to chronicle an item of Irish news that has nothing to do with the violence of party politics or party feeling, and that shows how worthy women are of that higher culture and education which has been so tardily and, in some instances, so grudgingly granted to them.

The Empress of Japan* has been ordering a whole wardrobe of fashionable dresses in Paris for her own use and the use of her ladies-in-waiting. The chrysanthemum (the imperial flower of Japan) has suggested the tints of most of the Empress's own gowns, and in accordance with the colour-schemes of other flowers the rest of the costumes have been designed. The same steamer, however, that carries out the masterpieces of M Worth* and M Félix to the Land of the Rising Sun, also brings to the Empress a letter of formal and respectful remonstrance from the English Rational Dress Soceity.* I trust that, even if the Empress rejects the sensible arguments of this important Society, her own artistic feeling may induce her to reconsider her resolution to abandon Eastern for Western costume.

I hope that some of my readers will interest themselves in the Ministering Children's League,* for which Mr Walter Crane has done the beautiful and suggestive design of 'The Young Knight.' The best way to make children good is to make them happy, and happiness seems to me an essential part of Lady Meath's* admirable scheme.

LITERARY AND OTHER NOTES III[1]

MADAME RISTORI's 'Etudes et Souvenirs' (Paul Ollendorff: Paris) is one of the most delightful books on the stage that has appeared since Lady Martin's* charming volume on the Shakespearian heroines. It is often said that actors leave nothing behind them but a

[1] January 1888. Madame Ristori, *Etudes et Souvenirs* (London, 1888); Elizabeth Rachel Chapman, *The New Purgatory and Other Poems* (London, 1887); Lady Augusta Noel, *Hithersea Mere* (London, 1887); Alice Corkran, *Margery Merton's Girlhood* (London, 1888); Emily Pfeiffer, *Women and Work* (London, 1888); *Treasures of Art and Song*, ed. Robert Ellice Mack (London, 1887); Frederic E. Weatherly, *Rhymes and Roses*, ill. Ernest Wilson and St Clair Simons (London, 1888); Dora Havers, *Cape Town Dicky*, ill. Alice Havers (London, 1888); Oliver Goldsmith, *The Deserted Village*, ill. Charles Gregory and John Hines (London and New York, 1888).

barren name and a withered wreath; that they subsist simply upon the applause of the moment; that they are ultimately doomed to the oblivion of old play-bills; and that their art, in a word, dies with them, and shares their own mortality. 'Chippendale the cabinet-maker,' says the clever author of 'Obiter Dicta,' 'is more potent than Garrick* the actor. The vivacity of the latter no longer charms (save in Boswell); the chairs of the former still render rest impossible in a hundred homes.' This view, however, seems to me to be exaggerated. It rests on the assumption that acting is simply a mimetic art, and takes no account of its imaginative and intellectual basis. It is quite true, of course, that the personality of the player passes away, and with it that pleasure-giving power by virtue of which the arts exist. Yet the artistic method of a great actor survives. It lives on in tradition, and becomes part of the science of a school. It has all the intellectual life of a principle. In England, at the present moment, the influence of Garrick on our actors is far stronger than that of Reynolds on our painters of portraits, and if we turn to France it is easy to discern the tradition of Talma, but where is the tradition of David?*

Madame Ristori's memoirs, then, have not merely the charm that always attaches to the autobiography of a brilliant and beautiful woman, but have also a definite and distinct artistic value. Her analysis of the character of Lady Macbeth, for instance, is full of psychological interest, and shows us that the subtleties of Shakespearian criticism are not necessarily confined to those who have views on weak endings and rhyming tags, but may also be suggested by the art of acting itself. The author of 'Obiter Dicta' seeks to deny to actors all critical insight and all literary appreciation. The actor, he tells us, is art's slave, not her child, and lives entirely outside literature, 'with its words for ever on his lips, and none of its truths engraven on his heart.' But this seems to me to be a harsh and reckless generalisation. Indeed, so far from agreeing with it, I would be inclined to say that the mere artistic process of acting, the translation of literature back again into life, and the presentation of thought under the conditions of action, is in itself a critical method of a very high order; nor do I think that a study of the careers of our great English actors will really sustain the charge of want of literary appreciation. It may be true that actors pass too quickly away from the form, in order to get at the feeling that gives the form beauty and colour, and that, where the literary critic studies the language, the actor looks simply for the life; and yet, how well the great actors have appreciated that marvellous music of words which in Shakespeare, at any rate, is so vital an element of poetic power, if indeed it be not equally so in the case of all who have any claim to be regarded as true poets. 'The sensual life of verse,' says Keats, in a dramatic criticism published in *The Champion*, 'springs warm from the lips of Kean, and to one learned in Shakespearian hieroglyphics, learned in the spiritual portion of those lines to which Kean adds a sensual grandeur, his tongue must seem to have robbed the Hybla bees and left them honeyless.'* This particular feeling, of which Keats speaks, is familiar to all who have heard Salvini,* Sarah Bernhardt, Ristori, or any of the great artists of our day, and it is a feeling that one cannot, I think, gain merely by reading the passage to oneself. For my own part I must confess that it was not until I heard Sarah Bernhardt in *Phèdre** that I absolutely realised the sweetness of the music of Racine. As for Mr Birrell's statement that actors have the words of literature for ever on their lips, but none of its truths engraved on their hearts, all that one can say is that, if it be true, it is a defect which actors share with the majority of literary critics.

The account Madame Ristori gives of her own struggles, voyages and adventures, is very pleasant reading indeed. The child of poor actors, she made her first appearance when she was three months old, being brought on in a hamper as a New Year's gift to a selfish old gentleman who would not forgive his daughter for having married for love. As, however, she began to cry long before the hamper was opened, the comedy became a farce, to the immense amusement of the public. She next appeared in a mediæval melodrama, being then three years of age, and was so terrified at the machinations of the villain that she ran away at the most critical moment. However, her stage-fright seems to have soon disappeared, and we find her playing Silvio Pellico's *Francesca da Rimini* at fifteen, and at eighteen making her *début* as Marie Stuart.* At this time the naturalism of the French method was gradually displacing the artificial elocution and academic poses of the Italian school of acting. Mme Ristori seems to have tried to combine simplicity with style, and the passion of nature with the self-restraint of the artist. '*J'ai voulu fondre les deux manières,*' she tells us, '*car je sentais que toutes choses étant susceptibles de progrès, l'art dramatique aussi était appelé à subir des* *transformations.*'* The natural development, however, of the Italian drama was almost arrested by the ridiculous censorship of plays then existing in each town under Austrian or Papal rule. The slightest allusion to the sentiment of nationality or the spirit of freedom was prohibited. Even the word *patria* was regarded as treasonable, and Mme Ristori tells us an amusing story of the indignation of a censor who was asked to license a play, in which a dumb man returns home after an absence of many years, and on his entrance upon the stage makes gestures expressive of his joy in seeing his native land once more. 'Gestures of this kind,' said the censor, 'are obviously of a very revolutionary tendency, and cannot possibly be allowed. The only gestures that I could think of permitting would be gestures expressive of a dumb man's delight in scenery generally.' The stage directions were accordingly altered, and the word 'landscape' substituted for 'native land'! Another censor was extremely severe on an unfortunate poet who had used the expression 'the beautiful Italian sky,' and explained to him that 'the beautiful Lombardo-Venetian sky' was the proper official expression to use. Poor Gregory in *Romeo and Juliet* had to be rechristened, because Gregory is a name dear to the Popes; and the—

> 'Here I have a pilot's thumb,
> Wrecked as homeward he did come,'

of the first witch in Macbeth was ruthlessly struck out as containing an obvious allusion to the steersman of St Peter's bark.* Finally, bored and bothered by the political and theological Dogberrys* of the day, with their inane prejudices, their solemn stupidity, and their entire ignorance of the conditions necessary for the growth of sane and healthy art, Mme Ristori made up her mind to leave the stage. She, however, was extremely anxious to appear once before a Parisian audience, Paris being at that time the centre of dramatic activity, and after some consideration left Italy for France in the year 1855. There she seems to have been a great success, particularly in the part of Myrrha; classical without being cold, artistic without being academic, she brought to the interpretation of the character of Alfieri's* great heroine the colour-element of passion, the form-element of style. Jules Janin was loud in his praises, the Emperor begged Ristori to join the troupe of the Comédie Francaise, and Rachel,* with the strange narrow jealousy of her nature, trembled for her laurels.

Myrrha was followed by Marie Stuart, and Marie Stuart by Medea. In the latter part Mme Ristori excited the greatest enthusiasm. Ary Scheffer designed her costumes for her; and the Niobe* that stands in the Uffizzi Gallery at Florence, suggested to Mme Ristori her famous pose in the scene with the children. She would not consent, however, to remain in France, and we find her subsequently playing in almost every country in the world from Egypt to Mexico, from Denmark to Honolulu. Her representations of classical plays seem to have been always immensely admired. When she played at Athens, the King offered to arrange for a performance in the beautiful old theatre of Dionysos, and during her tour in Portugal she produced *Medea* before the University of Coimbra. Her description of the latter engagement is extremely interesting. On her arrival at the University, she was received by the entire body of the undergraduates, who still wear a costume almost mediæval in character. Some of them came on the stage in the course of the play as the handmaidens of Creusa,* hiding their black beards beneath heavy veils, and as soon as they had finished their parts they took their places gravely among the audience, to Madame Ristori's horror, still in their Greek dress, but with their veils thrown back, and smoking long cigars. '*Ce n'est pas la première fois,*' she says, '*que j'ai dû empêcher, par un effort de volonté, la tragédie de se terminer en farce.*'* Very interesting, also, is her account of the production of Montanelli's *Camma*,* and she tells an amusing story of the arrest of the author by the French police on the charge of murder, in consequence of a telegram she sent to him in which the words 'body of the victim' occurred. Indeed, the whole book is full of cleverly written stories, and admirable criticisms on dramatic art. I have quoted from the French version, which happens to be the one that lies before me, but whether in French or Italian the book is one of the most fascinating autobiographies that has appeared for some time, even in an age like ours when literary egotism has been brought to such an exquisite pitch of perfection.

'The New Purgatory and Other Poems' (Fisher Unwin), by Miss E. R. Chapman, is, in some respects, a very remarkable little volume. It used to be said that women were too poetical by nature to make great poets, too receptive to be really creative, too well satisfied with mere feeling to search after the marble splendour of form. But we must not judge of woman's poetic power by her achievements in days when education was denied to her, for where there is no faculty of expression no art is possible. Mrs Browning, the first great English poetess, was also an admirable scholar, though she may not have put the accents on her Greek, and even in those poems that seem most remote from classical life, such as 'Aurora Leigh,'* for instance, it is not difficult to trace the fine literary influence of a classical training. Since Mrs Browning's time, education has become, not the privilege of a few women, but the inalienable inheritance of all; and, as a natural consequence of the increased faculty of expression thereby gained, the women poets of our day hold a very high literary position. Curiously enough, their poetry is, as a rule, more distinguished for strength than for beauty; they seem to love to grapple with the big intellectual problems of modern life; science, philosophy and metaphysics form a large portion of their ordinary subject-matter; they leave the triviality of triolets to men, and try to read the writing on the wall, and to solve the last secret of the Sphinx. Hence Robert Browning, not Keats, is their idol; 'Sordello' moves them more than the 'Ode on a Grecian Urn'; and all Lord Tennyson's magic and music seems to them as nothing compared with the psychological subtleties of 'The Ring and the Book,' or the pregnant questions stirred in the dialogue between Blougram and Gigadibs.* Indeed, I remember hearing a charming young Girtonian, forgetting for a moment the exquisite lyrics in 'Pippa Passes,' and the superb blank verse of 'Men and Women,' state quite seriously that the reason she admired the author of 'Red-cotton Night-cap Country'* was that he had headed a reaction against beauty in poetry!

Miss Chapman is probably one of Mr Browning's disciples. She does not imitate him, but it is easy to discern his influence on her verse; and she has caught something of his fine, strange faith. Take, for instance, her poem, 'A Strong-minded Woman':—

> 'See her? Oh, yes!—Come this way—hush! this way,
>   Here she is lying,
> Sweet—with the smile her face wore yesterday,
>   As she lay dying.
> Calm, the mind-fever gone, and, praise God! gone
>   All the heart-hunger;
> Looking the merest girl at forty-one—
>   You guessed her younger?
> Well, she'd the flower-bloom that children have,

Was lithe and pliant,
With eyes as innocent blue as they were brave,
  Resolved, defiant.
Yourself—you worship art! Well, at that shrine
  She too bowed lowly,
Drank thirstily of beauty, as of wine,
  Proclaimed it holy.
But could you follow her when, in a breath,
  She knelt to science,
Vowing to truth true service to the death,
  And heart-reliance?
Nay,—then for you she underwent eclipse,
  Appeared as alien
As once, before he prayed, those ivory lips
  Seemed to Pygmalion.

Hear from your heaven, my dear, my lost delight,
  You who were woman
To your heart's heart, and not more pure, more white,
  Than warmly human.
How shall I answer? How express, reveal
  Your true life-story?
How utter, if they cannot guess—not feel
  Your crowning glory?
This way. Attend my words. The rich, we know,
  Do into heaven
Enter but hardly; to the poor, the low,
  God's kingdom's given.
Well, there's another heaven—a heaven on earth—
  (That's love's fruition)
Whereto a certain lack—a certain dearth—
  Gains best admission.
Here, too, she was too rich—ah, God! if less
  Love had been lent her!—
Into the realm of human happiness
  These look—not enter.'

Well, here we have, if not quite an echo, at least a reminiscence of
the metre of 'The Grammarian's Funeral;'* and the peculiar blending
together of lyrical and dramatic forms, seems essentially characteristic of Mr Browning's method. Yet there is a distinct personal note
running all through the poem, and true originality is to be found
rather in the use made of a model than in the rejection of all models

and masters. *Dans l'art comme dans la nature on est toujours fils de quelqu'un,** and we should not quarrel with the reed if it whispers to us the music of the lyre. A little child once asked me if it was the nightingale who taught the linnets how to sing.

Miss Chapman's other poems contain a great deal that is interesting. The most ambitious is 'The New Purgatory,' to which the book owes its title. It is a vision of a strange garden in which, cleansed and purified of all stain and shame, walk Judas of Cherioth, Nero the Lord of Rome, Ysabel the wife of Ahab,* and others, around whose names cling terrible memories of horror, or awful splendours of sin. The conception is fine, but the treatment is hardly adequate. There are, however, some good strong lines in it, and, indeed, almost all of Miss Chapman's poems are worth reading, if not for their absolute beauty, at least for their intellectual intention.

Nothing is more interesting than to watch the change and development of the art of novel-writing in this nineteenth century—'this so-called nineteenth century,' as an impassioned young orator once termed it, after a contemptuous diatribe against the evils of modern civilisation. In France they have had one great genius, Balzac, who invented the modern method of looking at life; and one great artist, Flaubert,* who is the impeccable master of style; and to the influence of these two men we may trace almost all contemporary French fiction. But in England we have had no schools worth speaking of. The fiery torch lit by the Brontës has not been passed on to other hands; Dickens has influenced only journalism; Thackeray's delightful superficial philosophy, superb narrative power, and clever social satire have found no echoes; nor has Trollope left any direct successors behind him—a fact which is not much to be regretted, however, as, admirable though Trollope undoubtedly is for rainy afternoons and tedious railway journeys, from the point of view of literature he is merely the perpetual curate of Pudlington Parva.* As for George Meredith, who could hope to reproduce him? His style is chaos illumined by brilliant flashes of lightning. As a writer he has mastered everything, except language; as a novelist he can do everything, except tell a story; as an artist he is everything, except articulate.* Too strange to be popular, too individual to have imitators, the author of 'Richard Feverel'* stands absolutely alone. It is easy to disarm criticism, but he has disarmed the disciple. He gives us his philosophy through the medium of wit, and is never so pathetic as when he is humorous. To turn truth into a paradox is not difficult, but George Meredith makes all his paradoxes truths, and no Theseus can thread his labyrinth, no Œdipus* solve his secret.

However, it is only fair to acknowledge that there are some signs of a school springing up amongst us. This school is not native, nor does it seek to reproduce any English master. It may be described as the result of the realism of Paris filtered through the refining influence of Boston. Analysis, not action, is its aim; it has more psychology than passion, and it plays very cleverly upon one string, and this is the commonplace.

As a reaction against this school, it is pleasant to come across a novel like Lady Augusta Noel's* 'Hithersea Mere' (Macmillan and Co.). If this story has any definite defect, it comes from its delicacy and lightness of treatment. An industrious Bostonian* would have made half a dozen novels out of it, and have had enough left for a serial. Lady Augusta Noel is content to vivify her characters, and does not care about vivisection; she suggests rather than explains; and she does not seek to make life too obviously rational. Romance, picturesqueness, charm—these are the qualities of her book. As for its plot, it has so many plots that it is difficult to describe them. We have the story of Rhona Somerville, the daughter of a great popular preacher, who tries to write her father's life, and, on looking over his papers and early diaries, finds struggle where she expected calm, and doubt where she looked for faith, and is afraid to keep back the truth, and yet dares not publish it. Rhona is quite charming; she is like a little flower that takes itself very seriously, and she shows us how thoroughly nice and natural a narrow-minded girl may be. Then we have the two brothers, John and Adrian Mowbray. John is the hard-working, vigorous clergyman, who is impatient of all theories, brings his faith to the test of action, not of intellect, lives what he believes, and has no sympathy for those who waver or question—a thoroughly admirable, practical, and extremely irritating man. Adrian is the fascinating *dilettante*, the philosophic doubter, a sort of romantic rationalist with a taste for art. Of course, Rhona marries the brother who needs conversion, and their gradual influence on each other is indicated by a few subtle touches. Then we have the curious story of Olga, Adrian Mowbray's first love. She is a wonderful and mystical

girl, like a little maiden out of the Sagas,* with the blue eyes and fair
hair of the North. An old Norwegian nurse is always at her side, a
sort of Lapland witch who teaches her how to see visions and to
interpret dreams. Adrian mocks at this superstition, as he calls it, but
as a consequence of disregarding it, Olga's only brother is drowned
skating, and she never speaks to Adrian again. The whole story is
told in the most suggestive way, the mere delicacy of the touch
making what is strange seem real. The most delightful character in
the whole book, however, is a girl called Hilary Marston, and hers
also is the most tragic tale of all. Hilary is like a little woodland faun,
half Greek and half gipsy; she knows the note of every bird, and the
haunt of every animal; she is terribly out of place in a drawing-room,
but is on intimate terms with every young poacher in the district;
squirrels come and sit on her shoulder, which is pretty, and she
carries ferrets in her pockets, which is dreadful; she never reads a
book, and has not got a single accomplishment, but she is fascinating
and fearless, and wiser, in her own way, than any pedant or book-
worm. This poor little English Dryad* falls passionately in love with a
great blind helpless hero, who regards her as a sort of pleasant tom-
boy; and her death is most touching and pathetic. Lady Augusta
Noel has a charming and winning style, her descriptions of Nature
are quite admirable, and her book is one of the most pleasantly-
written novels that has appeared this winter.

Miss Alice Corkran's* 'Margery Merton's Girlhood' (Blackie
and Son) has the same lightness of touch and grace of treatment.
Though ostensibly meant for young people, it is a story that all can
read with pleasure, for it is true without being harsh, and beautiful
without being affected, and its rejection of the stronger and more
violent passions of life is artistic rather than ascetic. In a word, it is a
little piece of true literature, as dainty as it is delicate, and as sweet as
it is simple. Margery Merton is brought up in Paris by an old maiden
aunt, who has an elaborate theory of education, and strict ideas
about discipline. Her system is an excellent one, being founded on
the science of Darwin* and the wisdom of Solomon, but it comes to
terrible grief when put into practice; and finally she has to procure a
governess, Madame Réville, the widow of a great and unappreciated
French painter. From her Margery gets her first feeling for art, and
the chief interest of the book centres round a competition for an art

scholarship, into which Margery and the other girls of the convent school enter. Margery selects Joan of Arc as her subject; and, rather to the horror of the good nuns, who think that the saint should have her golden aureole, and be as gorgeous and as ecclesiastical as bright paints and bad drawing can make her, the picture represents a common peasant girl, standing in an old orchard, and listening in ignorant terror to the strange voices whispering in her ear. The scene in which she shows her sketch for the first time to the art master and the Mother Superior is very cleverly rendered indeed, and shows considerable dramatic power.

Of course, a good deal of opposition takes place, but ultimately Margery has her own way and, in spite of a wicked plot set on foot by a jealous competitor, who persuades the Mother Superior that the picture is not Margery's own work, she succeeds in winning the prize. The whole account of the gradual development of the conception in the girl's mind, and the various attempts she makes to give her dream its perfect form, is extremely interesting and, indeed, the book deserves a place among what Sir George Trevelyan* has happily termed 'the art-literature' of our day. Mr Ruskin in prose, and Mr Browning in poetry, were the first who drew for us the workings of the artist soul, the first who led us from the painting or statue to the hand that fashioned it, and the brain that gave it life. They seem to have made art more expressive for us, to have shown us a passionate humanity lying behind line and colour. Theirs was the seed of this new literature, and theirs, too, is its flower; but it is pleasant to note their influence on Miss Corkran's little story, in which the creation of a picture forms the dominant *motif*.

Mrs Pfeiffer's 'Women and Work' (Trübner and Co.) is a collection of most interesting essays on the relation to health and physical development of the higher education of girls, and the intellectual or more systematised effort of woman. Mrs Pfeiffer, who writes a most admirable prose style, deals in succession with the sentimental difficulty, with the economic problem, and with the arguments of physiologists. She boldly grapples with Professor Romanes,* whose recent article in the *Nineteenth Century*, on the leading characters which mentally differentiate men and women, attracted so much attention, and produces some very valuable statistics from America, where the influence of education on health has been most carefully studied. Her book is a most important contribution to the discussion of one of the great social problems of our day. The extended activity of women is now an accomplished fact; its results are on their trial; and Mrs Pfeiffer's excellent essays sum up the situation very completely, and show the rational and scientific basis of the movement more clearly and more logically than any other treatise I have as yet seen.

It is interesting to note that many of the most advanced modern ideas on the subject of the education of women are anticipated by Defoe in his wonderful Essay upon Projects,* where he proposes that a college for women should be erected in every county in England, and ten colleges of the kind in London. 'I have often thought of it,' he says, 'as one of the most barbarous customs in the world that we deny the advantages of learning to women. Their youth is spent to teach them to stitch and sew, or make baubles. They are taught to read, indeed, and perhaps to write their names or so, and that is the height of a woman's education. And I would but ask any who slight the sex for their understanding, "What is a man (a gentleman I mean) good for that is taught no more?" What has the woman done to forfeit the privilege of being taught? Shall we upbraid women with folly when it is only the error of this inhuman custom that hindered them being made wiser?' Defoe then proceeds to elaborate his scheme for the foundation of women's colleges, and enters into minute details about the architecture, the general curriculum, and the discipline. His suggestion that the penalty of death should be inflicted on any man who ventured to make a proposal of marriage to any of the girl students during term time possibly suggested the plot of Lord Tennyson's 'Princess,'* so its harshness may be excused, and in all other respects his ideas are admirable. I am glad to see that this curious little volume forms one of the National Library series. In its anticipations of many of our most modern inventions it shows how thoroughly practical all dreamers are.

I am sorry to see that Mrs Fawcett* deprecates the engagement of ladies of education as dressmakers and milliners, and speaks of it as being detrimental to those who have fewer educational advantages. I myself would like to see dressmaking regarded not merely as a learned profession, but as a fine art. To construct a costume that will be at once rational and beautiful requires an accurate knowledge of the principles of proportion, a thorough acquaintance with the laws of health, a subtle sense of colour, and a quick appreciation of the proper use of materials, and the proper qualities of pattern and design. The health of a nation depends very largely on its mode of dress; the artistic feeling of a nation should find expression in its costume quite as much as in its architecture; and just as the upholstering tradesman has had to give place to the decorative artist, so the ordinary milliner, with her lack of taste and lack of knowledge, her foolish fashions and her feeble inventions, will have to make way for the scientific and artistic dress designer. Indeed, so far from it being wise to discourage women of education from taking up the profession of dressmakers, it is exactly women of education who are needed, and I am glad to see in the new technical college for women at Bedford, millinery and dressmaking are to be taught as part of the ordinary curriculum. There has also been a Society of Lady Dressmakers started in London for the purpose of teaching educated girls and women, and the Scientific Dress Association is, I hear, doing very good work in the same direction.

I have received some very beautiful specimens of Christmas books from Messrs Griffith and Farran. 'Treasures of Art and Song,' edited by Robert Ellice Mack, is a real *édition de luxe* of pretty poems and pretty pictures; and 'Through the Year' is a wonderfully artistic calendar.

Messrs Hildesheimer and Faulkner have also sent me 'Rhymes and Roses,' illustrated by Ernest Wilson and St Clair Simmons; 'Cape Town Dicky,' a child's book, with some very lovely pictures by Miss Alice Havers; a wonderful edition of 'The Deserted Village,'* illustrated by Mr Charles Gregory and Mr Hines; and some really charming Christmas cards, those by Miss Alice Havers, Miss Edwards, and Miss Dealy being especially good.

The most perfect and the most poisonous of all modern French poets once remarked that a man can live for three days without bread, but that no one can live for three days without poetry. This, however, can hardly be said to be a popular view, or one that commends itself to that curiously uncommon quality which is called common sense. I fancy that most people, if they do not actually prefer a salmi to a sonnet,* certainly like their culture to repose on a basis of good cookery, and as there is something to be said for this attitude, I am glad to see that several ladies are interesting themselves in cookery classes. Mrs Marshall's brilliant lectures are, of course, well known, and besides her there is Mme Lebour-Fawssett, who holds weekly classes in Kensington. Mme Fawssett is the author of an admirable little book, entitled 'Economical French Cookery for Ladies,'* and I am glad to hear that her lectures are so successful. I was talking the other day to a lady who works a great deal at the East End of London, and she told me that no small part of the permanent misery of the poor is due to their entire ignorance of the cleanliness and economy necessary for good cooking.

The Popular Ballad Concert Society has been reorganised under the name of the Popular Musical Union. Its object will be to train the working classes thoroughly in the enjoyment and performance of music, and to provide the inhabitants of the crowded districts of the East-end with concerts and oratorios, to be performed as far as possible by trained members of the working classes; and, though money is urgently required, it is proposed to make the Society to a certain degree self-supporting by giving something in the form of high-class concerts in return for subscriptions and donations. The whole scheme is an excellent one, and I hope that the readers of THE WOMAN'S WORLD will give it their valuable support. Mrs Ernest Hart is the secretary, and the treasurer is the Rev S. Barnett.

LITERARY AND OTHER NOTES IV[1]

'CANUTE THE GREAT' (George Bell and Sons), by Michael Field,* is in many respects a really remarkable work of art. Its tragic element is to be found in life, not in death; in the hero's psychological development, not in his moral declension or in any physical calamity; and

[1] February 1888. Michael Field, *Canute the Great* (London, 1887); Frances Martin, *Life of Elizabeth Gilbert* (London, 1887); Louise Chandler Moulton, *Ourselves and Our Neighbours* (London, 1887); T. H. Penguin, *Warring Angels* (London, 1887); Mrs De Courcy Laffan, *A Song of Jubilee and Other Poems* (London, 1887); Bella Duffy, *Life of Madame de Staël* (London, 1887); John Evelyn, *Life of Mrs Godolphin*, ed. William Harcourt of Nuneham (London, 1888).

the author has borrowed from modern science the idea that in the evolutionary struggle for existence the true tragedy may be that of the survivor. Canute, the rough generous Viking, finds himself alienated from his gods, his forefathers, his very dreams. With centuries of Pagan blood in his veins, he sets himself to the task of becoming a great Christian governor and lawgiver to men; and yet he is fully conscious that, while he has abandoned the noble impulses of his race, he still retains that which in his nature is most fierce or fearful. It is not by faith that he reaches the new creed, nor through gentleness that he seeks after the new culture. The beautiful Christian woman whom he has made queen of his life and lands teaches him no mercy, and knows nothing of forgiveness. It is sin and not suffering that purifies him—mere sin itself. 'Be not afraid,' he says in the last great scene of the play:—

> 'Be not afraid;
> I have learnt this, sin is a mighty bond
> 'Twixt God and man. Love that has ne'er forgiven
> Is virgin and untender; spousal passion
> Becomes acquainted with life's vilest things,
> Transmutes them, and exalts. Oh, wonderful,
> This touch of pardon,—all the shame cast out;
> The heart a-ripple with the gaiety,
> The leaping consciousness that Heaven knows all,
> And yet esteems us royal. Think of it—
> The joy, the hope!'

This strange and powerful conception is worked out in a manner as strong as it is subtle; and, indeed, almost every character in the play seems to suggest some new psychological problem. The mere handling of the verse is essentially characteristic of our modern introspective method, as it presents to us, not thought in its perfected form, but the involutions of thought seeking for expression. We seem to witness the very workings of the mind, and to watch the passion struggling for utterance. In plays of this kind (plays that are meant to be read, not to be acted) it must be admitted that we often miss that narrative and descriptive element which in the epic is so great a charm, and, indeed, may be said to be almost essential to the perfect literary presentation of any story. This element the Greek managed to retain by the introduction of chorus and messenger; but we seem to have been unable to invent any substitute for it. That there is here a distinct loss cannot, I think, be denied. There is something harsh, abrupt, and inartistic in such a stage-direction as 'Canute strangles Edric, flings his body into the stream, and gazes out.' It strikes no dramatic note, it conveys no picture, it is meagre and inadequate. If acted it might be fine; but as read, it is unimpressive. However, there is no form of art that has not got its limitations, and though it is sad to see the action of a play relegated to a formal footnote, still there is undoubtedly a certain gain in psychological analysis and psychological concentration.

It is a far cry from the Knutlinga Saga* to Rossetti's note-book, but Michael Field passes from one to the other without any loss of power. Indeed, most readers will probably prefer 'The Cup of Water,' which is the second play in this volume, to the earlier historical drama. It is more purely poetical; and if it has less power, it has certainly more beauty. Rossetti conceived the idea of a story in which a young king falls passionately in love with a little peasant girl who gives him a cup of water, and is by her beloved in turn, but being betrothed to a noble lady, he yields her in marriage to his friend, on condition that once a year—on the anniversary of their meeting— she brings him a cup of water. The girl dies in childbirth, leaving a daughter who grows into her mother's perfect likeness, and comes to meet the king when he is hunting. Just, however, as he is about to take the cup from her hand, a second figure, in her exact likeness, but dressed in peasant's clothes, steps to her side, looks in the king's face, and kisses him on the mouth. He falls forward on his horse's neck, and is lifted up dead. Michael Field has struck out the supernatural element so characteristic of Rossetti's genius, and in some other respects modified for dramatic purposes material Rossetti left unused. The result is a poem of exquisite and pathetic grace. Cara, the peasant girl, is a creation as delicate as it is delightful, and it deserves to rank beside the Faun of 'Callirhöe.'* As for the young king who loses all the happiness of his life through one noble moment of unselfishness, and who recognised as he stands over Cara's dead body that

> '——women are not chattels,
> To deal with as one's generosity
> May prompt or straiten . . .'

and that

'—we must learn
To drink life's pleasures if we would be pure,'

he is one of the most romantic figures in all modern dramatic work. Looked at from a purely technical point of view, Michael Field's verse is sometimes lacking in music, and has no sustained grandeur of movement; but it is extremely dramatic, and its method is admirably suited to express those swift touches of nature and sudden flashes of thought which are Michael Field's distinguishing qualities. As for the moral contained in these plays, work that has the rich vitality of life has always something of life's mystery also; it cannot be narrowed down to a formal creed, nor summed up in a platitude; it has many answers, and more than one secret.

Miss Frances Martin's 'Life of Elizabeth Gilbert'* (Macmillan and Co.) is an extremely interesting book. Elizabeth Gilbert was born at a time when, as her biographer reminds us, kindly and intelligent men and women could gravely implore the Almighty to 'take away' a child merely because it was blind; when they could argue that to teach the blind to read, or to attempt to teach them to work, was to fly in the face of Providence; and her whole life was given to the endeavour to overcome this prejudice and superstition; to show that blindness, though a great privation, is not necessarily a disqualification; and that blind men and women can learn, labour, and fulfil all the duties of life. Before her day all that the blind were taught was to commit texts from the Bible to memory. She saw that they could learn handicrafts, and be made industrious and self-supporting. She began with a small cellar in Holborn, at the rent of eighteenpence a week, but before her death she could point to large and well-appointed workshops in almost every city of England where blind men and women are employed, where tools have been invented by or modified for them, and where agencies have been established for the sale of their work. The whole story of her life is full of pathos and of beauty. She was not born blind, but lost her sight through an attack of scarlet fever when she was three years old. For a long time she could not realise her position, and we hear of the little child making earnest appeals to be taken 'out of the dark room,' or to have a candle lighted; and once she whispered to her father, 'If I am a very good little girl, may I see my doll to-morrow?' However, all memory of vision seems to have faded from her before she left the sick-room, though, taught by those around her, she soon began to take an imaginary interest in colour, and a very real one in form and texture. An old nurse is still alive who remembers making a pink frock for her when she was a child, her delight at its being pink and her pleasure in stroking down the folds; and when in 1835 the young Princess Victoria visited Oxford with her mother, Bessie, as she was always called, came running home, exclaiming, 'Oh, mamma, I have seen the Duchess of Kent, and she had on a brown silk dress.' Her youthful admiration of Wordsworth was based chiefly upon his love of flowers, but also on personal knowledge. When she was about ten years old, Wordsworth went to Oxford to receive the honorary degree of D.C.L. from the University. He stayed with Dr Gilbert, then Principal of Brasenose, and won Bessie's heart the first day by telling at the dinner table how he had almost leapt off the coach in Bagley Wood to gather the blue veronica. But she had a better reason for remembering that visit. One day she was in the drawing-room alone, and Wordsworth entered. For a moment he stood silent before the blind child, the little sensitive face, with its wondering, inquiring look, turned towards him. Then he gravely said, 'Madam, I hope I do not disturb you.' She never forgot that 'Madam'—grave, solemn, almost reverential.

As for the great practical work of her life, the amelioration of the condition of the blind, Miss Martin gives a wonderful account of her noble efforts and her noble success; and the volume contains a great many interesting letters from eminent people, of which the following characteristic note from Mr. Ruskin is not the least interesting:—

'Denmark Hill, 2nd September, 1871.
'MADAM,—I am obliged by your letter, and I deeply sympathise with the objects of the institution over which you preside. But one of my main principles of work is that every one must do their best and spend their all in their own work, and mine is with a much lower race of sufferers than you plead for—with those who "have eyes and see not."—I am, Madam, your faithful servant,   "J. RUSKIN." '

Miss Martin is a most sympathetic biographer, and her book should be read by all who care to know the history of one of the remarkable women of our century.

'Ourselves and Our Neighbours' (Ward and Downey) is a pleasant volume of social essays from the pen of one of the most graceful and attractive of all American poetesses, Mrs Louise Chandler Moulton.* Mrs Moulton, who has a very light literary touch, discusses every important modern problem—from Society rose-buds and old bachelors, down to the latest fashions in bonnets and in sonnets. The best chapter in the book is that entitled 'The Gospel of Good Gowns,' which contains some very excellent remarks on the ethics of dress. Mrs Moulton sums up her position in the following passage:—

'The desire to please is a natural characteristic of unspoiled womanhood. "If I lived in the woods, I should dress for the trees," said a woman widely known for taste and for culture. Every woman's dress should be, and if she has any ideality will be, an expression of herself. . . . The true gospel of dress is that of fitness and taste. Pictures are painted, and music is written, and flowers are fostered, that life may be made beautiful. Let women delight our eyes like pictures, be harmonious as music, and fragrant as flowers, that they also may fulfil their mission of grace and of beauty. By companionship with beautiful thoughts shall their tastes be so formed that their toilets will never be out of harmony with their means or their position. They will be clothed almost as unconsciously as the lilies of the field; but each one will be herself, and there will be no more uniformity in their attire than in their faces.'

The modern Dryad who is ready to 'dress for the trees' seems to me a charming type; but I hardly think that Mrs Moulton is right when she says that the woman of the future will be clothed 'almost as unconsciously as the lilies of the field.' Possibly, however, she means merely to emphasise the distinction between dressing and dressing-up, a distinction which is often forgotten.

'Warring Angels' (J. Fisher Unwin) is a very sad and suggestive story. It contains no impossible heroine and no improbable hero, but is simply a faithful transcript from life, a truthful picture of men and women as they are. Darwin could not have enjoyed it, as it does not end happily. There is, at least, no distribution of cakes and ale in the last chapter. But, then, scientific people are not always the best judges of literature. They seem to think that the sole aim of art should be to amuse, and had they been consulted on the subject would have banished Melpomene from Parnassus. It may be admitted, however, that not a little of our modern art is somewhat harsh and painful. Our Castaly* is very salt with tears, and we have bound

the brows of the Muses with cypress and with yew. We are often told
that we are a shallow age,* yet we have certainly the saddest literature
of all the ages, for we have made Truth and not Beauty the aim of art,
and seem to value imitation more than imagination. This tendency
is, of course, more marked in fiction than it is in poetry. Beauty of
form is always in itself a source of joy; the mere *technique* of verse has
an imaginative and spiritual element; and life must, to a certain
degree, be transfigured before it can find its expression in music. But
ordinary fiction, rejecting the beauty of form in order to realise the
facts of life, seems often to lack the vital element of delight, to miss
that pleasure-giving power in virtue of which the arts exist. It would
not, however, be fair to regard 'Warring Angels' simply as a specimen of literary photography. It has a marked distinction of style, a
definite grace and simplicity of manner. There is nothing crude in it,
though it is to a certain degree inexperienced; nothing violent,
though it is often strong. The story it has to tell has frequently been
told before, but the treatment makes it new; and Lady Flower, for
whose white soul the angels of good and evil are at war, is admirably
conceived, and admirably drawn.

'A Song of Jubilee and Other Poems' (Kegan Paul, Trench, and
Co.) contains some pretty, picturesque verses. Its author is Mrs De
Courcy Laffan, who, under the name of Mrs Leith Adams,* is well
known as a novelist and storywriter. The Jubilee Ode is quite as good
as most of the Jubilee Odes* have been, and some of the short poems
are graceful. This from 'The First Butterfly' is pretty:—

> 'O little bird without a song! I love
> Thy silent presence, floating in the light—
> A living, perfect thing, when scarcely yet
> The snow-white blossom crawls along the wall,
> And not a daisy shows its star-like head
> Amid the grass.'

Miss Bella Duffy's 'Life of Madame de Staël' forms part of that
admirable 'Eminent Women Series' which is so well edited by Mr
John H. Ingram.* There is nothing absolutely new in Miss Duffy's
book, but this was not to be expected. Unpublished correspondence,
that delight of the eager biographer, is not to be had in the case of
Madame de Staël, the De Broglie family* having either destroyed or

successfully concealed all the papers which might have revealed any facts not already in the possession of the world. Upon the other hand, the book has the excellent quality of condensation, and gives us in less than two hundred pages a very good picture of Madame de Staël and her day. Miss Duffy's criticism of 'Corinne'* is worth quoting:

' "Corinne" is a classic of which everybody is bound to speak with respect. The enormous admiration which it exacted at the time of its appearance may seem somewhat strange in this year of grace; but then it must be remembered that Italy was not the over-written country it has since become. Besides this, Madame de Staël was the most conspicuous person-age of her day. Except Chateaubriand, she had nobody to dispute with her the palm of literary glory in France. Her exile, her literary circle, her courageous opinions, had kept the eyes of Europe fixed on her for years, so that any work from her pen was sure to excite the liveliest curiosity.

' "Corinne" is a kind of glorified guide-book, with some of the qualities of a good novel. It is very long-winded, but the appetite of the age was robust in that respect, and the highly-strung emotions of the hero and heroine could not shock a taste which had been formed by the *Sorrows of Werther*.* It is extremely moral, deeply sentimental, and of a deadly earn-estness—three characteristics which could not fail to recommend it to a dreary and ponderous generation, the most deficient in taste that ever trod the earth.

'But it is artistic in the sense that the interest is concentrated from first to last on the central figure, and the drama, such as it is, unfolds itself naturally from its starting point, which is the contrast between the characters of Oswald and Corinne.'

The 'dreary and ponderous generation, the most deficient in taste that ever trod the earth,' seems to me a somewhat exaggerated mode of expression, but 'glorified guide-book' is a not unfelicitous descrip-tion of the novel that once thrilled Europe. Miss Duffy sums up her opinion of Madame de Staël as a writer in the following passage:—

'Her mind was strong of grasp and wide in range, but continuous effort fatigued it. She could strike out isolated sentences alternately brilliant, exhaustive, and profound, but she could not link them to other sentences so as to form an organic whole. Her thought was definite singly, but vague as a whole. She always saw things separately, and tried to combine them arbitrarily, and it is generally difficult to follow out any idea of hers from its origin to its end. Her thoughts are like pearls of price profusely scat-tered, or carelessly strung together, but not set in any design. On closing one of her books, the reader is left with no continuous impression. He has been dazzled and delighted, enlightened also by flashes; but the horizons disclosed have vanished again, and the outlook is enriched by no new vistas.

'Then she was deficient in the higher qualities of the imagination. She could analyse, but not characterise; construct, but not create. She could take one defect like selfishness, or one passion like love, and display its workings; or she could describe a whole character, like Napoleon's, with marvellous penetration; but she could not make her personages talk, or act like human beings. She lacked pathos, and had no sense of humour. In short, hers was a mind endowed with enormous powers of comprehension, and an amazing richness of ideas, but deficient in perception of beauty, in poetry, and in true originality. She was a great social personage, but her influence on literature was not destined to be lasting, because, in spite of foreseeing too much, she had not the true prophetic sense of proportion, and confused the things of the present with those of the future—the accidental with the enduring.'

I cannot but think that in this passage Miss Duffy rather under-rates Madame de Staël's influence on the literature of the nineteenth century. It is true that she gave our literature no new form, but she was one of those who gave it a new spirit, and the romantic movement owes her no small debt. However, a biography should be read for its pictures more than for its criticisms, and Miss Duffy shows a remarkable narrative power, and tells with a good deal of *esprit* the wonderful adventures of the brilliant woman whom Heine* termed 'a whirlwind in petticoats.'

Mr. Harcourt's reprint of John Evelyn's 'Life of Mrs Godolphin'* (Sampson Low and Co.) is a welcome addition to the list of charming library books. Mr Harcourt's grandfather, the Archbishop of York, himself John Evelyn's great-great-grandson, inherited the manuscript from his distinguished ancestor, and in 1847 entrusted it for publication to Samuel Wilberforce,* then Bishop of Oxford. As the book has been for a long time out of print, this new edition is sure to awake fresh interest in the life of the noble and virtuous lady whom John Evelyn so much admired. Margaret Godolphin was one of the Queen's Maids of Honour at the Court of Charles II,* and was distinguished for the delicate purity of her nature, as well as for her high intellectual attainments. Some of the extracts Evelyn gives from her Diary seem to show an austere, formal, almost ascetic spirit; but it was inevitable that a nature so refined as hers should have turned in horror from such ideals of life as were presented by men like Buckingham and Rochester, like Etheridge, Killigrew, and Sedley,* like the King himself, to whom she could scarcely bring herself to speak. After her marriage she seems to have become happier and brighter, and her early death makes her a pathetic and interesting figure in the history of the time. Evelyn can see no fault in her, and his life of her is the most wonderful of all panegyrics.

Amongst the Maids of Honour mentioned by John Evelyn is Frances Jennings, the elder sister of the great Duchess of Marlborough.* Miss Jennings, who was one of the most beautiful women of her day, married first Sir George Hamilton, brother of the author of the 'Mémoires de Grammont,' and afterwards Richard Talbot, who was made Duke of Tyrconnel by James II.* William's successful occupation of Ireland,* where her husband was Lord Deputy, reduced her to poverty and obscurity, and she was probably the first Peeress who ever took to millinery as a livelihood. She had a dressmaker's shop in the Strand, and, not wishing to be detected, sat in a white mask and a white dress, and was known by the name of the 'White Widow.'

I was reminded of the Duchess when I read Miss Emily Faithfull's admirable article in *Galignani** on 'Ladies as Shopkeepers.' 'The most daring innovation in England at this moment,' says Miss Faithfull, 'is the lady shopkeeper. At present but few people have had the courage to brave the current social prejudice. We draw such fine distinctions between the wholesale and retail traders that our cotton-spinners, calico-makers, and general merchants seem to think that they belong to a totally different sphere, from which they look down on the lady who has had sufficient brains, capital, and courage to open a shop. But the old world moves faster than it did in former days, and before the end of the nineteenth century it is probable that a gentlewoman will be recognised in spite of her having entered on commercial pursuits, especially as we are growing accustomed to see scions of our noblest families on our Stock Exchange and in tea-merchants' houses; one Peer of the realm is now doing an extensive business in coals, and another is a cab proprietor.' Miss Faithfull then proceeds to give a most interesting account of the London dairy opened by the Hon Mrs Maberley, of Madame Isabel's millinery establishment, and of the wonderful work done by Miss Charlotte Robinson, who has recently been appointed Decorator to the Queen. 'About three years ago,' Miss Faithfull tells us, Miss Robinson came to Manchester, and opened a shop in King Street, and, regardless of that bugbear which terrifies most women—the loss of social status— she put up her own name over the door, and without the least self-assertion quietly entered into competition with the sterner sex. The result has been eminently satisfactory. This year Miss Robinson has exhibited at Saltaire* and at Manchester, and next year she proposes to exhibit at Glasgow, and, possibly, at Brussels. At first she had some difficulty in making people understand that her work is really commercial, not charitable; she feels that, until a healthy public opinion is created, women will pose as 'destitute ladies,' and never take a dignified position in any calling they adopt. Gentlemen who earn their own living are not spoken of as 'destitute,' and we must banish this idea in connection with ladies who are engaged in an equally honourable manner. Miss Faithfull concludes her most valuable article as follows:— 'The more highly educated our women of business are, the better for themselves, their work, and the whole community. Many of the professions to which ladies have hitherto turned are overcrowded, and when once the fear of losing social position is boldly disregarded, it will be found that commercial life offers a variety of more or less lucrative employments to ladies of birth and capital, who find it more congenial to their tastes and requirements to invest their money and spend their energies in a business which yields a fair return rather than sit at home content with a scanty pittance.'

I myself entirely agree with Miss Faithfull, though I feel that there is something to be said in favour of the view put forward by Lady Shrewsbury in THE WOMAN'S WORLD, and a great deal to be said in favour of Mrs Joyce's* scheme for emigration. Mr Walter Besant,* if we are to judge from his last novel, is of Lady Shrewsbury's way of thinking.

I hope that some of my readers will be interested in Miss Beatrice Crane's* little poem, 'Blush-roses,' for which her father, Mr Walter Crane, has done so lovely and graceful a design. Mrs Simon, of Birkdale Park, Southport, tells me that she offered a prize last term

at her school for the best sonnet on any work of art. The poems were
sent to Professor Dowden, who awarded the prize to the youthful
authoress of the following sonnet on Mr Watts's* picture of 'Hope':—

'"HOPE"

'She sits with drooping form and fair bent head,
Low-bent to hear the faintly-sounding strain
That thrills her with the sweet uncertain pain
Of timid trust and restful tears unshed.
Around she feels vast spaces. Awe and dread
Encompass her. And the dark doubt she fain
Would banish, sees the shuddering fear remain,
And ever presses near with stealthy tread.

'But not for ever will the misty space
Close down upon her meekly-patient eyes;
The steady light within them soon will ope
Their heavy lids, and then the sweet fair face,
Uplifted in a sudden glad surprise,
Will find the bright reward which comes to Hope.'

I myself am rather inclined to prefer this sonnet on Mr Watts's
'Psyche.' The sixth line is deficient; but, in spite of the faulty *tech-nique*, there is a great deal that is suggestive in it:—

'"PSYCHE"

'Unfathomable boundless mystery,
Last work of the Creator, deathless, vast,
Soul—essence moulded of a changeful past;
Thou art the offspring of Eternity;
Breath of his breath, by his vitality
Engendered, in his image cast,
Part of the Nature-song whereof the last
Chord soundeth never in the harmony.
"Psyche"! Thy form is shadowed o'er with pain
Born of intensest longing, and the rain
Of a world's weeping lieth like a sea
Of silent soundless sorrow in thine eyes.
Yet grief is not eternal, for clouds rise
From out the ocean everlastingly.'

I have to thank Mr William Rossetti for kindly allowing me to
reproduce Dante Gabriel Rossetti's drawing of the authoress of

'Goblin Market;' and thanks are also due to Mr Lafayette, of Dublin, for the use of his photograph of H.R.H. the Princess of Wales in her Academic Robes as Doctor of Music, which served as our frontispiece last month, and to Messrs Hills and Saunders,* of Oxford, and Mr Lord and Mr Blanchard, of Cambridge, for a similar courtesy in the case of the article on 'Greek Plays at the Universities.'

LITERARY AND OTHER NOTES V[1]

THE Princess Emily Ruete of Oman and Zanzibar,* whose efforts to introduce women doctors into the East are so well known, has just published a most interesting account of her life, under the title of 'Memoirs of an Arabian Princess' (Ward and Downey). The Princess is the daughter of the celebrated Sejid Saîd, Imam of Mesket and Sultan of Zanzibar, and her long residence in Germany has given her the opportunity of comparing Eastern with Western civilisation. She writes in a very simple and unaffected manner; and though she has many grievances against her brother, the present Sultan (who seems never to have forgiven her for her conversion to Christianity and her marriage with a German subject), she has too much tact, *esprit*, and good humour to trouble her readers with any dreary record of family quarrels and domestic differences. Her book throws a great deal of light on the question of the position of women in the East, and shows that much of what has been written on this subject is quite inaccurate. One of the most curious passages is that in which the Princess gives an account of her mother:—

'My mother was a Circassian by birth, who in early youth had been torn away from her home. Her father had been a farmer, and she had always lived peacefully with her parents and her little brother and sister. War broke out suddenly, and the country was overrun by marauding bands. On their approach, the family fled into an underground place, as my mother called it—she probably meant a cellar, which is not known in Zanzibar. Their place of refuge was, however, invaded by a merciless horde, the parents were slain, and the children carried off by three mounted Arnauts.

[1] March 1888. Princess Emily Ruete of Oman and Zanzibar, *Memoirs of an Arabian Princess* (London, 1888); Mrs Oliphant, *Makers of Venice* (London, 1887); Mabel Robinson, *The Plan of Campaign* (London, 1888); Harriet Waters Preston, *A Year in Eden* (London, 1886); *The Englishwoman's Year-Book, 1888* (London, 1888); Isabel Southall, *Rachel and Other Poems* (Birmingham, 1887).

'She came into my father's possession when quite a child, probably at the tender age of seven or eight years, as she cast her first tooth in our house. She was at once adopted as playmate by two of my sisters, her own age, with whom she was educated and brought up. Together with them she learnt to read, which raised her a good deal above her equals, who, as a rule, became members of our family at the age of sixteen or eighteen years, or older still, when they had outgrown whatever taste they might once have had for schooling. She could scarcely be called pretty; but she was tall and shapely, had black eyes, and hair down to her knees. Of a very gentle disposition, her greatest pleasure consisted in assisting other people, in looking after and nursing any sick person in the house; and I well remember her going about with her books from one patient to another, reading prayers to them.

'She was in great favour with my father, who never refused her anything, though she interceded mostly for others; and when she came to see him, he always rose to meet her half-way —a distinction he conferred but very rarely. She was as kind and pious as she was modest, and in all her dealings frank and open. She had another daughter besides myself, who had died quite young. Her mental powers were not great, but she was very clever at needlework. She had always been a tender and loving mother to me, but this did not hinder her from punishing me severely when she deemed it necessary.

'She had many friends at Bet-il-Mtoni, which is rarely to be met with in an Arab harem. She had the most unshaken and firmest trust in God. When I was about five years old, I remember a fire breaking out in the stables close by, one night while my father was at his city residence. A false alarm spread over the house that we, too, were in imminent danger; upon which the good woman hastened to take me on her arm, and her big kurân (we pronounce the word thus) on the other, and hurried into the open air. On the rest of her possessions she set no value in this hour of danger.'

Here is a description of Schesade, the Sultan's second legitimate wife:—

'She was a Persian Princess of entrancing beauty, and of inordinate extravagance. Her little retinue was composed of one hundred and fifty cavaliers, all Persians, who lived on the ground floor; with them she hunted and rode in the broad day—rather contrary to Arab notions. The Persian women are subjected to quite a Spartan training in bodily exercise; they enjoy great liberty, much more so than Arab women, but they are also more rude in mind and action.

'Schesade is said to have carried on her extravagant style of life beyond bounds; her dresses, cut always after the Persian fashion, were literally covered with embroideries of pearls. A great many of these were picked up nearly every morning by the servants in her rooms, where she had dropped them from her garments, but the Princess would never take any of these precious jewels back again. She did not only drain my father's exchequer most wantonly, but violated many of our sacred laws; in fact, she had only married him for his high station and wealth, and had loved some one else all the time. Such a state of things could, of course, only end in a divorce; fortunately Schesade had no children of her own. There is a rumour still current among us that beautiful Schesade was observed, some years after this event, when my father carried on war in Persia, and had the good fortune of taking the fortress of Bender Abbâs on the Persian Gulf, heading her troops, and taking aim at the members of our family herself.'

Another of the remarkable women mentioned by the Princess was her stepmother, Azze-bint-Zef, who seems to have completely ruled the Sultan, and to have settled all questions of home and foreign policy; while her great-aunt, the Princess Asche, was regent of the empire during the Sultan's minority, and was the heroine of the siege of Mesket. Of her the Princess gives the following account:—

'Dressed in man's clothes, she inspected the outposts herself at night, she watched and encouraged the soldiers in all exposed places, and was saved several times only by the speed of her horse in unforeseen attacks. One night she rode out, oppressed with care, having just received information that the enemy was about to attempt an entrance into the city by means of bribery that night, and with intent to massacre all; and now she went to convince herself of the loyalty of her troops. Very cautiously she rode up to a guard, requesting to speak to the "Akîd" (the officer in charge), and did all in her power to seduce him from his duty by great offers of reward on the part of the besiegers. The indignation of the brave man, however, completely allayed her fears as to the fidelity of the troops, but the experiment nearly cost her her own life. The soldiers were about to massacre the supposed spy on the spot, and it required all her presence of mind to make good her escape.

'The situation grew, however, to be very critical at Mesket. Famine at last broke out, and the people were well-nigh distracted, as no assistance or relief could be expected from without. It was therefore decided to attempt a last sortie in order to die at least with glory. There was just sufficient powder left for one more attack, but there was no more lead for either guns or muskets. In this emergency the regent ordered iron nails and pebbles to be used in place of balls. The guns were loaded with all the old iron and brass that could be collected, and she opened her treasury to have bullets made out of her own silver dollars. Every nerve was strained, and the sally succeeded beyond all hope. The enemy was completely taken by surprise and fled in all directions, leaving more than half their men dead and wounded on the field. Mesket was saved, and, delivered out of her deep distress, the brave woman knelt down on the battlefield and thanked God in fervent prayer.

'From that time her government was a peaceful one, and she ruled so wisely that she was able to transfer to her nephew, my father, an empire so unimpaired as to place him in a position to extend the empire by the conquest of Zanzibar. It is to my great-aunt, therefore, that we owe, and not to an inconsiderable degree, the acquisition of this second empire.

'She, too, was an Eastern woman!'

All through her book the Princess protests against the idea that Oriental women are degraded or oppressed, and in the following passage she points out how difficult it is for foreigners to get any real information on the subject:—

'The education of the children is left entirely to the mother, whether she be legitimate wife or purchased slave, and it constitutes her chief happiness. Some fashionable mothers in Europe shift this duty on to the nurse, and, by-and-by, on the governess, and are quite satisfied with looking up their children, or receiving their visits, once a day. In France the child is sent to be nursed in the country, and left to the care of strangers. An Arab mother, on the other hand, looks continually after her children. She watches and nurses them with the greatest affection, and never leaves them as long as they may stand in need of her motherly care, for which she is rewarded by the fondest filial love.

'If foreigners had more frequent opportunities to observe the cheerfulness, the exuberance of spirits even, of Eastern women, they would soon and more easily be convinced of the untruth of all those stories afloat about the degraded, oppressed, and listless state of their life. It is impossible to gain a true insight into the actual domesticity in a few moments' visit; and the conversation carried on, on those formal occasions, hardly deserves that name; there is barely more than the exchange of a few commonplace remarks—and it is questionable if even these have been correctly interpreted.

'Notwithstanding his innate hospitality, the Arab has the greatest possible objection to having his home pried into by those of another land and creed. Whenever, therefore, a European lady called on us, the enormous circumference of her hoops (which were the fashion then, and took up the entire width of the stairs) was the first thing to strike us dumb with wonder; after which, the very meagre conversation generally confined itself on both sides to the mysteries of different costumes; and the lady retired as wise as she was when she came, after having been sprinkled over with ottar of roses, and being the richer for some parting presents. It is true she had entered a Harem; she had seen the much-pitied Oriental ladies (though only through their veils); she had with her own eyes seen our dresses, our jewellery, the nimbleness with which we sat down on the floor—and that was all. She could not boast of having seen more than any other foreign lady who had called before her. She is conducted upstairs and downstairs, and is watched all the time. Rarely she sees more than the reception room, and more rarely still can she guess or find out who the veiled lady is with whom she conversed. In short, she has had no opportunity whatsoever of learning anything of domestic life, or the position of Eastern women.'

No one who is interested in the social position of women in the East should fail to read these pleasantly-written memoirs. The Princess is herself a woman of high culture, and the story of her life is as instructive as history, and as fascinating as fiction.

Mrs Oliphant's* 'Makers of Venice' (Macmillan and Co.) is an admirable literary *pendant* to the same writer's charming book on Florence, though there is a wide difference between the beautiful Tuscan city and the sea-city of the Adriatic. Florence, as Mrs Oliphant points out, is a city full of memories of the great figures of the past. The traveller cannot pass along her streets without treading in the very traces of Dante,* without stepping on soil made memorable by footprints never to be effaced. The greatness of the surroundings, the palaces, churches, and frowning mediæval castles in the midst of the city, are all thrown into the background by the greatness, the individuality, the living power and vigour of the men who are their originators, and at the same time their inspiring soul. But when we turn to Venice the effect is very different. We do not think of the makers of that marvellous city, but rather of what they made. The idealised image of Venice herself meets us everywhere. The mother is not overshadowed by the too great glory of any of her sons. In her records the city is everything—the republic, the worshipped ideal of a community in which every man for the common glory seems to have been willing to sink his own. We know that Dante stood within the red walls of the arsenal, and saw the galleys making and mending, and the pitch flaming up to heaven; Petrarch came to visit the great Mistress of the Seas, taking refuge there, 'in this city, true home of the human race,' from trouble, war and pestilence outside;

and Byron,* with his facile enthusiasms and fervent eloquence, made his home for a time in one of the stately, decaying palaces; but with these exceptions no great poet has ever associated himself with the life of Venice. She had architects, sculptors, and painters, but no singer of her own. The arts through which she gave her message to the world were visible and imitative. Mrs Oliphant, in her bright picturesque style, tells the story of Venice pleasantly and well. Her account of the two Bellinis is especially charming; and the chapters on Titian and Tintoret* are admirably written. She concludes her interesting and useful history with the following words, which are well worthy of quotation, though I must confess that the 'alien modernisms' trouble me not a little:

'The critics of recent days have had much to say as to the deterioration of Venice in her new activity, and the introduction of alien modernisms, in the shape of steamboats and other new industrial agents into her canals and lagoons. But in this adoption of every new development of power, Venice is only proving herself the most faithful representative of the vigorous republic of old. Whatever prejudice or angry love may say, we cannot doubt that the Michiels, the Dandolos, the Foscari, the great rulers who formed Venice, had steamboats existed in their day, serving their purpose better than their barges and *peati*, would have adopted them without hesitation, without a thought of what any critics might say. The wonderful new impulse which has made Italy a great power has justly put strength and life before those old traditions of beauty, which made her not only the "woman country" of Europe, but a sort of Odalisque trading upon her charms, rather than the nursing mother of a noble and independent nation. That in her recoil from that somewhat degrading position, she may here and there have proved too regardless of the claims of antiquity, we need not attempt to deny; the new spring of life in her is too genuine and great to keep her entirely free from this evident danger. But it is strange that any one who loves Italy, and sincerely rejoices in her amazing resurrection, should fail to recognise how venial is this fault.'

Miss Mabel Robinson's last novel, 'The Plan of Campaign' (Vizetelly and Co.), is a very powerful study of modern political life. As a concession to humanity, each of the politicians is made to fall in love, and the charm of their various romances fully atones for the soundness of the author's theory of rent. Miss Robinson dissects, describes, and discourses with keen scientific insight and minute observation. Her style, though somewhat lacking in grace, is, at its best, simple and strong. Richard Talbot and Elinor Fetherston are admirably conceived and admirably drawn, and the whole account of the murder of Lord Roeglass is most dramatic.

'A Year in Eden' (T. Fisher Unwin), by Harriet Waters Preston,* is a chronicle of New England life, and is full of the elaborate subtlety of the American school of fiction. The Eden in question is the little village of Pierpont, and the Eve of this provincial paradise is a beautiful girl called Monza Middleton, a fascinating, fearless creature, who brings ruin and misery on all who love her. Miss Preston writes an admirable prose style, and the minor characters in the book are wonderfully lifelike and true.

'The Englishwoman's Year-Book' (Hatchards) contains a really extraordinary amount of useful information on every subject connected with woman's work. In the census taken in 1831 (six years before the Queen ascended the Throne), no occupation whatever was specified as appertaining to women, except that of domestic service, but in the census of 1881, the number of occupations mentioned as followed by women is upwards of three hundred and thirty. The most popular occupations seem to be those of domestic service, school teaching, and dressmaking; the lowest numbers on the list are those of bankers, gardeners, and persons engaged in scientific pursuits. Besides these, the 'Year-Book' makes mention of stockbroking and conveyancing as professions that women are beginning to adopt. The historical account of the literary work done by Englishwomen in this century, as given in the 'Year-Book,' is curiously inadequate, and the list of women's magazines is not complete, but in all other respects the publication seems a most useful and excellent one.

Wordsworth, in one of his interesting letters to Lady Beaumont,* says that it is 'an awful truth that there neither is nor can be any genuine enjoyment of poetry among nineteen out of twenty of those persons who live or wish to live in the broad light of the world— among those who either are, or are striving to make themselves, people of consideration in society,' adding that the mission of poetry is 'to console the afflicted; to add sunshine to daylight by making the happy happier; to teach the young and the gracious of every age to see, to think, and feel, and, therefore, to become more actively and securely virtuous.'* I am, however, rather disposed to think that the age in which we live is one that has a very genuine enjoyment of poetry, though we may no longer agree with Wordsworth's ideas on the subject of the poet's proper mission; and it is interesting to note that this enjoyment manifests itself by creation even more than by criticism. To realise the popularity of the great poets, one should turn to the minor poets and see whom they follow, what master they select, whose music they echo. At present, there seems to be a reaction in favour of Lord Tennyson, if we are to judge by 'Rachel and Other Poems' (Cornish Brothers) which is a rather remarkable little volume in its way. The poem that gives its title to the book is full of strong lines and good images; and, in spite of its Tennysonian echoes, there is something attractive in such verses as the following:—

'Day by day along the Orient faintly glows the tender dawn,
Day by day the pearly dewdrops tremble on the upland lawn:

'Day by day the star of morning pales before the coming ray,
And the first faint streak of radiance brightens to the perfect day.

'Day by day the rosebud gathers to itself, from earth and sky,
Fragrant stores and ampler beauty, lovelier form and deeper dye:

'Day by day a richer crimson mantles in its glowing breast—
Every golden hour conferring some sweet grace that crowns the rest.

'And thou canst not tell the moment when the day ascends her throne,
When the morning star hath vanished, and the rose is fully blown.

'So each day fulfils its purpose, calm—unresting—strong and sure,
Moving onward to completion, doth the work of God endure.

'How unlike man's toil and hurry! how unlike the noise, the strife,
All the pain of incompleteness, all the weariness of life!

'Ye look upward and take courage. He who leads the golden hours,
Feeds the birds, and clothes the lily, made these human hearts of ours.

'Knows their need and will supply it, manna falling day by day,
Bread from heaven, and food of angels, all along the desert way.'

The Secretary of the International Technical College at Bedford has issued a most interesting prospectus of the aims and objects of the Institution. The College seems to be intended chiefly for ladies who have completed their ordinary course of English studies, and it will be divided into two departments, Educational and Industrial. In the latter, classes will be held for various decorative and technical arts, and for wood-carving, etching, and photography, as well as sick-nursing, dressmaking, cookery, physiology, poultry-rearing, and the cultivation of flowers. The curriculum certainly embraces a wonderful amount of subjects, and I have no doubt that the College will supply a real want.

The Ladies' Employment Society has been so successful that it has moved to new premises in Park Street, Grosvenor Square, where there are some very pretty and useful things for sale. The children's smocks are quite charming, and seem very inexpensive. The subscription to the Society is one guinea a year, and a commission of five per cent. is charged on each thing sold.

Miss May Morris,* whose exquisite needle-work is well known, has just completed a pair of curtains for a house in Boston. They are amongst the most perfect specimens of modern embroidery that I have seen, and are from Miss Morris's own design. I am glad to hear that Miss Morris has determined to give lessons in embroidery. She has a thorough knowledge of the art, her sense of beauty is as rare as it is refined, and her power of design is quite remarkable.

Mrs Jopling's life-classes for ladies have been such a success that a similar class has been started in Chelsea by Mr Clegg Wilkinson at the Carlyle Studios, King's Road. Mr Wilkinson (who is a very brilliant young painter) is strongly of opinion that life should be studied from life itself, and not from that abstract presentation of life which we find in Greek marbles—a position which I have always held very strongly myself.

The portrait of Mrs Craik that appeared in the January number of THE WOMAN'S WORLD was taken from a photograph by Mr Buchanan Wollaston, of Chislehurst, who most kindly allowed us to reproduce it.

A NOTE ON SOME MODERN POETS[1]

'IF I were king,' says Mr Henley,* in one of his most modest rondeaus,

> 'Art should aspire, yet ugliness be dear;
> Beauty, the shaft, should speed with wit for feather;
> And love, sweet love, should never fall to sere,
>   If I were king.'

And these lines contain, if not the best criticism of his own work, certainly a very complete statement of his aim and motive as a poet. His little 'Book of Verses' (David Nutt) reveals to us an artist who is seeking to find new methods of expression and has not merely a delicate sense of beauty and a brilliant fantastic wit, but a real passion also for what is horrible, ugly, or grotesque. No doubt, everything that is worthy of existence is worthy also of art—at least, one would like to think so—but while echo or mirror can repeat for us a beautiful thing, to artistically render a thing that is ugly requires the most exquisite alchemy of form, the most subtle magic of transformation. To me there is more of the cry of Marsyas than of the singing of Apollo in the earlier poems of Mr Henley's volume, the 'Rhymes and Rhythms in Hospital,'* as he calls them. But it is impossible to deny their power. Some of them are like bright, vivid pastels; others like charcoal drawings, with dull blacks and murky whites; others like etchings with deeply-bitten lines, and abrupt contrasts, and clever colour-suggestions. In fact, they are like anything and everything, except perfected poems—that they certainly are not. They are still in the twilight. They are preludes, experiments, inspired jottings in a note-book, and should be heralded by a design of 'Genius Making Sketches.' Rhyme gives architecture as well as melody to verse; it gives that delightful sense of limitation which in all the arts is so pleasurable, and is, indeed, one of the secrets of perfection; it will whisper, as a French critic has said, 'things unexpected and charming, things with strange and remote relations to each other,' and bind them together in indissoluble bonds of beauty; and in his constant rejection of rhyme, Mr Henley seems to me to have abdicated half

---

[1] December 1888. W. E. Henley, *A Book of Verse* (London, 1888); William Sharp, *Romantic Ballads and Poems of Phantasy* (London, 1888); Agnes Mary Frances Robinson, *Poems, Ballads and a Garden Play* (London, 1888); Dinah Craik, *Poems* (London, 1888).

his power. He is a *roi en exil* who has thrown away some of the strings of his lute, a poet who has forgotten the fairest part of his kingdom.

However, all work criticises itself. Here is one of Mr Henley's inspired jottings. According to the temperament of the reader, it will serve either as a model or as the reverse:—

> 'As with varnish red and glistening
> Dripped his hair; his feet were rigid;
> Raised, he settled stiffly sideways:
> You could see the hurts were spinal.
>
> 'He had fallen from an engine,
> And been dragged along the metals.
> It was hopeless, and they knew it;
> So they covered him, and left him.
>
> 'As he lay, by fits half sentient,
> Inarticulately moaning,
> With his stockinged feet protruded
> Sharp and awkward from the blankets,
>
> 'To his bed there came a woman;
> Stood and looked, and sighed a little,
> And departed without speaking,
> As himself a few hours after.
>
> 'I was told she was his sweetheart.
> They were on the eve of marriage.
> She was quiet as a statue,
> But her lip was gray and writhen.'

In this poem, the rhythm, and the music, such as it is, are obvious—perhaps a little too obvious. In the following I see nothing but ingeniously printed prose. It is a description—and a very accurate one—of a scene in a hospital ward. The medical students are supposed to be crowding round the doctor. What I quote is only a fragment, but the poem itself is a fragment:—

> 'So shows the ring
> Seen, from behind, round a conjuror
> Doing his pitch in the street.
> High shoulders, low shoulders, broad shoulders, narrow ones,
> Round, square, and angular, serry and shove;
> While from within a voice,
> Gravely and weightily fluent,

Sounds; and then ceases; and suddenly
(Look at the stress of the shoulders!)
Out of a quiver of silence,
Over the hiss of the spray,
Comes a low cry, and the sound
Of breath quick intaken through teeth
Clenched in resolve. And the master
Breaks from the crowd, and goes,
Wiping his hands,
To the next bed, with his pupils
Flocking and whispering behind him.

'Now one can see.
Case Number One
Sits (rather pale) with his bedclothes
Stripped up, and showing his foot
(Alas, for God's image!)
Swaddled in wet white lint
Brilliantly hideous with red.'

Théophile Gautier once said that Flaubert's style was meant to be read, and his own style to be looked at. Mr Henley's unrhymed rhythms form very dainty designs, from a typographical point of view. From the point of view of literature, they are a series of vivid concentrated impressions with a keen grip of fact, a terrible actuality, and an almost masterly power of picturesque presentation. But the poetic form—what of that?

Well, let us pass to the later poems, to the rondels and rondeaus, the sonnets and quatorzains, the echoes and the ballades. How brilliant and fanciful this is! The Toyokuni colour-print* that suggested it could not be more delightful. It seems to have kept all the wilful fantastic charm of the original:—

'Was I a Samurai renowned,
Two-sworded, fierce, immense of bow?
A histrion angular and profound?
A priest? a porter?—Child, although
I have forgotten clean, I know
That in the shade of Fujisan,
What time the cherry-orchards blow,
I loved you once in old Japan.

'As here you loiter, flowing-gowned
And hugely sashed, with pins a-row

Your quaint head as with flamelets crowned,
Demure, inviting—even so,
When merry maids in Miyako
To feel the sweet o' the year began,
And green gardens to overflow,
I loved you once in old Japan.

'Clear shine the hills; the rice-fields round
Two cranes are circling; sleepy and slow,
A blue canal the lake's blue bound
Breaks at the bamboo bridge; and lo!
Touched with the sundown's spirit and glow,
I see you turn, with flirted fan,
Against the plum-tree's bloomy snow . . .
I loved you once in old Japan!'

'ENVOY.

'Dear, 'twas a dozen lives ago;
But that I was a lucky man
The Toyokuni here will show:
I loved you—once—in old Japan!'

This rondel, too—how light it is, and graceful!—

'We'll to the woods and gather may
Fresh from the footprints of the rain;
We'll to the woods, at every vein
To drink the spirit of the day.

'The winds of spring are out at play,
The needs of spring in heart and brain.
We'll to the woods and gather may
Fresh from the footprints of the rain.

'The world's too near her end, you say?
Hark to the blackbird's mad refrain!
It waits for her, the vast Inane?
Then, girls, to help her on the way
We'll to the woods and gather may.'

There are fine verses, also, scattered through this little book; some
of them very strong, as—

'Out of the night that covers me,
    Black as the pit from pole to pole,

I thank whatever gods may be
    For my unconquerable soul.

'It matters not how strait the gate,
    How charged with punishments the scroll,
I am the master of my fate:
    I am the captain of my soul.'

Others with a true touch of romance, as—

'Or ever the knightly years were gone
    With the old world to the grave,
I was a king in Babylon,
    And you were a Christian slave.'

And here and there we come across such felicitous phrases as—

'In the sand
The gold prow-griffin claws a hold,'

or—

'The spires
Shine and are changed,'

And many other graceful or fanciful lines, even 'the green sky's minor thirds' being perfectly right in its place, and a very refreshing bit of affectation in a volume where there is so much that is natural.

However, Mr Henley is not to be judged by samples. Indeed, the most attractive thing in the book is no single poem that is in it, but the strong humane personality that stands behind both flawless and faulty work alike, and looks out through many masks, some of them beautiful, and some grotesque, and not a few misshapen. In the case with most of our modern poets, when we have analysed them down to an adjective, we can go no further, or we care to go no further; but with this book it is different. Through these reeds and pipes* blows the very breath of life. It seems as if one could put one's hand upon the singer's heart and count its pulsations. There is something wholesome, virile, and sane about the man's soul. Anybody can be reasonable, but to be sane is not common; and sane poets are as rare as blue lilies, though they may not be quite so delightful.

'Let the great winds their worst and wildest blow,
    Or the gold weather round us mellow slow;

> We have fulfilled ourselves, and we can dare,
> And we can conquer, though we may not share
> In the rich quiet of the afterglow,
>   What is to come,'

is the concluding stanza of the last rondeau—indeed, of the last poem in the collection, and the high, serene temper displayed in these lines serves at once as keynote and keystone to the book. The very lightness and slightness of so much of the work, its careless moods and casual fancies, seem to suggest a nature that is not primarily interested in art—a nature, like Sordello's,* passionately enamoured of life, one to which lyre and lute are things of less importance. From this mere joy of living, this frank delight in experience for its own sake, this lofty indifference, and momentary unregretted ardours, come all the faults and all the beauties of the volume. But there is this difference between them—the faults are deliberate, and the result of much study; the beauties have the air of fascinating impromptus. Mr Henley's healthy, if sometimes misapplied, confidence in the myriad suggestions of life gives him his charm. He is made to sing along the highways, not to sit down and write. If he took himself more seriously his work would become trivial.*

Mr William Sharp* takes himself very seriously and has written a preface to his 'Romantic Ballads and Poems of Phantasy' (Walter Scott), which is, on the whole, the most interesting part of his volume. We are all, it seems, far too cultured, and lack robustness. There are those amongst us, says Mr Sharp, 'who would prefer a dexterously-turned triolet to such apparently uncouth measures as "Thomas the Rhymer" or the ballad of Clerk Saunders,'* and 'who would rather listen to the drawing-room music of the Villanelle than to the wild harp-playing by the mill-dams o' Binnorie, or the sough of the night-wind o'er drumly Allan water.' Such an expression as 'the drawing-room music of the Villanelle' is not very happy, and I cannot imagine any one with the smallest pretensions to culture preferring a dexterously turned triolet to a fine imaginative ballad, as it is only the Philistine who ever dreams of comparing works of art that are absolutely different in motive, in treatment, and in form. If English Poetry is in danger—and, according to Mr Sharp, the poor nymph is in a very critical state—what she has to fear is not the fascination of dainty metre or delicate form, but the predominance of the intellectual spirit over the spirit of beauty. Lord Tennyson dethroned Wordsworth as a literary influence, and later on Mr Swinburne filled all the mountain valleys with echoes of his own song. The influence to-day is that of Mr Browning. And as for the triolets, and the rondels, and the careful study of metrical subtleties, these things are merely the signs of a desire for perfection in small things, and of the recognition of poetry as an art. They have had certainly one good result—they have made our minor poets readable, and have not left us entirely at the mercy of geniuses.

But, says Mr Sharp, every one is far too literary; even Rossetti is too literary. What we want is simplicity and directness of utterance; these should be the dominant characteristics of poetry. Well, is that quite so certain? Are simplicity and directness of utterance absolute essentials for poetry? I think not. They may be admirable for the drama, admirable for all those imitative forms of literature that claim to mirror life in its externals and its accidents, admirable for quiet narrative, admirable in their place; but their place is not everywhere. Poetry has many modes of music; she does not blow through one pipe alone. Directness of utterance is good, but so is the subtle recasting of thought into a new and delightful form. Simplicity is good, but complexity, mystery, strangeness, symbolism, obscurity even, these have their value. Indeed, properly speaking, there is no such thing as Style; there are merely styles, that is all.

One cannot help feeling also that everything that Mr. Sharp says in his preface was said at the beginning of the century by Wordsworth,* only where Wordsworth called us back to nature, Mr Sharp invites us to woo romance. Romance, he tells us, is 'in the air.' A new romantic movement is imminent: 'I anticipate,' he says, 'that many of our poets, especially those of the youngest generation, will shortly turn towards the "ballad" as a poetic vehicle, and that the next year or two will see much romantic poetry.'

The ballad! Well, Mr Andrew Lang some months ago signed the death-warrant of the ballade, and—though I hope that in this respect Mr Lang resembles the Queen in 'Alice in Wonderland,'* whose bloodthirsty orders were by general consent never carried into execution—it must be admitted that the number of ballades given to us by some of our poets was, perhaps, a little excessive. But the ballad? 'Sir Patrick Spens,'* 'Clerk Saunders,' 'Thomas the Rhymer'—are

these to be our archetypes, our models, the sources of our inspiration? They are certainly great imaginative poems. In Chatterton's
'Ballad of Charity,' Coleridge's 'Rhyme of the Ancient Mariner,' the
'La Belle Dame sans Merci' of Keats, the 'Sister Helen' of Rossetti,*
we can see what marvellous works of art the spirit of old romance
may fashion. But to preach a spirit is one thing, to propose a form is
another. It is true that Mr Sharp warns the rising generation against
imitation. A ballad, he reminds them, does not necessarily denote a
poem in quatrains and in antique language. But his own poems, as I
think will be seen later on, are, in their way, warnings, and show the
danger of suggesting any definite 'poetic vehicle.' And, further, are
simplicity and directness of utterance really the dominant characteristics of these old imaginative ballads that Mr Sharp so enthusiastic-
ally, and, in some particulars, so wisely praises? It does not seem to
me to be so. We are always apt to think that the voices which sang at
the dawn of poetry were simpler, fresher, and more natural than
ours, and that the world which the early poets looked at, and
through which they walked, had a kind of poetical quality of its
own, and could pass, almost without changing, into song. The snow
lies thick now upon Olympus, and its scraped sides are bleak and
barren, but once, we fancy, the white feet of the Muses brushed the
dew from the anemones in the morning, and at evening came Apollo
to sing to the shepherds in the vale. But in this we are merely
lending to other ages what we desire, or think we desire, for our
own. Our historical sense is at fault. Every century that produces
poetry is, so far, an artificial century, and the work that seems to us
the most natural and simple product of its time is probably the
result of the most deliberate and self-conscious effort. For Nature is
always behind the age. It takes a great artist to be thoroughly
modern.

Let us turn to the poems, which have really only the preface to
blame for their somewhat late appearance. The best is undoubtedly
'The Weird of Michael Scott,' and these stanzas are a fair example of
its power:—

> 'Then Michael Scott laughed long and loud:
> "Whan shone the mune ahint yon cloud
> I speered the towers that saw my birth—
> Lang, lang, sall wait my cauld grey shroud,
> Lang cauld and weet my bed o' earth!"

'But as by Stair he rode full speed
His horse began to pant and bleed;
"Win hame, win hame, my bonnie mare,
Win hame if thou wouldst rest and feed,
Win hame, we're nigh the House of Stair!" '

'But with a shrill heart-bursten yell
The white horse stumbled, plunged, and fell,
And loud a summoning voice arose,
"Is't White-Horse Death that rides frae Hell,
Or Michael Scott that hereby goes?"'

' "Ah, Laird of Stair, I ken ye weel!
Avaunt, or I your saul sall steal,
An' send ye howling through the wood
A wild man-wolf—aye, ye maun reel
An' cry upon your Holy Rood!" ' '

There is a good deal of vigour, no doubt, in these lines; but one cannot help asking whether this is to be the common tongue of the future Renaissance of Romance. Are we all to talk Scotch, and to speak of the moon as the 'mune,' and the soul as the 'saul'? I hope not. And yet if this Renaissance is to be a vital, living thing, it must have its linguistic side. Just as the spiritual development of music, and the artistic development of painting, have always been accompanied, if not occasioned, by the discovery of some new instrument or some fresh medium, so, in the case of any important literary movement, half of its strength resides in its language. If it does not bring with it a rich and novel mode of expression, it is doomed either to sterility or to imitation. Dialect, archaisms and the like, will not do. Take, for instance, another poem of Mr Sharp's, a poem which he calls 'The Deith-Tide':—

'The weet saut wind is blawing
Upon the misty shore:
As, like a stormy snawing,
The deid go streaming o'er:—
    The wan drown'd deid sail wildly
    Frae out each drumly wave:
    It's O and O for the weary sea,
    And O for a quiet grave.'

This is simply a very clever *pastiche*, nothing more, and our language is not likely to be permanently enriched by such words as 'weet,' 'saut,' 'blawing,' and 'snawing.' Even 'drumly,' an adjective of which Mr Sharp is so fond that he uses it both in prose and verse, seems to me to be hardly an adequate basis for a new romantic movement.

However, Mr Sharp does not always write in dialect. 'The Son of Allan' can be read without any difficulty, and 'Phantasy' can be read with pleasure. They are both very charming poems in their way, and none the less charming because the cadences of the one recall 'Sister Helen,' and the motive of the other reminds us of 'La Belle Dame sans Merci.' But those who wish thoroughly to enjoy Mr Sharp's poems should not read his preface; just as those who approve of the preface should avoid reading the poems. I cannot help saying that I think the preface a great mistake. The work that follows it is quite inadequate, and there seems little use in heralding a dawn that rose long ago, and proclaiming a Renaissance whose first-fruits, if we are to judge them by any high standard of perfection, are of so ordinary a character.

Miss Mary Robinson* has also written a preface to her little volume—'Poems, Ballads, and a Garden Play' (T. Fisher Unwin)—but the preface is not very serious, and does not propose any drastic change or any immediate revolution in English literature. Miss Robinson's poems have always the charm of delicate music and graceful expression; but they are perhaps weakest where they try to be strong, and certainly least satisfying where they seek to satisfy. Her fanciful flower-crowned Muse, with her tripping steps and pretty wilful ways, should not write Antiphons to the Unknowable,* or try to grapple with abstract intellectual problems. Hers is not the hand to unveil mysteries, nor hers the strength for the solving of secrets. She should never leave her garden, and as for her wandering out into the desert to ask the Sphinx questions, that should be sternly forbidden to her. Dürer's 'Melencolia,'* that serves as the frontispiece to this dainty book, looks sadly out of place. Her seat is with the sibyls, not with the nymphs. What has she to do with shepherdesses piping about Darwinism and 'The Eternal Mind'?*

However, if the 'Songs of the Inner Life' are not very successful, the 'Spring Songs' are delightful. They follow each other like wind-blown petals, and make one feel how much more charming flower is than fruit, apple-blossom than apple. There are some artistic temperaments that should never come to maturity, that should always remain in the region of promise, and should dread autumn with its harvesting more than winter with its frosts. Such seems to me the temperament that this volume reveals. The first poem of the second series, 'La Belle au Bois Dormant,' is worth all the more serious and thoughtful work, and has far more chance of being remembered. It is not always to high aim and lofty ambition that the prize is given. If Daphne* had gone to meet Apollo, she would never have known what laurels are.

From these fascinating spring lyrics and idylls we pass to the romantic ballads. One artistic faculty Miss Robinson certainly possesses—the faculty of imitation. There is an element of imitation* in all the arts, it is to be found in literature as much as in painting, and the danger of valuing it too little is almost as great as the danger of setting too high a value upon it. To catch by dainty mimicry the very mood and manner of antique work, and yet to retain that touch of modern passion without which the old form would be dull and empty; to win from long-silent lips some faint echo of their music, and to add to it a music of one's own; to take the mode and fashion of a bygone age, and to experiment with it and search curiously for its possibilities; there is a pleasure in all this. It is a kind of literary acting, and has something of the charm of the art of the stage-player. And how well, on the whole, Miss Robinson does it! Here is the opening of the ballad of Rudel:—

> 'There was in all the world of France
>   No singer half so sweet:
> The first note of his viol brought
>   A crowd into the street.
>
> 'He stepped as young, and bright, and glad
>   As Angel Gabriel.
> And only when we heard him sing
>   Our eyes forgot Rudel.
>
> 'And as he sat in Avignon,
>   With princes at their wine,
> In all that lusty company
>   Was none so fresh and fine.

> 'His kirtle's of the Arras-blue,
>   His cap of pearls and green;
> His golden curls fall tumbling round
>   The fairest face I've seen.

How Gautier would have liked this from the same poem!—

> 'Hew the timbers of sandal-wood,
>   And planks of ivory;
> Rear up the shining masts of gold,
>   And let us put to sea.

> 'Sew the sails with a silken thread
>   That all are silken too;
> Sew them with scarlet pomegranates
>   Upon a sheet of blue.

> 'Rig the ship with a rope of gold
>   And let us put to sea.
> And now, good-bye to good Marseilles,
>   And hey for Tripoli!'

The ballad of the Duke of Gueldres's wedding is very clever:

> ' "O welcome, Mary Harcourt,
>   Thrice welcome, lady mine;
> There's not a knight in all the world
>   Shall be as true as thine.

> ' "There's venison in the aumbry, Mary,
>   There's claret in the vat;
> Come in, and breakfast in the hall
>   Where once my mother sat!"

> 'O red, red is the wine that flows,
>   And sweet the minstrel's play,
> But white is Mary Harcourt
>   Upon her wedding-day.

> O many are the wedding guests
>   That sit on either side;
> But pale below her crimson flowers
>   And homesick is the bride.

Miss Robinson's critical sense is at once too sound and too subtle to allow her to think that any great Renaissance of Romance will necessarily follow from the adoption of the ballad-form in poetry;

but her work in this style is very pretty and charming, and 'The Tower of St Maur,' which tells of the father who built up his little son in the wall of his castle in order that the foundations should stand sure, is admirable in its way. The few touches of archaism in language that she introduces are quite sufficient for their purpose, and though she fully appreciates the importance of the Celtic spirit in literature, she does not consider it necessary to talk of 'blawing' and 'snawing.' As for the garden play, 'Our Lady of the Broken Heart,' as it is called, the bright, birdlike snatches of song that break in here and there—as the singing does in 'Pippa Passes'—form a very welcome relief to the somewhat ordinary movement of the blank verse, and suggest to us again where Miss Robinson's real power lies. Not a poet in the true creative sense, she is still a very perfect artist in poetry, using language as one might use a very precious material and producing her best work by the rejection of the great themes and large intellectual motives that belong to fuller and richer song. When she essays such themes, she certainly fails. Her instrument is the reed, not the lyre. Only those should sing of Death whose song is stronger than Death is.

The collected poems of the author of 'John Halifax, Gentleman' (Macmillan and Co.), have a pathetic interest as the artistic record of a very gracious and comely life. They bring us back to the days when Philip Bourke Marston was young—'Philip, my King,' as she called him in the pretty poem of that name; to the days of the Great Exhibition, with the universal piping about peace; to those later terrible Crimean days, when Alma and Balaclava* were words on the lips of our poets; and to days when Leonora was considered a very romantic name.

'Leonora, Leonora,
How the word rolls—*Leonora*.
Lion-like in full-mouthed sound,
Marching o'er the metric ground,
With a tawny tread sublime.
So your name moves, Leonora,
Down my desert rhyme.'

Mrs Craik's best poems are, on the whole, those that are written in blank verse; and these, though not prosaic, remind one that prose

was her true medium of expression. But some of the rhymed poems
have considerable merit. These may serve as examples of Mrs
Craik's style:

'A SKETCH

'Dost thou thus love me, O thou all beloved,
In whose large store the very meanest coin
Would out-buy my whole wealth? Yet here thou comest
Like a kind heiress from her purple and down
Uprising, who for pity cannot sleep,
But goes forth to the stranger at her gate—
The beggared stranger at her beauteous gate—
And clothes and feeds; scarce blest till she has blest.

'But dost thou love me, O thou pure of heart,
Whose very looks are prayers? What couldst thou see
In this forsaken pool by the yew-wood's side,
To sit down at its bank, and dip thy hand,
Saying, "It is so clear!"—and lo! erelong,
Its blackness caught the shimmer of thy wings,
Its slimes slid downward from thy stainless palm,
Its depths grew still, that there thy form might rise.'

'THE NOVICE

'It is near morning. Ere the next night fall
   I shall be made the bride of heaven. Then home
   To my still marriage-chamber I shall come,
And spouseless, childless, watch the slow years crawl.

'These lips will never meet a softer touch
   Than the stone crucifix I kiss; no child
   Will clasp this neck. Ah, virgin-mother mild,
Thy painted bliss will mock me overmuch.

'This is the last time I shall twist the hair
   My mother's hand wreathed, till in dust she lay:
   The name, her name given on my baptism day,
This is the last time I shall ever bear.

'O weary world, O heavy life, farewell!
   Like a tired child that creeps into the dark
   To sob itself asleep, where none will mark,—
So creep I to my silent convent cell.

> 'Friends, lovers whom I loved not, kindly hearts
> Who grieve that I should enter this still door,
> Grieve not. Closing behind me evermore,
> Me from all anguish, as all joy, it parts.'

The volume chronicles the moods of a sweet and thoughtful nature, and though many things in it may seem somewhat old-fashioned, it is still very pleasant to read, and has a faint perfume of withered rose-leaves about it.

SOME LITERARY NOTES[1]

'The various collectors of Irish folk-lore,' says Mr W. B. Yeats* in his charming little book 'Fairy and Folk Tales of the Irish Peasantry' (Walter Scott) 'have, from our point of view, one great merit, and from the point of view of others, one great fault. They have made their work literature rather than science, and told us of the Irish peasantry rather than of the primitive religion of mankind, or whatever else the folk-lorists are on the gad after. To be considered scientists they should have tabulated all their tales in forms like grocers' bills—item the fairy king, item the queen. Instead of this they have caught the very voice of the people, the very pulse of life, each giving what was most noticed in his day. Croker and Lover,* full of the ideas of harum-scarum Irish gentility, saw everything humorised. The impulse of the Irish literature of their time came from a class that did not—mainly for political reasons—take the populace seriously, and imagined the country as a humorist's Arcadia; of its passion, its gloom, its tragedy, they knew nothing. What they did was not wholly false; they merely magnified an irresponsible type, found oftenest among boatmen, carmen, and gentlemen's servants, into the type of a whole nation, and created the stage Irishman. The writers of 'Forty-eight, and the famine combined, burst their bubble. Their work had the dash as well as the shallowness of an ascendant and idle class; and, in Croker, is touched everywhere with beauty—a gentle Arcadian beauty. Carleton,* a peasant born, has in many of his stories,

[1] February 1889. *Fairy and Folk Tales of the Irish Peasantry*, ed. W. B. Yeats (London, 1888); Violet Fane, *The Story of Helen Davenant* (London, 1889); Anna Kingsford, *Dreams and Dream-Stories* (London, 1888); Amy Levy, *The Romance of a Shop* (London, 1888); Margaret Lee, *Faithful and Unfaithful* (London, 1889).

more especially in his ghost stories, a much more serious way with him, for all his humour. Kennedy,* an old bookseller in Dublin, who seems to have had a something of genuine belief in the fairies, comes next in time. He has far less literary faculty, but is wonderfully accurate, giving often the very words in which the stories were told. But the best book since Croker is Lady Wilde's "Ancient Legends." The humour has all given way to pathos and tenderness. We have here the innermost heart of the Celt in the moments he has grown to love through years of persecution, when, cushioning himself about with dreams, and hearing fairy-songs in the twilight, he ponders on the soul and on the dead. Here is the Celt, only it is the Celt dreaming.'

Into a volume of very moderate dimensions, and of extremely moderate price, Mr Yeats has collected together the most characteristic of our Irish folk-lore stories, grouping them together according to subject. First come the 'Trooping Fairies.' The peasants say that these are fallen angels who were not good enough to be saved, nor bad enough to be lost; but the Irish antiquarians see in them the gods of Pagan Ireland, who, when no longer worshipped and fed with offerings, dwindled away in the popular imagination, and now are only a few spans in height. Their chief occupations are feasting, fighting, making love, and playing the most beautiful music. They have only one industrious person amongst them, the *Leprachaun* (the Little Shoemaker). It is his duty to repair their shoes when they wear them out with dancing. Mr Yeats tells us that near the village of Ballisodare is a little woman who lived amongst them seven years. When she came home she had no toes; she had danced them all off. On May Eve, every seventh year, they fight for the harvest, for the best ears of grain belong to them. An old man informed Mr Yeats that he saw them fight once, and that they tore the thatch off a house. Had any one else been near they would merely have seen a great wind whirling everything into the air as it passed. When the wind drives the leaves and straws before it, that is the fairies, and the peasants take off their hats and say 'God bless them.' When they are gay, they sing. Many of the most beautiful tunes of Ireland are only their music, caught up by eavesdroppers. No prudent peasant would hum 'The Pretty Girl Milking the Cow'* near a fairy rath, for they are jealous, and do not like to hear their songs on clumsy mortal life. Blake* once saw a fairy's funeral. But this, as Mr Yeats points out,

must have been an English fairy, for the Irish fairies never die; they
are immortal.

Then come the 'Solitary Fairies;' amongst them we find the little
Leprachaun mentioned above. He has grown very rich, as he possesses all the treasure-crocks buried in war-time. In the early part of
this century, according to Croker, they used to show in Tipperary a
little shoe forgotten by the fairy shoemaker. Then there are two
rather disreputable little fairies—the *Cluricaun*, who gets intoxicated
in gentlemen's cellars, and 'The Red Man,' who plays unkind practical jokes. The *Fear-Gorta* (Man of Hunger) is an emaciated
phantom who goes through the land in time of famine, begging an
alms and bringing good luck to the giver. The *Water-Sheerie* is own
brother to the English Jack-o'-Lantern. The *Leanhaun Shee* (fairy
mistress) seeks the love of mortals. If they refuse, she must be their
slave; if they consent, they are hers, and can only escape by finding
another to take their place. The fairy lives on their life, and they
waste away. Death is no escape from her. She is the Gaelic Muse, for
she gives inspiration to those she persecutes. The Gaelic poets die
young, for she is restless, and will not let them remain long on earth.
The *Pooka* is essentially an animal spirit, and some have considered
him the forefather of Shakespeare's 'Puck.' He lives on solitary
mountains, and among old ruins 'grown monstrous with much soli-
tude,' and is of the race of the nightmare. He has many shapes—is
now a horse, now a goat, now an eagle. Like all spirits, he is only half
in the world of form. The Banshee does not care much for our
democratic levelling tendencies; she only loves old families, and
despises the *parvenu* or the *nouveau riche*. When more than one
Banshee is present, and they wail and sing in chorus, it is for the
death of some holy or great one. An omen that sometimes accom-
panies the Banshee is an immense black coach, mounted by a coffin,
and drawn by headless horses driven by a *Dullahan*. A *Dullahan* is
the most terrible thing in the world. In 1807 two of the sentries
stationed outside St James's Park saw one climbing the railings, and
died of fright. Mr Yeats suggests that they are possibly descended
from that Irish giant who swam across the Channel with his head in
his teeth.

Then come the stories of ghosts, of saints and priests, and of
giants. The ghosts live in a state intermediary between this
world and the next. They are held there by some earthly longing or

affection, or some duty unfulfilled, or anger against the living; they are those who are too good for hell, and too bad for heaven. Sometimes they take the forms of insects, especially that of butterflies. The author of 'The Parochial Survey of Ireland'* heard a woman say to a child who was chasing a butterfly, 'How do you know it is not the soul of your grandfather?' On November Eve they are abroad, and dance with the fairies. As for the saints and priests, there are no martyrs in the stories. That ancient chronicler Giraldus Cambrensis* taunted the Archbishop of Cashel, because no one in Ireland had received the crown of martyrdom. 'Our people may be barbarous,' the prelate answered, 'but they have never lifted their hands against God's saints; but now that a people have come amongst us who know how to make them' (it was just after the English invasion) 'we shall have martyrs plentifully.' The giants were the old Pagan heroes of Ireland, who grew bigger and bigger, just as the gods grew smaller and smaller. The fact is they did not wait for offerings; they took them *vi et armis*.

Some of the prettiest stories are those that cluster round *Tír-nan-Og*. This is the Country of the Young, 'for age and death have not found it; neither tears nor loud laughter have gone near it.' One man has gone there and returned. The bard, Oisen—who wandered away on a white horse, moving on the surface of the foam with his fairy Niamh—lived there three hundred years, and then returned looking for his comrades. The moment his foot touched the earth his three hundred years fell on him, and he was bowed double, and his beard swept the ground. He described his sojourn in the Land of Youth to St. Patrick before he died. Since then, according to Mr Yeats, 'many have seen it in many places: some in the depths of lakes, and have heard rising therefrom a vague sound of bells; more have seen it far off on the horizon, as they peered out from the western cliffs. Not three years ago a fisherman imagined that he saw it.'

Mr Yeats has certainly done his work very well. He has shown great critical capacity in his selection of the stories, and his little introductions are charmingly written. It is delightful to come across a collection of purely imaginative work, and Mr Yeats has a very quick instinct in finding out the best and the most beautiful things in Irish folk-lore. I am also glad to see that he has not confined himself entirely to prose, but has included Allingham's* lovely poem on the fairies:

'Up the airy mountain,
  Down the rushy glen,
We daren't go a hunting
  For fear of little men;
Wee folk, good folk,
  Trooping all together;
Green jacket, red cap,
  And white owl's feather.

'Down along the rocky shore
  Some make their home;
They live on crispy pancakes
  Of yellow tide-foam;
Some in the reeds
  Of the black mountain lake,
With frogs for their watch-dogs
  All night awake.

'High on the hill-top
  The old king sits,
He is now so old and grey
  He's nigh lost his wits.
With a bridge of white mist
  Colunkill he crosses,
On his stately journeys
  From Slieveleague to Rosses;
Or going up with music,
  On cold starry nights,
To sup with the Queen
  Of the gay Northern Lights.'

All lovers of fairy-tales and folk-lore should get this little book.
'The Horned Women,' 'The Priest's Soul,'* and 'Teig O'Kane,' are
really marvellous in their way; and, indeed, there is hardly a single
story that is not worth reading and thinking over.

The wittiest writer in France at present is a woman. That clever,
that *spirituelle grande dame*, who has adopted the pseudonym of
'Gyp',* has in her own country no rival. Her wit, her delicate and
delightful *esprit*, her fascinating modernity, and her light happy
touch, give her a unique position in that literary movement which
has taken for its object the reproduction of contemporary life. Such
books as 'Autour du Mariage,' 'Autour du Divorce,' and 'Le Petit

Bob,'* are, in their way, little playful masterpieces, and the only work
in England that we could compare with them is Violet Fane's 'Edwin
and Angelina Papers.'* To the same brilliant pen which gave us these
wise and witty studies of modern life we owe now a more serious,
more elaborate production. 'Helen Davenant' (Chapman and Hall) is
as earnestly wrought out as it is cleverly conceived. If it has a fault, it
is that it is too full of matter. Out of the same material a more
economical writer would have made two novels and half a dozen
psychological studies for publication in American magazines.
Thackeray once met Bishop Wilberforce at dinner at Dean Stanley's,*
and, after listening to the eloquent prelate's extraordinary flow and
fund of stories, remarked to his neighbour, 'I could not afford to
spend at that rate.' Violet Fane is certainly lavishly extravagant of
incident, plot, and character. But we must not quarrel with richness
of subject-matter at a time when tenuity of purpose and meagreness
of motive seem to be becoming the dominant notes of contemporary
fiction. The side-issues of the story are so complex that it is difficult,
almost impossible, to describe the plot in any adequate manner. The
interest centres round a young girl, Helen Davenant by name, who
contracts a private and clandestine marriage with one of those mysterious and fascinating foreign noblemen who are becoming so
invaluable to writers of fiction, either in narrative or dramatic form.
Shortly after the marriage her husband is arrested for a terrible
murder committed some years before in Russia, under the evil influence of occult magic and mesmerism. The crime was done in a
hypnotic state, and, as described by Violet Fane, seems much more
probable than the actual hypnotic experiments recorded in scientific
publications. This is the supreme advantage that fiction possesses
over fact. It can make things artistically probable, can call for
imaginative and realistic credence, can, by force of mere style, com-
pel us to believe. The ordinary novelists, by keeping close to the
ordinary incidents of commonplace life, seem to me to abdicate half
their power. Romance, at any rate, welcomes what is wonderful; the
temper of wonder is part of her own secret; she loves what is strange
and curious. But besides the marvels of occultism and hypnotism,
there are many other things in 'Helen Davenant' that are worthy of
study. Violet Fane writes an admirable style. The opening chapter of
the book, with its terrible poignant tragedy, is most powerfully written, and I cannot help wondering that the clever authoress cared to

abandon, even for a moment, the superb psychological opportunity that this chapter affords. The touches of nature, the vivid sketches of high life, the subtle renderings of the phases and fancies of society, are also admirably done. 'Helen Davenant' is certainly clever, and shows that Violet Fane can write prose that is as good as her verse, and can look at life not merely from the point of view of the poet, but also from the standpoint of the philosopher, the keen observer, the fine social critic. To be a fine social critic is no small thing, and to be able to incorporate in a work of fiction the results of such careful observation is to achieve what is out of the reach of many. The difficulty under which the novelists of our day labour seems to me to be this: if they do not go into society, their books are unreadable; and if they do go into society, they have no time left for writing. However, Violet Fane has solved the problem.

'The chronicles which I am about to present to the reader are not the result of any conscious effort of the imagination. They are, as the title-page indicates, records of dreams occurring at intervals during the last ten years, and transcribed, pretty nearly in the order of their occurrence, from my diary. Written down as soon as possible after awaking from the slumber during which they presented themselves, these narratives, necessarily unstudied in style and wanting in elegance of diction, have at least the merit of fresh and vivid colour; for they were committed to paper at a moment when the effect and impress of each successive vision were strong and forceful on the mind. . . .

'The most remarkable features of the experiences I am about to record are the methodical consecutiveness of their sequences, and the intelligent purpose disclosed alike in the events witnessed and in the words heard or read. . . . I know of no parallel to this phenomenon, unless in the pages of Bulwer Lytton's romance entitled 'The Pilgrims of the Rhine,'* in which is related the story of a German student endowed with so marvellous a faculty of dreaming, that for him the normal conditions of sleeping and waking became reversed; his true life was that which he lived in his slumbers, and his hours of wakefulness appeared to him as so many uneventful and inactive intervals of arrest, occurring in an existence of intense and vivid interest which was wholly passed in the hypnotic state. . . .

'During the whole period covered by these dreams I have been busily and almost continuously engrossed with scientific and literary pursuits, demanding accurate judgment and complete self-possession and rectitude of mind. At the time when many of the most vivid and remarkable visions occurred, I was following my course as a student at the Paris Faculty of

Medicine, preparing for examinations, daily visiting hospital wards as dresser, and attending lectures. Later, when I had taken my degree, I was engaged in the duties of my profession and in writing for the Press on scientific subjects. Neither had I ever taken opium, haschish, or other dream-producing agent. A cup of tea or coffee represents the extent of my indulgences in this direction. I mention these details in order to guard against inferences which might otherwise be drawn as to the genesis of my faculty.

'It may, perhaps, be worthy of notice that by far the larger number of the dreams set down in this volume occurred towards dawn; sometimes even, after sunrise, during a "second sleep." A condition of fasting, united possibly with some subtle magnetic or other atmospheric state, seems, therefore, to be that most open to impressions of the kind.'

This is the account given by the late Dr Anna Kingsford* of the genesis of her remarkable volume, 'Dreams and Dream-Stories' (George Redway); and certainly some of the stories, especially those entitled 'Steepside,' 'Beyond the Sunset,' and 'The Village of Seers,' are well worth reading, though not intrinsically finer, either in motive or idea, than the general run of magazine stories. No one who had the privilege of knowing Mrs Kingsford, who was one of the brilliant women of our day, can doubt for a single moment that these tales came to her in the way she describes; but to me the result is just a little disappointing. Perhaps, however, I expect too much. There is no reason whatsoever why the imagination should be finer in hours of dreaming than in its hours of waking. Mrs Kingsford quotes a letter written by Jamblichus to Agathocles,* in which he says: 'The soul has a twofold life, a lower and a higher. In sleep the soul is liberated from the constraint of the body, and enters, as an emancipated being, on its divine life of intelligence. The nobler part of the mind is thus united by abstraction to higher natures, and becomes a participant in the wisdom and foreknowledge of the gods. . . . The night-time of the body is the day-time of the soul.' But the great masterpieces of literature and the great secrets of wisdom have not been communicated in this way; and even in Coleridge's case, though 'Kubla Khan'* is wonderful, it is not more wonderful, while it is certainly less complete, than 'The Ancient Mariner.'

As for the dreams themselves, which occupy the first portion of the book, their value of course depends chiefly on the value of the truths or predictions which they are supposed to impart. I must confess that most modern mysticism seems to me to be simply a method of imparting useless knowledge in a form that no one can understand. Allegory, parable, and vision have their high artistic uses, but their philosophical and scientific uses are very small. However, here is one of Mrs. Kingsford's dreams. It has a pleasant quaintness about it:—

THE WONDERFUL SPECTACLES

'I was walking alone on the sea-shore. The day was singularly clear and sunny. Inland lay the most beautiful landscape ever seen; and far off were ranges of tall hills, the highest peaks of which were white with glittering snows. Along the sands by the sea came towards me a man accoutred as a postman. He gave me a letter. It was from you. It ran thus:—

' "I have got hold of the earliest and most precious book extant. It was written before the world began. The text is easy enough to read; but the notes, which are very copious and numerous, are in such minute and obscure characters that I cannot make them out. I want you to get for me the spectacles which Swedenborg used to wear; not the smaller pair—those he gave to Hans Christian Andersen*—but the large pair, and these seem to have got mislaid. I think they are Spinoza's make. You know, he was an optical-glass maker by profession, and the best we ever had. See if you can get them for me."

'When I looked up after reading this letter I saw the postman hastening away across the sands, and I cried out to him, "Stop! how am I to send the answer? Will you not wait for it?"

'He looked round, stopped, and came back to me.

' "I have the answer here," he said, tapping his letter-bag, "and I shall deliver it immediately."

' "How can you have the answer before I have written it?" I asked. "You are making a mistake."

' "No," he said. "In the city from which I come the replies are all written at the office, and sent out with the letters themselves. Your reply is in my bag."

' "Let me see it," I said. He took another letter from his wallet, and gave it to me. I opened it, and read, in my own handwriting, this answer, addressed to you:—

' "The spectacles you want can be bought in London; but you will not be able to use them at once, for they have not been worn for many years, and they sadly want cleaning. This you will not be able to do yourself in London, because it is too dark there to see well, and because your fingers are not small enough to clean them properly. Bring them here to me, and I will do it for you."

'I gave this letter back to the postman. He smiled and nodded at me; and then I perceived, to my astonishment, that he wore a camel's-hair tunic round his waist. I had been on the point of addressing him—I know not why—as *Hermes*.* But I now saw that he must be John the Baptist;* and in my fright at having spoken to so great a Saint I awoke.'

Mr Maitland, who edits the present volume, and who was joint-author with Mrs Kingsford of that curious book, 'The Perfect Way,'* states in a footnote that in the present instance the dreamer knew nothing of Spinoza at the time, and was quite unaware that he was an optician; and the interpretation of the dream, as given by him, is that the spectacles in question were intended to represent Mrs Kingsford's remarkable faculty of intuitional and interpretative perception. For a spiritual message fraught with such meaning, the mere form of this dream seems to me somewhat ignoble, and I cannot say that I like the blending of the postman with St John the Baptist. However, from a psychological point of view, these dreams are interesting, and Mrs Kingsford's book is undoubtedly a valuable addition to the literature of the mysticism of the nineteenth century.

'The Romance of a Shop' (T. Fisher Unwin), by Miss Amy Levy,* is a more mundane book, and deals with the adventures of some young ladies who open a photographic studio in Baker Street, to the horror of some of their fashionable relatives. It is so brightly and pleasantly written that the sudden introduction of a tragedy into it seems violent and unnecessary. It lacks the true tragic temper, and without this temper in literature all misfortunes and miseries seem somewhat mean and ordinary. With this exception the book is admirably done, and the style is clever and full of quick observation. Observation is perhaps the most valuable faculty for a writer of fiction. When novelists reflect and moralise, they are, as a rule, dull. But to observe life with keen vision and quick intellect, to catch its many modes of expression, to seize upon the subtlety, or satire, or dramatic quality of its situations, and to render life for us with some spirit of distinction and fine selection—this, I fancy, should be the aim of the modern realistic novelist. It would be, perhaps, too much to say that Miss Levy has distinction; this is the rarest quality in modern literature, though not a few of its masters are modern; but she has many other qualities which are admirable.

'Faithful and Unfaithful' (Macmillan and Co.) is a powerful but not very pleasing novel. However, the object of most modern fiction is not to give pleasure to the artistic instinct, but rather to portray life vividly for us, to draw attention to social anomalies, and social forms of injustice. Many of our novelists are really pamphleteers, reformers masquerading as story-tellers, earnest sociologists seeking to mend as well as to mirror life. The heroine, or rather martyr, of Miss Margaret Lee's story is a very noble and graciously Puritanic American girl, who is married at the age of eighteen to a man whom she insists on regarding as a hero. Her husband cannot live in the high rarefied atmosphere of idealism with which she surrounds him; her firm and fearless faith in him becomes a factor in his degradation. 'You are too good for me,' he says to her in a finely conceived scene at the end of the book; 'we have not an idea, an inclination, or a passion in common. I'm sick and tired of seeming to live up to a standard that is entirely beyond my reach and my desire. We make each other miserable! I can't pull you down, and for ten years you have been exhausting yourself in vain efforts to raise me to your level. The thing must end!' He asks her to divorce him, but she refuses. He then abandons her, and availing himself of those curious facilities for breaking the marriage-tie that prevail in the United States, succeeds in divorcing her without her consent, and without her knowledge. The book is certainly characteristic of an age so practical and so literary as ours, an age in which all social reforms have been preceded and have been largely influenced by fiction. 'Faithful and Unfaithful' seems to point to some coming change in the marriage-laws of America.

EXPLANATORY NOTES

The Explanatory Notes indicate Wilde's reuse of quotations or ideas from the journalism in other forums such as his critical essays. In this way, I highlight the extent to which Wilde reworked his journalistic material throughout his *œuvre*. I have used the following versions of the texts:

'Shakespeare and Stage Costume', *The Nineteenth Century*, 17 (1885), 800–18.

'The Decay of Lying', *The Nineteenth Century*, 25 (1889), 35–56.

'The True Function and Value of Criticism I', *The Nineteenth Century*, 28 (1890), 123–47.

'The True Function and Value of Criticism II', *The Nineteenth Century*, 28 (1890), 435–59.

'The Critic as Artist', in *Intentions* (London, 1891).

'The Decay of Lying', in *Intentions* (London, 1891).

'The Truth of Masks', in *Intentions* (London, 1891).

'The Soul of Man Under Socialism', *Fortnightly Review*, 49 (1891), 292–319.

'A Few Maxims for the Instruction of the Over-Educated', *The Saturday Review*, 78 (1894), 533–4.

'Phrases and Philosophies for the Use of the Young', *The Chameleon*, 1 (1894), 1–3.

Abbreviation

Letters   *The Complete Letters of Oscar Wilde*, ed. Merlin Holland and Rupert Hart-Davis (London, 2002).

PALL MALL GAZETTE

3   *The 'Girl Graduate'*: a report that described Wilde's lecture on dress appeared in the *Pall Mall Gazette* on 2 October 1884. The anonymous letter from 'The Girl Graduate' responding to the report was published in the *Pall Mall Gazette* on 7 October 1884. 'The Girl Graduate' argued against flat shoes and 'cumbrous, uncomely, and hybrid' divided skirts, instead advocating freedom of expression in clothing.

   Stygian mud: here Wilde describes the muddy streets of London as being like the mud of the river Styx, a river in Hades in Greek mythology.

   vertugadin . . . 'dress improver': the vertugadin was a French-style hooped skirt like a farthingale. The 'dress improver' was a kind of bustle designed to accentuate the bottom and slim the waist.

   Henry VI: (1421–71), king of England (1422–61, 1470–1).

4   *Mr Wentworth Huyshe*: Huyshe's response to Wilde's ideas appeared in the *Pall Mall Gazette* on 3 October 1884. He argued against Wilde's proposed modifications to Greek costume, suggesting that women 'will

never consent to loose-waists and flat feet, not though a greater apostle than Mr Wilde rose from the dead'.

Dr Jaeger: Gustav Jaeger (1832–1917), German hygienist and dress reformer. He advocated a system of hygienic woollen clothing that was popularized in Britain by George Bernard Shaw.

Mr E. W. Godwin . . . Health Exhibition: Edward William Godwin (1833–86), architect, theatrical designer, and archaeologist. Godwin designed the Wildes' house at 16 Tite Street. The project was fraught with difficulties and Wilde was forced to take legal action against his builders (*Letters*, p. 263). Godwin had a formative influence on Wilde's thinking about archaeological realism in the theatre, interior design, and dress reform. Rehashed versions of Godwin's ideas appeared unacknowledged in Wilde's lectures. The International Health Exhibition opened on 8 May 1884. Its aim was to demonstrate the effects of food, dress, and living conditions on a healthy lifestyle. Godwin contributed a pamphlet to the exhibition entitled *Dress, and its relation to health and culture* (1884).

5 *a macaroni . . . first Charles*: in contrast to Huyshe, who had praised eighteenth-century costume, Wilde accentuates his admiration of seventeenth-century dress by favouring all things seventeenth century. So he prefers the style of the cavalier who supported Charles I (1600–49) in the Civil War to the eighteenth-century dandy macaroni who affected foreign styles during the reign of George III (1738–1820). He approves of the aristocratic paintings of Sir Anthony Vandyke (1599–1641), court painter to Charles I, but not the portraits of Sir Thomas Lawrence (1769–1830) who was court painter to George III.

6 *Mr Whistler*: James Abbott McNeill Whistler (1834–1903), American painter notorious as a dandy and wit. Whistler and Wilde were friends until early 1890 when Whistler accused Wilde of plagiarism in a letter to the editor of *Truth*. Wilde responded angrily, accusing Whistler of being 'ill-bred and ignorant'. The Ten O'Clock lecture was an attack on the art critic John Ruskin's (1819–1900) belief in the moral purpose of art. Whistler had earlier taken Ruskin to court for libel when Ruskin suggested that Whistler was 'flinging a pot of paint into the public's face'. Whistler received a farthing's damages. Wilde takes the opportunity presented by the review to engage with Whistler's ideas on art.

miniature Mephistopheles, mocking the majority!: Wilde characterizes Whistler as a little devil encouraging the audience to discard their beautiful things in favour of the cultivation of ugliness.

7 *Velasquez*: Diego Rodríguez de Silva y Velázquez (1599–1660), Spanish painter noted for the realism of his portraits.

Crystal Palace: a building of glass and iron designed by Joseph Paxton (1801–65) to house the Great Exhibition of 1851. It was destroyed by fire in 1936.

7 *Carot's letters*: Wilde probably means the letters of the French landscape painter Jean Baptiste Corot (1796–1875). In 'The True Function and Value of Criticism II' (1890), Wilde states that Corot felt that the landscape was 'but a mood of his own mind'.

Fusiyama: the dormant volcano in Japan also known as Mount Fuji. Mount Fuji was a common image in the Japanese art so admired by Whistler.

8 *Parthenon*: a temple on the Acropolis in Athens, Greece, dedicated to the goddess Athena.

Edgar Allan Poe . . . Paul Delaroche: Edgar Allan Poe (1809–49), American writer and poet. Wilde greatly admired Poe and visited his house during his tour of America in 1882. He called Poe a 'marvellous lord of rhythmic expression' in 'To Read or Not to Read' (p. 13). Charles Baudelaire (1821–67), French poet. His *Fleurs du mal* (1857) is now a classic of French verse although he was fined for offending public morals with a number of poems in the first edition. Wilde admired Baudelaire and wrote to Robert Ross from prison that 'if I spend my future life reading Baudelaire in a café I shall be leading a more natural life than if I take to hedger's work or plant cacao in mud-swamps' (*Letters*, p. 790). Benjamin West (1738–1820), American historical painter and portraitist. Paul Hippolyte Delaroche (1797–1859), French painter and portraitist. Wilde explained his choice of West and Delaroche in a letter to Whistler of 23 February 1885. They both 'recklessly took to lecturing on Art' and 'as of their works, nothing at all remains, I conclude that they explained themselves away' (*Letters*, p. 250).

a man can live for three days without bread . . . an aphorism of Baudelaire's: a version of this quotation appears in Baudelaire's essay 'Conseils aux jeunes littérateurs' (1846). It reads: 'Quoi d'étonnant, d'ailleurs, puisque tout homme bien portant peut se passer de manger pendant deux jours,—de poésie, jamais?' ('How surprising that any healthy man can go without food for two days—without poetry, never'). Wilde may have quoted from memory, hence his inaccuracy.

salmi: a stew made from game birds in which the bird is part-roasted then cooked in wine or port.

9 *ortolans*: small birds eaten as delicacies. They are usually eaten whole in a single bite with the bird's head hanging from the diner's mouth.

turned, for her iniquities, into a pillar of that salt: Lot's wife was turned into a pillar of salt for looking back as she and Lot fled the destruction of Sodom (Genesis 19).

10 *back-hendl . . . Alexandre Dumas*: back-hendl is fried, breaded chicken. Kulibatsch is a pie with meat, fish, or vegetables. Alexandre Dumas (1802–70), French novelist and playwright, best known for *The Count of Monte Cristo* (1844–5) and *The Three Musketeers* (1844).

pompono . . . Delmonico's: pompono (or pompano) is a species of fish with a smooth silver skin and sweet white meat. Delmonico's is a famous restaurant in New York where Wilde dined during his 1882 lecture tour.

the Yosemité Valley: valley in the Sierra Nevada mountains, California.

A Handbook to Marriage: the author of the book, Edward Hardy, was an assistant master at Portora Royal School, which Wilde attended from 1864 to 1871.

Socrates . . . Artemus Ward: Socrates (469–399 BC), Greek philosopher. He wrote nothing but Plato preserved his teaching methods of critical dialogue. Wilde made use of the dialogue form in 'The Decay of Lying' (1889) and 'The True Function and Value of Criticism I and II' (1890). Artemus Ward was the pseudonym of the American humorous moralist Charles Farrar Browne (1834–67), who contributed to *Punch*.

Dr Johnson . . . Lord Chancellor: Samuel Johnson (1709–84), essayist, biographer, lexicographer, and wit. The Lord Chancellor is the cabinet minister who is head of the judiciary in England and Wales and Speaker of the House of Lords. James Boswell (1740–95) records Johnson's proposition about the Lord Chancellor in his *Life of Samuel Johnson* (1791).

Lord Verulam: Francis Bacon (1561–1626), statesman and philosopher. In his essay 'Of Marriage and Single Life' (1625) Bacon noted: 'Certainly the best works, and of greatest merit for the public, have proceeded from unmarried or childless men; which both in affection and means, have married and endowed the public.'

11 *Solomon owed all his wisdom to the number of his wives*: Solomon, King of Israel (c.970–930 BC). The Bible tells that he had seven hundred wives and three hundred concubines (1 Kings 11) and that his fall was the result of his love of many strange women.

Bismarck . . . Mahommed: Prince Otto van Bismarck (1815–98), German statesman and Prime Minister of Prussia (1862–90). In 1871 he became the first chancellor of the German Reich. He married Johanna von Puttkamer in 1847 and wrote of her, 'she it is who has made me what I am.' John Stuart Mill (1806–73), philosopher and economist. Mill married Harriet Taylor in 1851. She was, in his view, the chief inspiration of his philosophy and he dedicated his essay 'On Liberty' (1859) to her. Muhammad (c.570–632), prophet and founder of the Muslim religion. His first wife, Khadija (c.555–619), was an ardent supporter of her husband and was the first convert to Islam.

Lord Beaconsfield: Benjamin Disraeli (1804–81), politician, Prime Minister (1868, 1874–80), and novelist. He married Mary Anne Wyndham Lewis in 1839 and made no secret of the fact that he married her for money. He was therefore disappointed to find that her income died with her. He is purported to have said of his wife: 'She is an excellent creature, but she can never remember which came first, the Greeks or the Romans.' Wilde showed his admiration for Disraeli in a draft review of Disraeli's correspondence written in 1886. In it he described Disraeli's life as 'the most brilliant of paradoxes'. See Anya Clayworth and Ian Small, eds., ' "Amiel and Lord Beaconsfield": An Unpublished Review by Oscar Wilde', *English Literature in Transition 1880–1920*, 39 (1996), 284–97.

11 *Archbishop Whately*: Richard Whately (1787–1863), professor of political economy and archbishop of Dublin.

Girton and Nuneham: Girton College, Cambridge was the first college to be opened to women, in 1869. Nuneham probably refers to Newnham College, Cambridge, also for women, which opened in 1876.

ormolu inkstands covered with sham onyxes: an inkstand coloured gold with an alloy to make it look gilded and covered with false onyx. The implication is that these are wedding presents that one would not wish to receive.

Murray . . . bliss: John Murray (1808–92), publisher and travel writer. Murray published a long and profitable series of guidebooks, some of which he wrote himself. Karl Baedeker (1801–59), German editor and publisher. Baedeker published the popular travel guidebooks, which still retain his name.

12 *TO READ, OR NOT TO READ*: the title given to Wilde's letter by the *Gazette* is a parody of Hamlet's famous line 'To be, or not to be' (*Hamlet*, II. i).

Cicero's Letters . . . Grote's History of Greece: Marcus Tullius Cicero (106–43 BC), Roman prose writer. Cicero's letters to his friend Atticus were discovered in 1345 and are a valuable record of Latin prose and contemporary life. Gaius Suetonius Tranquillus (Suetonius) (AD *c.*70–*c.*140), Roman biographer. His aim was to bring out the moral character of his subjects as well as their private lives. Giorgio Vasari (1511–74), Italian painter, architect, and author of *The Lives of the Most Excellent Italian Architects, Painters and Sculptors* (1550 and 1568), one of the main sources for the history of Italian art in the nineteenth century. Benvenuto Cellini (1500–71), Italian goldsmith, sculptor, and author. Sir John Mandeville, the ostensible author of the famous book of *Travels* which first appeared in 1356–7. The book claims to be a geographical and ethical guide for pilgrims to the Holy Land and is widely seen as a prototype of the popular genre of the fabulous travel book. Marco Polo (1254–1324), Italian member of a patrician family who wrote an account of his travels on an embassy from the Pope to Kublai, Grand Khan of Tartary. Louis de Rouvroy, duc de Saint-Simon (1675–1755), French chronicler and memorialist. Saint-Simon's *Mémoires* (21 vols., 1829–30) are an incomparable record of his life at court in the latter part of Louis XIV's reign. Theodor Mommsen (1817–1903), German historian and politician. His major historical work was *The History of Rome* (1854–85), which sought to demythologize Rome. George Grote (1794–1871), banker, MP, and historian. Grote's eight-volume *History of Greece* (1846–56) was an immediate success.

Plato . . . Keats: Plato (*c.*428–348 BC), Greek philosopher famous for the profundity of his thought. Many of his works appeared in the form of dialogues, also favoured by Wilde in some of his critical essays. John Keats (1795–1821), poet. Wilde greatly admired Keats, calling him in his 1882 lecture, 'The English Renaissance', 'the pure and serene artist'. Wilde wrote a number of poems and articles about Keats and was given a manuscript of the poet's 'Sonnet on Blue'.

Thomson's Seasons . . . Lewes' History of Philosophy: James Thomson (1700–48), poet. Thomson's *The Seasons* (1726–30) is a popular and influential work that moved eighteenth-century poetry away from the urbanity of the work of Alexander Pope (1688–1744). Samuel Rogers (1763–1855), poet and art collector; *Italy* (1822–8) was a collection of verse tales. William Paley (1743–1805), philosopher. Paley's *Evidences of Christianity* (1794) finds evidence for the existence of God in the designs of nature. Wilde described the book in 'The Decay of Lying' (1889) as 'behind the age'. Wilde rejects all the works of all the Christian Fathers apart from St Augustine (354–430), whose most famous writings are *Confessions* (*c.*400), a spiritual autobiography, and *De civitate dei*, a vindication of the Christian Church. Wilde rejects John Stuart Mill's seminal modification of Benthamite utilitarianism in his essay 'Utilitarianism' (1861) and his economic ideas from *Principles of Political Economy* (1848) in favour of Mill's essay on the freedom and rights of the individual, 'On Liberty'. Wilde later wrote his own essay in support of the individual, 'The Soul of Man Under Socialism' (1891). Voltaire, pseudonym of François-Marie Arouet (1694–1778), French satirist, novelist, historian, poet, and dramatist. Voltaire was the universal genius of the Enlightenment. Joseph Butler (1692–1752), theologian. In his *Analogy of Religion* (1736) Butler argues that belief in immortality, revelation, and miracles is as reasonable as the beliefs upon which religion was founded. Sir Alexander Grant (1826–84), translator. Grant produced a translation of Aristotle for the Ancient Classics for English Readers series in 1870. David Hume (1711–76), Scottish philosopher and historian; his *History of England* (1754–62) was a best-seller. George Henry Lewes (1817–78), biographer, essayist, and scientist. Lewes's *Biographical History of Philosophy* (1845–6) was a popular history of philosophy.

nothing that one can learn is ever worth learning: Wilde reworked this aphorism into 'Education is an admirable thing, but it is well to remember from time to time that nothing that is worth knowing can be taught' in 'The True Function and Value of Criticism II' (1890). It then reappeared in 'A Few Maxims for the Instruction of the Over-Educated' (1894) as 'Education is an admirable thing. But it is well to remember from time to time that nothing that is worth knowing can be taught.'

University Extension Scheme: in the late nineteenth century, universities began to extend their educational resources to the general public in open lectures. The University of Cambridge, for example, provided extension lectures in provincial centres particularly to offer professional teaching and examinations to women. Lady Bracknell explains Gwendoline's absence to her father in *The Importance of Being Earnest* (1895) by claiming that she 'is attending a more than usually lengthy lecture by the University Extension Scheme'.

12 *the Greek Anthology*: a collection of 6,000 short elegiac poems by about 800 Greek writers (tenth–seventh century BC). A translation of the collection was published in 1864.

13 *Tanagra . . . Pheidian marbles*: Tanagra, a city in Boeotia where small terracotta statues were unearthed from tombs. Wilde describes Sybil Merton in 'Lord Arthur Savile's Crime' (1887) as 'like one of those delicate little figurines men find in the olive woods near Tanagra'. He goes on to elaborate on the construction of the statuettes in 'The True Function and Value of Criticism I' (1890): 'From the river valley he took the fine clay in his fingers, and, with a little tool of wood or bone, fashioned it into forms so exquisite that the people gave them to their dead as their playthings.' Mabel Chiltern in *An Ideal Husband* (1895) is also likened to 'a Tanagra statuette'. The Pheidian marbles were sculptures designed by Pheidias in 493 BC for the Parthenon in Athens.

Southey . . . Keble: Robert Southey (1774–1843), poet, playwright, and historian. He was made poet laureate in 1813 and was accused by many of betraying his Jacobin principles. Lord George Gordon Byron (1788–1824), poet and critic, roundly mocked Southey in *Don Juan* (1819–24) and *The Vision of Judgement* (1822). John Keble (1792–1866), poet and vicar. Keble's 1833 Assize Sermon on National Apostasy led others to write *Tracts for the Times* (1833) which saw the beginning of the Oxford Movement. Wilde probably 'elbows out' Southey and Keble for Edgar Allan Poe and Charles Baudelaire because they were both establishment figures.

The Curse of Kehama . . . the Christian Year: *The Curse of Kehama* (1810) was Southey's long Oriental poem. *The Christian Year* (1827) was Keble's volume of sacred verse.

All the Year Round . . . Balzac: *All the Year Round* was Dickens's weekly periodical that he edited from 1859 until his death. Honoré de Balzac (1799–1850), French novelist. Wilde praises the work of Balzac at length in 'The Decay of Lying' (1889). He goes as far as to suggest that 'the nineteenth century, as we know it, is largely an invention of Balzac' to support his argument that 'literature always anticipates life'.

'Comédie Humaine': (1827–47), a series of co-ordinated and connected novels and stories by Balzac. The Preface to the first collected edition sets out Balzac's grand design to give an authentic and comprehensive fictional representation of French society.

M Taine: Hippolyte Taine (1828–93), French philosopher, historian, and critic.

Buffon: Georges-Louis Leclerc, Comte de Buffon (1707–88), French naturalist. Buffon's *Histoire naturelle, générale et particulière* (1749–88) observed animals in their natural habitats.

M Zola's 'L'Assommoir' . . . *unimaginative realism and imaginative reality*: Émile Zola (1840–1902), French novelist and leading figure in naturalism. His *L'Assommoir* (1877) was set in the taverns of Paris. In 'The Decay of Lying' (1889) Wilde is disparaging of Zola, noting of his characters, 'They have their dreary vices, and their drearier virtues. The record of their lives is absolutely without interest. Who cares what happens to them?' However, Wilde does not criticize Zola on the grounds of morality, a common complaint about Zola at this time. Instead he notes that Zola 'is perfectly truthful, and describes things exactly as they happen. What more could any moralist desire?' *Illusions perdues*, a trilogy by Balzac consisting of *Les Deux Poètes* (1837), *Un Grand Homme de province à Paris* (1839), and *Les Souffrances de l'inventeur* (1843). Wilde's assertion that the distinction between Zola and Balzac is 'the distinction between unimaginative realism and imaginative reality' is taken from a footnote in Algernon Charles Swinburne's (1837–1909) *Study of Shakespeare* (1879) in which Swinburne also argues that Balzac is good and Zola is bad. Wilde reuses this sentence in 'The Decay of Lying' (1889).

14 *'All Balzac's characters . . . genius'*: the quotation from Baudelaire is also borrowed from Swinburne's *Study of Shakespeare*. Swinburne paraphrases a passage from Baudelaire's essay on Theophile Gautier (1859). This quotation is also used in 'The Decay of Lying' (1889).

Trollope: Anthony Trollope (1815–82), novelist. Trollope, like Balzac, made use of reappearing characters, so the comparison that Wilde makes between the two writers is a useful one.

Lucien de Rubempré . . . De Marsay: all characters from Balzac's novels. In 'The Decay of Lying' (1889), Wilde describes the death of Lucien de Rubempré, a character in *Illusions perdues*, as 'one of the greatest tragedies of my life'. It is possible that de Rubempré was one of the models for Dorian Gray. Le Père Goriot, a character in *Le Père Goriot* (1835). Ursule Mirouët, a character in *Ursule Mirouët* (1841). Marguerite Claës, a character in *Le Contrat de mariage* (1835). The Baron Hulot and Mme Marneffe, characters in *La Cousine Bette* (1846). Le cousin Pons, a character in *Le Cousin Pons* (1847). De Marsay, a character in *Le Père Goriot* and *Illusions perdues*.

15 *Mr Routledge . . . M. Poulet-Malassis*: George Routledge (1812–88), publisher and owner of the publishing house Routledge and Sons. Auguste Poulet-Malassis (1825–78), publisher. He published the first edition of Baudelaire's scandalous *Fleurs du mal*.

Mr Henry James took his 'Madonna of the Future': Henry James (1843–1916), novelist and essayist. James greatly admired Balzac, who he called 'the master of us all', and based *Madonna of the Future* (1879) on Balzac's techniques. Wilde and James were not on good terms, especially as Wilde's *The Importance of Being Earnest* (1895) ended up replacing James's *Guy Domville* (1895) at the St James' Theatre when James's play flopped. Wilde describes James in 'The Decay of Lying' (1889) as writing 'fiction as if it was a painful duty'.

15 *the translations are very unequal*: in most of his reviews of translations Wilde points out errors. In this particular review he showcases his own knowledge of French by picking out specific examples for criticism. His attention to detail here is characteristic of his own approach to translating.

16 *It is well printed, and nicely bound*: another observation commonly made by Wilde in reviews is about the appearance of the book. He paid a great deal of attention to the binding and paper of his own work and shows here an early interest in the appearance of the works of others.

Homer . . . Thespis: Homer (eighth century BC), Greek writer, supposed author of *The Iliad* and *The Odyssey*. In 'The True Function and Value of Criticism II' (1890) Wilde suggests that Homer's blindness might have been 'an artistic myth', 'serving to remind us, not merely that the great poet is always a seer, seeing not with the eyes of the body but with the eyes of the soul, but that he is a real singer also'. Thespis (sixth century BC), Greek dramatic and tragic poet, who introduced the idea of a single player on the Greek stage rather than a Chorus, hence the term thespian.

Mr G. R. Sims: George R. Sims (1847–1922), poet, journalist, and novelist. A characteristic feature of Sims's verse was his use of colloquial language.

the style of the Surrey Theatre: the Surrey Theatre in Blackfriars Street, London had a chequered career and was destroyed by fire three times. In the 1880s George Conquest (1837–1901), actor, playwright, and pantomimist, ran the theatre and made it famous for melodramas and pantomimes. Wilde's reference to the style of the Surrey Theatre may thus imply that the tramps' poetry has the low cultural quality of pantomime.

17 *'Facilis descensus Averno!'*: 'Easy is the way down to the Underworld', from Virgil's *Aeneid* (Book 6).

On est toujours fils de quelqu'un: 'One is always the son of somebody' or 'Everybody is somebody's son.' This is a key phrase used by Wilde to define his ideas about literary originality. It reappears in his editorial column for *The Woman's World* in January 1888 as: 'Dans l'art comme dans la nature on est toujours fils de quelqu'un' (p. 154). Wilde suggests in this review that ideas and language are finite and therefore there is no possibility for originality, only reinterpretation of old ideas. He goes on to develop this idea into a fuller argument in 'The True Function and Value of Criticism II' (1890) in which he says: 'No doubt Homer had old ballads and stories to deal with, as Shakespeare had chronicles and plays and novels from which to work, but they were merely his rough material. He took them and shaped them into song. They became his, because he made them lovely.'

Mr Matthew Arnold: (1822–88), poet, essayist, and critic. Wilde set out to engage with Arnold's 'The Function of Criticism at the Present Time' (1865) in 'The True Function and Value of Criticism I and II' (1890).

18 *Mr Marzials*: Frank Thomas Marzials (1840–1912), author and translator. Marzials's *Dickens* was part of Walter Scott's Great Writers series. Wilde had reviewed the previous volumes on the poets Samuel Taylor Coleridge (1772–1834) and Henry Wadsworth Longfellow (1807–82) for the *Pall Mall Gazette* on 27 March 1887. The title of this review—'Great Writers by Little Men'—is suggestive of his attitude to the series.

'Mr Vincent Crumules' (sic) . . . Mr Walter Scott's publications: Vincent Crummles is a character in Dickens's *Nicholas Nickleby* (1838–9). Walter Scott (1826–1910), publisher and owner of Walter Scott Publishing Co. Ltd.

amazing stump-campaign in America: a stump is a political speech, especially made on campaign tours. Wilde could be referring to the great success of Dickens's tour of America in 1842 that Marzials describes in detail. He could also, however, be alluding to Dickens's other purpose in visiting America, to campaign for the institution of an international copyright law.

19 *Micawber . . . Mrs Nickleby*: Micawber, a character in Dickens's *David Copperfield* (1849–50). Mrs Nickleby, a character in Dickens's *Nicholas Nickleby*.

Ferdinand and Miranda by the side of Caliban: all characters in Shakespeare's *The Tempest* (1611).

Cruikshank's illustrations: George Cruikshank (1792–1878), illustrator and caricaturist. Cruikshank had a long association with Dickens and illustrated works such as *Sketches by Boz* (1836) and *Oliver Twist* (1837).

20 *Lord Frederick Verisopht and Sir Mulberry Hawk*: both characters in *Nicholas Nickleby*.

Mr Pater: Walter Horatio Pater (1839–94), philosopher, essayist, and critic. The effect of Pater's work on Wilde is most clearly reflected in Wilde's comment in *De Profundis* (1897) that Pater's *Studies in the History of the Renaissance* (1873) 'has had such a strange influence over my life'. Wilde's review of *Imaginary Portraits* was his first of Pater's work. The review pleased Pater to the extent that he asked Wilde to review *Appreciations* (1889) in order that 'it may not fall into unsympathetic hands' (Lawrence Evans, ed., *Letters of Walter Pater* (Oxford, 1970), 106). Pater then returned the favour by reviewing *The Picture of Dorian Gray* (1890). However, he left his review so late that it had little impact on the ongoing debate about the novel's morality.

Sebastian Van Storck: one of Pater's characters in *Imaginary Portraits*. Van Storck is a seventeenth-century Dutch philosopher who broods on the thought of the earth cooling down forever from its cosmic heat.

Watteau: Jean-Antoine Watteau (1684–1721), French rococo painter. In the stage directions to *An Ideal Husband* (1895) Wilde describes Mrs

Marchmont and Lady Basildon as women Watteau 'would have loved' to paint.

21 *to him who saw Monna Lisa sitting among the rocks*: the *Mona Lisa* (*c.*1503) was painted by Leonardo da Vinci (1452–1519). Pater wrote about the *Mona Lisa* in *Studies in the History of the Renaissance* (1873).

peintre des fêtes galantes: Watteau invented the 'fêtes galantes', small pictures in which women and men play music and make love in soft dreamy parkland.

the Helder: Van Storck is drowned by a freak high tide in the shallow sea off Den Helder in North Holland.

Spinoza: Baruch de Spinoza (1632–77), philosopher. Spinoza's most famous work, *Ethics* (*c.*1665), argues that it is by goodness and piety that man reaches perfect happiness.

Dionysus: Greek god of wine, fruitfulness, and vegetation, worshipped in orgiastic rites.

a picture by Mantegna: Andrea Mantegna (1431–1506), Italian painter and engraver, noted especially for his frescoes.

22 *the late King of Bavaria*: Ludwig II, King of Bavaria (1845–86). He was a patron of the German composer, dramatist, and writer Richard Wagner (1813–83), but became a recluse and was deposed in 1886.

Aufklärung: enlightenment. The term is used generally to describe the philosophic, scientific, and rational spirit, freedom from superstition, scepticism, and faith in religious tolerance which characterized much of eighteenth-century Europe. Pater uses it in *Imaginary Portraits* in the story 'Duke Carl of Rosenmold'.

Herder . . . Goethe: Johann Gottfried Herder (1744–1803), German philosopher and critic who heavily influenced Goethe. Gotthold Ephraim Lessing (1729–81), German critic and dramatist. Lessing suggested in his criticism that German writers should look to Shakespeare and English models rather than the narrow conventions of the French classical school. Johann Wolfgang von Goethe (1749–1832), dramatist, critic, poet, and novelist.

23 *Mr Mahaffy*: the Revd John Pentland Mahaffy (1839–1919), Professor of Ancient History at Trinity College, Dublin, knighted in 1918. Mahaffy was Wilde's tutor and mentor at Trinity and took him on two trips to Europe, in 1875 and 1877. Mahaffy's politics with regard to Ireland were somewhat changeable. He was a Tory Unionist who was a friend of the future Conservative Prime Minister Arthur James Balfour (1848–1930), but he also had nationalist leanings. Wilde reviewed another of Mahaffy's books, *The Principles of the Art of Conversation*, for the *Pall Mall Gazette* on 16 December 1887.

Paper-Unionists . . . Primrose League: Paper-Unionists is a term used widely in the *Pall Mall Gazette*, probably with reference to unionists who signed covenants in defence of the union. Wilde seems to be using it here to refer to those politicians who sought to uphold the union without wanting to take responsibility for it. It is a phrase that Wilde also uses in relation to the poetry of John Cameron Grant in 'The Poet's Corner' (*Pall Mall Gazette*, 15 February 1888). The Primrose League was a conservative political organization founded in 1838 to commend Benjamin Disraeli's ideals of conservatism. The League sought to preserve the traditional freedoms of the British way of life and to improve the lot of the working people of the countryside. The League's emblem was a primrose, Disraeli's favourite flower.

Alexander: Alexander the Great (356–323 BC), King of Macedon who conquered most of the ancient world.

Tipperary . . . Mitchelstown: Wilde accuses Mahaffy of treating the world of the ancient Greeks as if it were Ireland of the nineteenth century. In 1848 Tipperary was the scene of a failed rebellion against the Act of Union. Mr Smith, or William Smith O'Brien (1803–64), was an MP and prominent member of the Young Ireland group who led the abortive 1848 rebellion. He was transported to Australia for his involvement in the rebellion but was subsequently pardoned. Joy Melville notes in *Mother of Oscar: The Life of Jane Francesca Wilde* (1994) that Smith O'Brien was a visitor to the Wildes' house in Dublin when Oscar was a child and that he was Oscar's earliest childhood hero. The Battle of Chaeronea took place in 338 BC: Philip of Macedonia and Alexander the Great conquered Greece by defeating the Athenians. Mitchelstown, County Cork was the site of a number of demonstrations against land evictions in 1887 led by the nationalist MP William O'Brien (1852–1928). On 9 September 1887 a further demonstration at Mitchelstown turned into a riot and the police shot three members of the public. The policemen concerned were found guilty of wilful murder, but as the hearing had taken place in a coroner's court their convictions were not upheld.

24 *Mr Balfour . . . Demosthenes*: as Chief Secretary for Ireland 1887–92, Balfour was nicknamed 'Bloody Balfour'. William O'Brien edited the nationalist paper *United Ireland* that promoted, despite the British government's attempts to stop it, the aims of the Irish Land League. O'Brien was imprisoned on several occasions and at the time this review was written was in prison for publishing details of Land League activities. Demosthenes (384–322 BC), an Athenian orator and statesman who resisted Philip of Macedon's imperial ambitions in a series of orations, the *Philippics*. He committed suicide rather than be put to death.

Herodotus . . . United Ireland: Herodotus (484–425 BC) Greek historian, often called the father of history and the father of lies. *United Ireland* was a newspaper founded in 1881 by the Home Rule Party leader Charles Stewart Parnell (1846–91) to promote the ideas of his party. It carried on the front of each issue a large provocative cartoon, at this time, usually of Arthur Balfour.

25 *Gladstone . . . Quinctius*: William Ewart Gladstone (1809–98), Liberal

Prime Minister 1868–74, 1880–85, 1886, 1892–4. Gladstone devoted much of his later career to securing Home Rule for Ireland. John Morley (1838–1923), journalist and close supporter of Gladstone. Morley was well known as the editor of a number of nineteenth-century periodicals including *The Fortnightly Review* and the *Pall Mall Gazette*. He was Chief Secretary for Ireland 1886, 1892–5. Quintus Marcius Philippus or Marcius (second century BC), Roman censor and consul. Titus Quinctius Flamininus or Quinctius (c.230–175 BC), Roman general and statesman.

25 *Belvedere Apollo . . . Perganene school*: the Belvedere Apollo is one of the most famous representations of the Greek god Apollo. The Artemis of the Vatican is a Greek sculpture of Artemis of Ephesus. The Dying Gaul is a celebrated classical statue showing a weary warrior supporting himself on one arm. The spelling of Perganene was incorrect in the original article and was corrected in the next day's *Gazette* to Pergamene. The Pergamene school of Hellenistic sculpture was associated with the town of Pergamum in Asia Minor.

   Aristophanes: (450–385 BC), Greek comic dramatist famous for his satirical plots on contemporary topics.

26 *Zeno . . . Pyrrho*: Zeno (335–262 BC), Greek philosopher and founder of the Stoic school in Athens. Epicurus (341–270 BC), Greek philosopher who held that the highest good is pleasure. Pyrrho (c.365–270 BC), Greek philosopher who founded scepticism.

   Laocoon: in Greek legend, Laocoön was the Trojan priest of Apollo who warned against accepting the Greek gift of the Trojan horse.

   Menander . . . Sheridan: Menander (c.342–292 BC), Greek comic dramatist. Richard Brinsley Sheridan (1751–1816), Irish dramatist.

   Jack Absolute . . . Charles Surface: Jack Absolute and Bob Acres are characters from Sheridan's *The Rivals* (1775). Charles Surface is a character in Sheridan's *School for Scandal* (1777).

   Philopoenen . . . Victor Emmanuel: the spelling of the original is incorrect and was corrected in the following day's *Gazette* to 'Philopoemen' Philopoemen (c.252–183 BC), Greek statesman and general. Giuseppe Garibaldi (1807–82), Italian soldier who fought for the unification of Italy. Antigonus Doson (d. 221 BC), king of Macedon. Victor Emmanuel II (1820–78), king of Italy 1861–78.

   Mr Shorthouse's 'John Inglesant' . . . Athenaeus: Joseph Henry Shorthouse (1834–1903), novelist. His historical novel *John Inglesant* (1881) is a religious intrigue set in the seventeenth century. Apollonius Rhodius (c.300 BC), Alexandrian poet who wrote the epic poem *The Voyage of the Argo*, also known as the *Argonautica*. Ptolemy Philadelphus (309–246 BC), king of Egypt (285–246 BC). Athenaeus of Naucratis (c. AD 200), Greek rhetorician.

27 *Theocritus . . . Four Gospels*: Theocritus (c.310–250 BC), Greek poet who wrote the first pastoral poems in Greek. The second Macedon war ended

with a Roman victory at the battle of Cynoscephalae. Lucian (*c.* AD 200), Greek writer noted especially for his satirical dialogues. Plutarch (*c.* AD 46–120), Greek biographer and philosopher, noted for his *Parallel Lives* of distinguished Greeks and Romans. The first four books of the New Testament,—Matthew, Mark, Luke, and John—are known as the Four Gospels.

Mr Wilfrid Blunt: Wilfrid Scawen Blunt (1840–1922), poet, diplomat, traveller, and anti-imperialist. Blunt was an acquaintance of Wilde's.

The 'Love Sonnets of Proteus': Blunt's 1875 volume of poetry.

Musset-like modernities: Wilde refers here to the French poet and play-wright Alfred de Musset (1810–57). His work was well known for its melancholy tone and anxiety.

'In Vinculis': *In Vinculis* ('in chains') was a sonnet sequence written by Blunt while imprisoned in Galway Gaol for participating in an illegal meeting.

28 *Mr Balfour*: Balfour and Blunt became enemies after Blunt published details of a conversation that he had had with Balfour on the subject of the imprisonment of the nationalist MP John Dillon (1851–1927). Balfour had told Blunt that the imprisonment of John Dillon would probably lead to Dillon's death, and had indicated that the Government were therefore going to press for imprisonment. See Elizabeth Longford, *A Pilgrimage of Passion: The Life of Wilfrid Scawen Blunt* (1973).

29 *'Defence of Philosophic Doubt'*: Balfour published *A Defence of Philosophic Doubt* in 1879.

30 *Mr Andrew Lang ... Mr Rider Haggard*: Andrew Lang (1844–1912), journalist, poet, Greek scholar, and man of letters. Sir Henry Rider Haggard (1856–1925), adventure novelist and author of *King Solomon's Mines* (1886). Lang was a good friend of Rider Haggard and they collaborated on *The World's Desire* in 1891.

when Leigh Hunt was in gaol: James Henry Leigh Hunt (1784–1859), essayist, journalist, and poet. In 1813 Hunt was imprisoned for two years for libelling the Prince Regent in his journal the *Examiner*. However, while in prison he was allowed to have his family with him, to continue to write and edit the *Examiner*, and to receive visits from his friends.

'ivories of speech,' to borrow one of Mr Pater's phrases: a phrase from Pater's *Marius the Epicurean* (1885).

Rémy Belleau's: (1528–77), French scholar and poet.

Henri Murger's: (1822–61), French author. Murger popularized the idea of the bohemian in his *Scènes de la vie de Bohème* (1847–9) upon which Puccini based his opera *La Bohème* (1896). Wilde refers to Murger as poor because he died destitute at the age of 38.

recently christened 'the Divine Amateur': the poet and editor William Ernest Henley (1849–1903) called Lang a 'Divine Amateur'. Wilde refers to Lang as the 'Divine Amateur' again in an essay 'English Poetesses' in *The Queen* (8 December 1888).

31 *Mr Wyke Bayliss*: later Sir Wyke Bayliss (1835–1906), art historian and President of the Royal Society of British Artists.

his predecessor in office: James McNeill Whistler was President 1886–7. Whistler caused controversy in the Society by his autocratic revamping of the galleries and invitations to foreign artists to exhibit with the Society. He was forced to resign. Wilde uses the first part of the review to criticize Whistler as well as commenting on Bayliss.

the old Puck to the fresh Prospero: Puck is a character in Shakespeare's *A Midsummer Night's Dream* (1595) and Prospero is a character in *The Tempest*. Puck is a mischievous comic character whereas Prospero is a powerful and mysterious magician. Wilde, while labelling Whistler as the comic Puck, prefers him to Bayliss's Prospero.

Mr Ruskin: Ruskin was Slade Professor of Art at Oxford University during Wilde's time as an undergraduate there. When *The Happy Prince and Other Tales* was published in 1888, Wilde sent Ruskin a copy. In his accompanying letter he wrote that he had 'learned nothing but what was good' from Ruskin (*Letters*, p. 349).

'Habakkuk est capable de tout': Habakkuk was a Hebrew prophet. This quotation meaning 'Habakkuk is capable of anything' has been attributed to Voltaire.

32 *the Pythia*: the priestess of Apollo at Delphi, who transmitted the oracles.

Corot's aphorism: this aphorism is also used by Wilde in 'The True Function and Value of Criticism II' (1890).

Mr Palgrave: Francis Turner Palgrave (1824–97), poet and critic. Palgrave's 'The Decline of Art' was published in *The Nineteenth Century*, 23 (1888), 71–92. Bayliss accuses Palgrave of lifting ideas from his *The Witness of Art* (1875) and tries to prove it by publishing a series of parallel passages.

33 *Florence Nightingale in the hospital at Scutari . . . Vivien*: Florence Nightingale (1820–1910), nurse. She was sent to Scutari during the Crimean War to inspect the military hospitals. Her work there dramatically cut mortality rates. Merlin and Vivien are both characters in Alfred Tennyson's (1809–92) *Idylls of the King* (1870). Vivien, filled with hatred for King Arthur and his court, seduces the aged Merlin and imprisons him in an oak.

Mr Barker's 'Waterloo Banquet' . . . Prince of Wales': Thomas Jones Barker (1815–82), a leading exponent in battle painting. William Powell Frith (1819–1909), painter. His *Marriage of the Prince of Wales* was painted in 1865.

Bezaleel: the artificer who executed works of art in connection with the tabernacle in the wilderness (Exodus 35).

Mr Stopford Brooke: Stopford Augustus Brooke (1832–1916), clergyman, man of letters, and socialist.

34 *Mr Edward Carpenter's*: (1844–1929), poet, essayist, and socialist.

Mr William Morris . . . Mr Walter Crane: William Morris (1834–96), poet, designer, and socialist. Wilde reviewed Morris's two-volume translation of Homer's *Odyssey* (1887) in the *Pall Mall Gazette* on 26 April 1887 and 24 November 1887. He also reviewed Morris's lecture on tapestry to the Arts and Crafts Exhibition in the paper on 2 November 1888. In 'The Garden of Eros' (1881), Wilde expresses his admiration for Morris, calling him 'our sweet and simple Chaucer's child'. Walter Crane (1845–1915), writer, designer, illustrator, and socialist. Crane was most famous for his illustrated books for children published by Macmillan and Co. With Jacomb Hood, Crane illustrated *The Happy Prince and Other Tales* (1888) for Wilde.

35 *Mr T. D. Sullivan's*: Timothy Daniel Sullivan (1827–1914), Irish Nationalist MP, mayor of Dublin, and composer of popular nationalist ballads. His most famous song was 'God Save Ireland', which commemorates the Manchester martyrs who were shot for the murder of a policeman while rescuing their leaders from custody in Manchester.

Mendelssohn . . . Moody and Sankey: Felix Mendelssohn (1809–47), German composer. Dwight Lyman Moody (1837–99) and Ira David Sankey (1840–1908), American evangelists. With Sankey as singer and organist, they carried on a revival campaign in England and America.

'Wacht am Rhein' . . . 'Marseillaise': 'Wacht am Rhein' or 'The Watch on the Rhine' (1840), a German patriotic song written by Max Schneckenburger. It was the battle song of the German army 1870–1. The 'Marseillaise' is the French national anthem. The words and music were composed by C. J. Roget de Lisle as a war song for the Rhine army of revolutionary France.

'Lillibulero' . . . Beethoven's Ninth Symphony: 'Lillibulero' is a song attributed to Lord Wharton satirizing the earl of Tyrconnel on the occasion of his going to Ireland in 1686–7 as James II's lieutenant. *Norma* (1831), a two-act opera by Vincenzo Bellini (1801–35). John Brown (1800–59), leader of the anti-slavery movement. He is commemorated in the well-known marching song 'John Brown's Body'. Ludwig van Beethoven (1770–1827), German composer. His Ninth Symphony was written in response to a commission from the Philharmonic Society of London.

the National Anthem in Shelley's version . . . 'Ye Banks and Braes of Bonny Doon': Percy Bysshe Shelley's (1792–1822) 'New National Anthem' (1819) was written after Peterloo when members of the burgeoning trade union movement were attacked by the cavalry. *The Voice of Toil* (1884) is a poem by William Morris. 'Ye Banks and Braes of Bonny Doon' is a line from 'Banks o' Doon' (1792), a song by the Scottish poet Robert Burns (1759–96).

35 *Victor Hugo*: (1802–85), French poet, novelist, and dramatist. His most famous works are *Notre-Dame de Paris* (1831) and *Les Misérables* (1862).

36 *The Reformation gained much from the use of popular hymns and hymn-tunes*: the Reformation saw the breaking of monopoly of Latin in Church hymns. Instead, worshippers were encouraged to sing in their own language.

   The walls of Thebes rose up to the sound of music: in Greek myth, the music of Amphion's lyre is supposed to have caused stones to move of their own accord to build the walls of Thebes.

   Blue books: blue books are parliamentary reports. Clearly the book that Wilde was reviewing was not a blue book but, by suggesting it was, Wilde links the Government with Froude's anti-Home Rule views.

   Mr Froude's heavy novel: James Anthony Froude (1818–94), historian and novelist. It is noteworthy that Wilde does not actually mention the title of the book until the final paragraph of the review.

   Their first practical leader is an Irish American: Wilde is probably alluding here to Charles Stewart Parnell, whose mother was American. It is interesting that Wilde refers to the Irish as 'they' rather than 'we'.

37 *Huguenots . . . recalled the Edict of Nantes*: Huguenots were French Protestants. The 1598 Edict of Nantes guaranteed them religious liberty, but the Edict was revoked by Louis XIV in 1685.

40 *Pecca fortiter, therefore, as Luther says*: Martin Luther (1483–1546), German leader of the Protestant reformation. '*Pecca fortiter*': sin strongly, from a letter (1521) from Luther to Melanchthon (1497–1560).

   'Robert Elsmere': Mary Augusta Ward's novel *Robert Elsmere* (1888) is about religious doubt. It was her most successful book but Wilde was critical of it, referring to it in 'The Decay of Lying' (1889) as 'a masterpiece of the "genre ennuyeux" '.

   Mr Swinburne: Algernon Charles Swinburne (1837–1909), poet. Wilde read Swinburne as early as his university days, writing to his friend William Ward on 10 July 1876 that he had had to be woken on the morning of his degree viva and was discovered in bed 'with Swinburne (a copy of)' (*Letters*, p. 20). In April 1895 Wilde was asked who he thought should be Poet Laureate and wrote in *The Idler* that 'Mr Swinburne is already the Poet Laureate of England'. Swinburne's first volume of *Poems and Ballads* (1866) was received with shock by some critics because of its preoccupation with masochism and *femmes fatales* and its repudiation of Christianity. However, other artists and writers admired it, including Dante Gabriel Rossetti (1828–82). Wilde's reference to Swinburne's poetry in this review as 'very perfect and very poisonous' therefore reflects the polarization of opinion about the 1866 volume. It is also a reworking of his reference to Baudelaire in 'Literary and Other Notes III' as 'the most perfect and the most poisonous of all modern French poets' (p. 119). This was the only review that Wilde wrote about Swinburne.

Marie Stuart . . . 'Bothwell': Wilde means Swinburne's poem *Mary Stuart* (1881). *Bothwell* (1874) is a verse drama also by Swinburne.

42 *clangours*: prolonged or repeated clanging noises.

Medea: in Greek legend, a sorceress who assisted Jason in obtaining the golden fleece from her father. When Jason deserted her for Glauce, daughter of the Corinthian King Creon, Medea killed Glauce, Creon, and her own two children and fled to Athens.

43 *threnody on John William Inchbold*: a threnody is an ode, speech, or song in lamentation for the dead. John William Inchbold (1830–88), landscape painter.

THE DRAMATIC REVIEW

44 *Shakespeare on Scenery*: Wilde reused material from this article for another essay on the subject of Shakespeare and the late nineteenth-century stage, 'Shakespeare and Stage Costume' for *The Nineteenth Century* in May 1885. Certain phrases are repeated word for word. Wilde went on to revise 'Shakespeare and Stage Costume' into 'The Truth of Masks' for his essay volume *Intentions* (1891). 'The Truth of Masks' dramatically reversed Wilde's arguments in both 'Shakespeare on Scenery' and 'Shakespeare and Stage Costume' and asserted the importance of illusion rather than reality. However, Wilde's final lines in 'The Truth of Masks' offer a typically Wildean qualification: 'Not that I agree with everything I have said in this essay. There is much with which I entirely disagree.'

Mr Irving . . . Hamlet: Henry Irving (1858–1905), actor-manager and owner of the Lyceum Theatre, London. *Much Ado About Nothing* (1598–9), a comedy by Shakespeare. Wilson Barrett (1846–1904), actor-manager who specialized mostly in melodramas. He ran the Lyric Theatre, London. *Hamlet* (1601), a tragedy by Shakespeare.

Messina . . . Elsinore: *Much Ado About Nothing* is set in Messina. The battlements of Elsinore are the setting for the opening of *Hamlet*.

the play, and the play only, is the thing: a corruption of Hamlet's line 'The play's the thing | Wherein I'll catch the conscience of the King' (*Hamlet*, II. ii). Wilde uses the line to imply that the play is not the only thing he's concerned with.

Henry V . . . smallness of the stage: *Henry V* (1599) is a historical drama by Shakespeare. In the opening scene of the play the Chorus asks the audience to 'pardon, gentles all, | The flat unraised spirit, that hath dar'd, | On this unworthy scaffold, to bring forth | So great an object' (*Henry V*, I. i). The Chorus goes on to urge the audience to 'piece out our imperfections with your thoughts' (I. i), in other words to use their imagination to flesh out the play.

45 *Princess's . . . Lyceum*: the Princess's Theatre in Oxford Street, London; the Lyceum Theatre in Wellington Street, London.

45 *Cleopatra's barge*: Wilde is referring to the famous speech by Enobarbus in Shakespeare's *Antony and Cleopatra* (1606–7) in which he describes Antony's first encounter with the Egyptian queen: 'The barge she sat in, | like a burnished throne, | Burned on the water: the poop was beaten gold; | Purple the sails, and so perfumed that | The winds were lovesick with them . . .' (*Antony and Cleopatra*, II. ii). Wilde suggests that if the barge was real it would never have survived, but that Shakespeare's descriptions do survive.

Nereid's: in Greek myth, nereids were sea nymphs who were the daughters of the sea god Nereus.

46 *beauty for beauty's sake*: a variation on the popular maxim, 'art for art's sake', which was popularized by Wilde in the early 1880s.

A painted door is more like a real door than a real door is itself: here Wilde suggests that art is capable of being more realistic than life itself, in other words that illusion is more real than reality. Wilde goes on to develop this argument further in 'The True Function and Value of Criticism I and II' (1890).

47 *Mr Beverley . . . Academicians*: William Roxby Beverley (1814–89), scene-painter. He opposed the innovation of 'built stuff' on the stage and assisted the development of the art of scene painting by his original methods and use of new inventions. William Telbin (1813–73), scene-painter. Academicians are members of the Royal Academy of Arts, which was founded in 1768 for the exhibition of works by contemporary artists.

R. A.'s whose total inability to paint we can see every May for a shilling: Wilde is referring to the annual exhibition at the Royal Academy that opened each May.

Miss Ellen Terry: Ellen Alice Terry (1847–1928), actress and leading lady at the Lyceum Theatre. Wilde wrote a number of sonnets describing Terry in theatrical parts such as Portia in *The Merchant of Venice* (1596). He admired the 'splendid artistic powers, and the nobleness and tenderness' (*Letters*, p. 81) of her acting.

a sheep has been sacrificed: Wilde is referring here to the original meaning of ovation. In William Smith's *Dictionary of Greek and Roman Antiquities* (1875), ovation or ovatio is explained as a celebration of a lesser triumph for a Roman general. The general would enter the city of Rome on foot rather than drawn by four horses and would have a myrtle rather than a laurel wreath. In his honour, a sheep was sacrificed rather than a bull.

49 *Melpomene . . . Thalia*: in Greek myth, Melpomene was the muse of tragedy and Thalia was the muse of comedy and pastoral poetry.

Mr Alexander's: George Alexander Gibb Samson (1858–1918), English actor-manager. He acted with Irving at the Lyceum until 1889 when he entered management on his own. He produced and starred in both *Lady Windermere's Fan* (1892) and *The Importance of Being Earnest* (1895) at the St James' Theatre. He was especially encouraging to Wilde when

Wilde first began writing plays. In a letter of 1894, Wilde described Alexander as a 'good wise friend' (*Letters*, p. 597).

Mr Norman Forbes: Norman Forbes-Robertson (1859–1932), actor and playwright. Forbes-Robertson was a friend of Wilde's and sent congratulations to him when Cyril Wilde was born in 1885. Later he tried to get Wilde to write a play for him.

Hazlitts: William Hazlitt (1778–1830), critic, theatre critic, and essayist. He produced a book about Shakespeare, *Characters of Shakespear's Plays* (1817).

out-Heroded Herod: Herod (*c.*73–4 BC), King of Judaea who ordered the Massacre of the Innocents in the latter part of his reign. Wilde is quoting from Hamlet's advice to the First Player: 'I would have such a fellow whipped for o'erdoing Termagant. It out-Herods Herod. Pray you avoid it' (*Hamlet*, III. ii). The term derives from the medieval mystery plays, in which Herod is presented as a ranting tyrant. Wilde also used this phrase to describe the author and editor Frank Harris (1856–1931) in a letter to Robert Ross in 1900 (*Letters*, p. 1188).

50 *boy's attire*: in Shakespeare's theatre, boys played all the female roles, therefore the Player Queen should have been a boy.

that disappointing Atlantic Ocean: Wilde is referring to his own reported comment that the Atlantic Ocean was 'rather disappointing' on his arrival in America in 1882. Irving and Terry had just returned from a tour of America with the Lyceum company. Wilde again refers to the Atlantic as 'disappointing' in a letter to George Alexander in 1894 (*Letters*, p. 610).

Henry IV: a historical play by Shakespeare (1597). This play was chosen to inaugurate the Oxford University Dramatic Society (OUDS) because the Vice Chancellor of the University, Benjamin Jowett (1817–93), had decreed that the Society could only perform Shakespeare. He also decreed that women must play the women's parts in the plays. Wilde attended the OUDS dinner after the performance and made a speech there.

by the banks of the Cam . . . Box and Cox: in other words in Cambridge. *Box and Cox* (1847), a farce by J. M. Morton adapted from two French vaudevilles. It was the *sine qua non* of amateur shows at this time.

51 *Isis . . . Cumnor cowslips*: Isis is the local name for the River Thames at Oxford. Ilyssus is the name of one of the two streams watering the Athenian plain from Mount Hymettus. In 'The True Function and Value of Criticism II' (1890), Wilde notes that 'By the Ilyssus, there were no tedious magazines about art, in which the industrious prattle of what they don't understand.' Colonos or Colonus is the hill town north of Athens where the Greek dramatist Sophocles (496–406 BC) was born. Pallas is another name for Athena. In Greek myth, Athena was a virgin goddess of wisdom and practical skills. Wilde alludes to Matthew Arnold's 'Thyrsis' (1866) when he mentions the Cumnor cowslips. In

Arnold's poem, the speaker laments that the goddess Proserpina never knew the beauty of the Cumner (*sic*) cowslips on the hills near Oxford. Wilde also mentions the Cumnor cowslips in 'The True Function and Value of Criticism I' (1890).

51 *archaeological accuracy*: Wilde's praise for the archaeological accuracy of the production highlights a popular movement in theatre at the time in which the study of architecture and costume was applied to theatre practice in order to produce a historically accurate and unified production. *The Dramatic Review* was in favour of archaeological realism and published many articles supporting it.

52 *Mr Mackinnon's*: Alan McKinnon, director of the production, and of all productions for OUDS until 1895. He later wrote a history of the society, *The Oxford Amateurs* (1910).

Mr Coleridge's: Hon. Gilbert D. Coleridge (1859–1953), one of the founding members of OUDS.

Mr Bourchier's: Arthur Bourchier (1863–1927), actor and founder of OUDS.

Kemble: John Philip Kemble (1757–1823), actor well known for stately parts such as this. He was in the last production of *Henry IV*, in 1815.

Mrs Woods . . . understood Welsh: Mrs H. G. Woods was the wife of the Bursar of Trinity College. Lady Edward Spencer Churchill sang Lady Mortimer's song in Welsh after coaching from the Celtic Professor.

53 *D.C.L.'s*: Doctor of Civil Law from Oxford University.

the crimson or the sheep-skin hood: hoods worn when graduating from Oxford with a doctoral degree.

Mr George Meredith . . . M Zola's 'formule scientifique': George Meredith (1828–1909), poet and novelist. Wilde noted of Meredith in 'The Decay of Lying' (1889): 'As a writer he has mastered everything, except language: as a novelist he can do everything, except language: as an artist he is everything except articulate.' In 'The True Function and Value of Criticism II' (1890), Wilde famously refers to Meredith as a 'prose-Browning'. Wilde's reference to Zola's 'formule scientifique' highlights the scientific naturalism which was the basis of Zola's approach to writing. Zola aimed to take a slice of life and place it under the microscope and examine it. This resulted in a carefully documented account of French middle- and working-class life.

Goldsmith: Oliver Goldsmith (1730–74), Irish playwright, novelist, and poet.

'The Vicar of Wakefield': a novel by Goldsmith (1766).

54 *The originality . . . annexes everything*: an idea that Wilde expands upon in 'The True Function and Value of Criticism I and II' (1890).

Mr Wills's Olivia: William Gorman Wills (1828–91), Irish dramatist who often wrote for the Lyceum. *Olivia* (1885) is his adaptation of Goldsmith's *The Vicar of Wakefield*.

55 *Mr Terriss*: William Charles James Lewin (1847–97), actor who made his name in *Olivia*.

Miss Emery's: Isabel Winifred Emery (1862–1924), actress.

the famous cherry orchard of the Théâtre-Français: the Théâtre-Français is the national theatre of France, founded in 1680. At the height of the fashion for realism in the theatre, a real cherry orchard was constructed on the stage.

Chiromancy: or cheiromancy, the science of the hand and palm-reading. Wilde later put the idea of cheiromancy at the centre of 'Lord Arthur Savile's Crime' (1887).

56 *Théophile Gautier's first novel*: Théophile Gautier (1811–72), French novelist, poet, and critic. His first novel was *Mademoiselle de Maupin* (1835). Wilde quotes Swinburne's 'Sonnet (with a copy of *Mademoiselle de Maupin*)' (1878) when he refers to the novel as 'that golden book of spirit and sense, | The holy writ of beauty'. In a letter of July 1882, Wilde complains about the heaviness of his luggage during his tour of America because he 'can't travel without Balzac and Gautier, and they take up so much room' (*Letters*, p. 175).

Coombe: the production of *As You Like It* (1600) took place in the grounds of Dr McGeagh's hydropathic institution at Coombe Woods near Kingston-upon-Thames. Some professional actors were used but friends of Godwin and Lady Archibald Campbell took other parts.

Lady Archiebald Campbell: Janey Sevilla Campbell (1846–1923), actress and pioneer in the production of pastoral plays. Lady Archie was a close friend of Whistler and of Godwin. Wilde published an article by her describing the production of *As You Like It* in his first number as editor of *The Woman's World* (1887).

57 *Mr Hermann Vezin*: (1829–1910), American actor. Wilde sent Vezin a copy of his first play, *Vera; Or, the Nihilists* (1880) and asked for 'any suggestions about situations or dialogue' (*Letters*, p. 99).

Mrs Plowden: Florence Plowden or Mrs Vyner Robinson (d. 1890).

Miss Calhoun: Eleanor Calhoun (1865–1927), American actress to whom Wilde sent a copy of *Vera; Or, the Nihilists* (1880) in 1889.

58 *Chelsea China Shepherdesses*: figurines made from white soft paste porcelain by the Chelsea China Works. By linking the costume of Phoebe to the Chelsea shepherdesses, Wilde alludes to the anachronism of the dress.

Rev. Arthur Batson: the Revd Arthur Wellesey Batson, conductor. Godwin had designed Batson's house. Batson argued with the Chorus leader during the production, causing the Chorus leader to write furiously to Godwin: 'Please beg Mr Batson to behave like a gentleman—tell him to leave off insulting the singers by caustic remarks . . . he walks without knocking into their bedrooms.'

58 *Mr Walsham*: Henry Walsham (d. 1898), singer and member of the D'Oyly Carte Opera Company.

to exchange Piccadilly for Parnassus: Wilde reuses this phrase in a letter to the poet Violet Fane (1843–1905). He notes: 'Besides, *you* live between Parnassus and Piccadilly: it is those who live in the country whom Nature deteriorates' (*Letters*, p. 324). It is interesting that Wilde reuses a phrase from a review in a letter: it is usually the other way round.

new theatre at Oxford: as a result of the growing interest in the University in amateur dramatics, a theatre was built to accommodate productions. This production of *Twelfth Night* (1601) was the first to be mounted in the new premises.

59 *Hazlitt says somewhere*: Hazlitt notes in *Characters of Shakespear's Plays* that 'If poor Malvolio's treatment afterwards is a little hard, poetical justice is done in the uneasiness which Olivia suffers on account of her mistaken attachment to Cesario, as her insensibility to the violence of the Duke's passion is atoned for by the discovery of Viola's concealed love of him.'

60 *Mr Adderley . . . Mr Coningsby Disraeli*: the Hon. James G. Adderley (1861–1942), pioneer of OUDS. Coningsby Disraeli (1867–1936), nephew of Benjamin Disraeli.

Slade Professorship: the art collector Felix Slade (1790–1868) endowed The Slade Professorship of Art at Oxford. It was the first professorship of its kind and its first holder was John Ruskin.

her riper age: this quotation is from 'Prologue to the University of Oxford' (1673) by John Dryden (1631–1700).

the Cenci: a verse tragedy (1819) by Shelley. The play's melodramatic plot was taken from the true story of Beatrice Cenci who was tried and executed for the murder of her violent father. The Lord Chamberlain banned the play, on the grounds of immorality, and Shelley was unable to get it produced in his lifetime. The Shelley Society arranged a private performance of the play in order to avoid the jurisdiction of the censor.

Edmund Kean . . . Miss O'Neill: Edmund Kean (c.1787–1833), tragic actor. Eliza O'Neill (1791–1872), Irish actress.

61 *and suffered consists*: this quotation and all those preceding it are from Shelley's Preface to *The Cenci* (1819). By using Shelley's own discussion of his play, Wilde avoids having to comment at length on the vexed question of the morality of *The Cenci*.

62 *Miss Alma Murray . . . Mr Leonard Outram's*: Alma Murray (1854–1945), tragic actress. Her portrayal of Beatrice in this production was her greatest triumph. Leonard S. Outram (d. 1901), playwright, director, and actor.

the Agamemnon . . . Eumenides: both plays are part of the *Oresteia* (458 BC) by the Greek dramatist Aeschylus (c.525–456 BC).

a circus: Godwin made use of the circular arena at Hengler's Circus in order to attempt to re-create the stage area of Greek theatre.

the temple of Bassae ... Troy: the temple of Bassae (*c.*425–420 BC) was dedicated to Apollo Epicurus and was probably designed by the Greek architect Ictinus (fifth century BC). Troy, an ancient city in Asia Minor, was the scene of the Trojan War.

63 *Miss Kinnaird*: Helen Kinnaird, opera singer who went on to work with the D'Oyly Carte Company.

Phrygian cap: a conical cap of soft material worn during ancient times that became a symbol of liberty during the French Revolution.

Mr Beerbohm-Tree: Sir Herbert Draper Beerbohm Tree (1853–1917), actor-manager. From 1887 to 1897, Tree was the lessee and manager of the Haymarket Theatre, where he produced two of Wilde's plays, *A Woman of No Importance* (1893) and *An Ideal Husband* (1895). Richard Ellmann notes that Tree stated that he produced *A Woman of No Importance* not with the help of Wilde but with his interference (Richard Ellmann, *Oscar Wilde* (London, 1988), 360).

64 *Mrs Jopling*: Louise Jopling (1843–1933), artist and art teacher.

Mrs Beerbohm-Tree's: Helen Maud Tree (1863–1937), actress. Mrs Tree appeared in her husband's production of *A Woman of No Importance* (1893).

Sardou ... Mr Burnand's: Victorien Sardou (1831–1908), French dramatist whose work was popular in the London theatres. George Bernard Shaw, who disliked Sardou's work, referred to it as 'Sardoodledom'. Sir Frances Cowley Burnand (1836–1917), editor of *Punch* and playwright. Burnand's play *The Colonel* (1881) satirized the Aesthetic movement and, in particular, the work of Godwin.

65 *Helena in Troas*: (1886), a play by the Irish dramatist and poet John Todhunter (1839–1916). Constance Wilde (1858–98) played a small role in the play and reviewed the production for *The Lady*.

THE COURT AND SOCIETY REVIEW

66 *Buffalo Bill ... Mrs Brown-Potter*: William Frederick Cody or Buffalo Bill (1846–1917), soldier and performer. Buffalo Bill's Wild West Show came to Britain for the first time in 1887 for Queen Victoria's Golden Jubilee. Cora Urquhart or Mrs James Brown-Potter (1859–1936), society lady turned actress. Her début was at the Haymarket Theatre, London on 29 March 1887. She later bought an option on Wilde's play scenario *Mr and Mrs Daventry* (1894).

Sandy Hook ... Delmonico's: the Sandy Hook lighthouse is a major landmark just outside New York. Wilde mentions Delmonico's in 'Dinners and Dishes' (pp. 8–10).

67 *Elevated Railway ... Bunker's Hill*: the first elevated railway was opened

in New York in 1868. The railroad was above street level on bridges reached by steps. The Battle of Bunker Hill (1775) was the first major pitched battle in the American War of Independence. Although the British troops forced the Americans from their positions, the battle gave impetus to the revolution.

68 *that they never talk seriously . . . except about amusements*: here Wilde uses the technique of reversal which made his wordplay so effective.

their inexperience: Wilde reverses the roles here and makes children wiser than their parents: this is a key feature of his early fairy-tales. For example, in 'The Selfish Giant' the child teaches the giant how to be a good man and the giant's transformation is rewarded by a revelation of Paradise. Parenting is always seen in the early stories from the point of view of the child.

69 *bien chausée et bien gantée*: well shod and with a good pair of gloves, i.e. well turned out.

70 *Boston*: it is interesting that Wilde uses Boston, birthplace of Edgar Allan Poe, as a place where 'an occasional lion' comes from.

the Row: the Rotten Row bridlepath in Hyde Park was the place to be seen in nineteenth-century London.

M Renan . . . Philistine: Ernest Renan (1823–92), French historian, archaeologist, and Hebraist. Wilde mentions Renan's classic work, *Vie de Jésus* (1863), as an influence as early as 1877. Arnold developed his theory that the English middle classes are predominantly philistine in *Culture and Anarchy* (1869).

71 *Ravenna . . . Verona*: Wilde visited Ravenna *en route* to Greece in March and April of 1877. He won the Newdigate Poetry Prize for 1878 with his poem about the city. Wilde also immortalized Verona in a sonnet, 'At Verona' (1881).

Don Quixote of common sense: Miguel de Cervantes Saavedra (1547–1616) was the author of *Don Quixote de la Mancha* (1605, 1615), the story of Don Quixote who has had his wits disordered by inordinate devotion to chivalric tales and travels round misinterpreting everything as relating to a chivalric romance. Wilde seems to be suggesting here that the American man does the same thing by interpreting everything according to its uses.

deplacé: out of place.

boys at Eton, or lads at Oxford: notice here that Wilde refers to himself as being part of a 'we' who attended Eton and Oxford, although he did not attend Eton. His use of these institutions is a social indicator of the audience for *The Court and Society Review*.

72 *boot-black*: a shoe-cleaner.

Benedict and Beatrice: characters from Shakespeare's *Much Ado About Nothing* who resist falling in love with one another although everyone else in the play realizes their mutual affection. Their relationship during the early part of the play is characterized by witty repartee. Wilde supposes that their marriage at the end of the play would have led them into other topics of conversation.

73 *Don Juan ... Georges Dandin*: Byron's *Don Juan* tells the story of the adventures and many love affairs of Don Juan of Seville. Wilde implies that America would not like the poem because of its celebration of Don Juan's conquests. Molière's *Georges Dandin or the Confounded Husband* (1668) tells the story of a tradesman who marries a nobleman's daughter and suffers many humiliations as a result. Wilde suggests that this play would be more to the taste of the American audience.

railway travelling: Wilde had done a considerable amount of travelling across America during his lecture tour of 1882 so was fully aware of the enormous size of the country. He complained on numerous occasions about the large distances he was travelling, remarking in a letter to his manager that he wished his tour were 'arranged more according to geographical convenience' (*Letters*, p. 146).

74 *Eve*: Wilde alludes here to Eve's desire in the Old Testament to taste the forbidden fruit which led to God ejecting Adam and Eve from the Garden of Eden.

Butterfly's Boswell: in the title of the review, Wilde refers to Dowdeswell as Boswell, thereby suggesting that Dowdeswell's account of Whistler is of comparable quality to Boswell's famous biographical accounts of Dr Johnson.

Every great man has . . . the biography: Wilde reused this sentence in 'The True Function and Value of Criticism I' (1890), changing the word 'usually' to 'invariably'. When he revised 'The True Function and Value of Criticism' for *Intentions* (1891) and renamed it 'The Critic as Artist', he made a further revision to the sentence, replacing 'usually' with 'always'. The final incarnation of the line was: 'Every great man nowadays has his disciples, and it is always Judas who writes the biography.'

Mr Walter Dowdeswell: Walter Dowdeswell's Gallery opened in 1878 in New Bond Street, London. Wilde also mentions 'Messrs Dowdeswell's Gallery' in 'The Decay of Lying' (1889).

75 *'Grattez le maître . . . le Tartare!'*: 'Scratch the master and you will find a Tartar!'

Velasquez . . . Gleyre: Whistler greatly admired Velázquez and aspired to emulate him. In Canto IX of *Don Juan*, Byron refers to the Duke of Wellington (1769–1852) as Vilainton: 'Oh, Wellington (or 'Vilainton'— for fame | Sounds the heroic syllables both ways).' Wilde is clearly alluding to the great military achievements of Wellington but hinting that Whistler could never have achieved the same. Charles Gleyre (1808–74), Swiss painter.

'White Girl' . . . Salon des Refusés: the *Symphony in White No. 1: The White Girl* (1862) was exhibited at the inaugural show of the Salon des Refusés in 1863. In 1863 there was such an outcry about the rejection of 2,800 canvases from the Salon de Paris show that Emperor Napoleon III

demanded that all submitted canvases must be shown. The Salon des Refusés was created to show the rejected pictures.

75 *cénacle . . . Suffolk Street*: *cénacle*: coterie. The Suffolk Street Galleries were the galleries of the Royal Society of British Artists.

76 *Othello . . . Lear*: characters in Shakespeare's tragedies *Othello* (1602) and *King Lear* (1606).

portraits are pure works of fiction: Wilde alludes here to Whistler's using his mistress Maud Franklin (1857–1941) as the model for a portrait of Mrs Frances Leyland (1834–1910).

77 *Butterfly's Barnum*: by referring to the extravagant advertisements of the American showman Phineas Taylor Barnum (1810–91), Wilde implicitly criticizes Dowdeswell's advertising of his own work on Whistler.

Oracles . . . bazaars: Wilde is alluding here to the passing of the times when oracles, prophets, and sibyls would be consulted seriously for information about the future. He implies that in his contemporary society, classical seers would only be used to tell fortunes and to predict the outcome of horse races.

Mr Mark Twain's: pseudonym of Samuel Langhorne Clemens (1835–1910), American writer famous for *The Adventures of Tom Sawyer* (1876) and *The Adventures of Huckleberry Finn* (1884). Twain's original article, 'English as She is Taught', drew on a manuscript he had received for his opinion. He liked the content of the manuscript so much that he chose to review it before it was even published.

wisdom from the lips of babes and sucklings: Wilde uses here a common revision of the lines from Psalms: 'Out of the mouth of very babes and sucklings hast thou ordained strength, because of thine enemies: that thou mightest still the enemy, and the avenger' (Psalm 8: 2). Wisdom has replaced strength in the common usage of this quotation.

the American child educates its father and mother: Wilde alludes here to his own article, 'The American Invasion' (see pp. 66–9), where he suggests that American children educate their parents.

the fallacy . . . anything else: Wilde refers here to the ongoing debate about extending the franchise to women. Although Wilde had elsewhere been supportive of women's suffrage (particularly as editor of *The Woman's World*), he labels it here a 'fallacy'. He links it to the concept of *egalité*, one of the cornerstone principles of the French Revolution of 1789. *Egalité*, in terms of the Revolution, was the doing away with privilege even at the cost of political liberty. Despite all the changes brought about by the French Revolution, when Napoleon Bonaparte became Emperor of France, *egalité* was compromised. The quotation with which Wilde follows this observation, though, clouds the issue slightly. 'Things which are equal to each other are unequal to anything else' could suggest that the equality of men and women in the franchise is wonderful because it is unlike anything else or that the equality of men and women is not useful because it merely causes other inequalities. Wilde therefore leaves his position unclear.

78 *The Stamp Act*: a law passed in 1765 by the British Parliament requiring all publications, legal and commercial documents in the American colonies to bear a tax stamp. It was the cause of widespread unrest in the colonies hence the irony of the child's definition.

   Bulwell . . . nearly one hundred years elapsed: Bulwell probably refers to the novelist Edward Bulwer Lytton (1831–91). Gibbon wrote *The History of the Decline and Fall of the Roman Empire* (1776–88), which was not a history of his travels in Italy. Wordsworth's poem was 'Intimations of Immortality from Recollections of Early Childhood' (1807), not 'imitations'. William Cullen Bryant (1794–1878), American poet. Geoffrey Chaucer (*c.*1343–1400), poet, described by some critics as the father of English poetry. Oliver Wendell Holmes (1809–94), writer and professor of anatomy and physiology. He was a very prolific rather than profligate writer. Wilde met Holmes on his tour of America in 1882. Charles Brontë: clearly the child is referring to the novelist Charlotte Brontë (1816–55) here. Alfred the Great (848–99), king of the West Saxons, was better known as a translator than as a novelist. Johnson is better known for his essays and lexicography rather than as a writer of fiction. Henry Wadsworth Longfellow (1807–82), American poet: his *Tales of a Wayside Inn* (1863) follows the form of Chaucer's *Canterbury Tales* (*c.*1387), but there is clearly more than a century between the two poets. Although Longfellow wrote some prose, he is more famous for his poetry. Wilde also met Longfellow on his 1882 tour of America.

79 *olfactory nerve*: the olfactory nerve contributes to the sense of smell rather than hearing.

   Brompton Buddhists: Wilde is probably referring here to Helena Petrovna Blavatsky (1831–91) and Henry Steel Olcott (1832–1907), who founded the Theosophical Society in 1875 and who both converted to Buddhism in 1881. Blavatsky was a controversial figure in London because in 1895 she was accused of fakery by the Society for Psychical Research.

   Mr Posket in 'The Magistrate': The Magistrate (1885), a farce by Arthur Wing Pinero (1855–1934) in which the magistrate, Mr Posket, gets unwittingly caught up in a web of deceit created by his wife and stepson.

   trouvaille . . . Mr Bradlaugh: *trouvaille*: a find or brainwave. Charles Augustus Vansittart Conybeare (1853–1919), radical Liberal MP for Camborne, Cornwall who was arrested for his protests about Irish Land reform. Charles Bradlaugh (1833–91), atheist MP whose refusal to take the parliamentary oath resulted in the denial of his seat for six years. Bradlaugh was put on trial with the writer Annie Besant (1847–1933) for circulating a pamphlet about contraception.

THE WOMAN'S WORLD

81 *Princess Christian ... Margravine of Bayreuth*: Princess Christian of Schleswig-Holstein (1846–1923), daughter of Queen Victoria. Margravine Wilhelmine Friederike Sophie von Bayreuth (1709–58), sister of Frederick the Great and founder of the Bayreuth Opera House later favoured by Wagner.

Frederick the Great: or Frederick II (1712–86), King of Prussia (1740–86).

Newton ... Rousseau: Sir Isaac Newton (1642–1727), mathematician, philosopher, astronomer, and physicist noted particularly for his three laws of motion and for his law of gravitation. John Locke (1632–1704), empiricist philosopher who argued against the divine right of kings in *Treatises of Government* (1690). Anthony Ashley Cooper, 3rd Earl of Shaftesbury (1671–1713), moral and aesthetic philosopher. Jean-Jacques Rousseau (1712–78), writer and philosopher whose best-known work is *Discours sur les sciences et les arts* (1750). Wilde noted of him in 'The True Function and Value of Criticism I' (1890), 'Humanity will always love Rousseau for having confessed his sins, not to a priest, but to the world.'

Carlyle: Thomas Carlyle (1795–1881), critic, journalist, and essayist. Carlyle was a friend of Wilde's parents and Wilde often quoted Carlyle in his letters. After Carlyle's death, Wilde bought and used his writing desk.

Her father: Frederick William I (1688–1740), King of Prussia (1713–40).

82 *the Queen ... Anspach*: Queen Sophie Dorothea (1687–1759), mother of Frederick the Great. The Margrave of Anspach married Wilhelmine's sister, Frederika.

my sister: Frederika Louisa (1714–34), later married the Margrave of Anspach.

83 *Peter the Great and his wife*: Peter the Great or Peter I (1672–1725), Tsar of Russia (1682–1725). He introduced many reforms to the country and founded the new capital of St Petersburg in 1703. His wife during this visit was probably his second wife, Catherine I (1684–1727), later Empress of Russia (1725–7). Catherine was of Lithuanian peasant stock hence the Margravine's comment about her 'low origin'.

84 *Monbijou*: a summerhouse belonging to the Queen in a suburb of Berlin.

85 *Telemachus ... Amelot de la Houssaye's 'Roman History'*: in Greek myth, Telemachus is the son of Odysseus and Penelope, who helped his father slay his mother's suitors. Abraham Nicolas Amelot de la Houssaye (1634–1706), French historian and publicist whose *Histoire du gouvernement de Venise* (1676) caused a scandal and resulted in his brief imprisonment in the Bastille.

Empress of Germany: Maria Theresa (1717–80), archduchess of Austria, queen of Hungary and Bohemia (1740–80).

87 *'Women's Voices'* . . . *Mrs William Sharp*: *Women's Voices* (1887) was an anthology which presented a rather more radical women's poetical canon than had hitherto been available. It contains poetry by a number of authors whom Wilde solicited for contributions to *The Woman's World*. Wilde does not comment upon the radical nature of the anthology at all, printing instead Mrs Sharp's own comments on the subject from her Preface to the collection and offering some suggestions of other poets who might have been added. As John Stokes notes, these suggestions were based on the Revd Alexander Dyce's *Specimens of British Poetesses* (1827) (John Stokes, 'Wilde the Journalist', in *The Cambridge Companion to Oscar Wilde*, ed. Peter Raby (Cambridge, 1997)). Wilde makes use of Sharp's potted biographies of the writers in her anthology. He reuses substantial passages from this part of the review for an article, 'English Poetesses' in *The Queen* magazine of December 1888. He makes use of the lists of women writers in particular, changing them only slightly by adding and rephrasing material. Elizabeth Abigail Sharp (active *c.*1870), biographer, anthologist, and wife of the writer and poet William Sharp (1855–1905). She contributed an article about Mrs Dinah Craik to *The Woman's World* in January 1888.

'Revenge' . . . *Queene of Jewry*: 'Revenge' is part of *The Tragedie of Mariam the Faire Queene of Jewry* (1602). This poem is somewhat of a revisionist text as rather than presenting Mariam as a selfish, manipulative woman it shows her nobility and her rebellious spirit. Lady Elizabeth Carew or Cary (1585–1639), poet.

Margaret, Duchess of Newcastle: Margaret Cavendish, Duchess of Newcastle (1623–73), poet and biographer. Samuel Pepys (1633–1703) dismissed her work as 'airy, empty, whimsical, and rambling'.

88 *'Friendship's Mystery'* . . . *'Nocturnal Reverie'*: 'Friendship's Mystery' (1667) by Katherine Philips, the 'Matchless Orinda' (1631–64), poet. 'A Song' (1677) by Aphra Behn (1640–89), dramatist and poet. 'Nocturnal Reverie' (1713) by Anne Finch, Countess of Winchilsea (1661–1720), poet.

Wordsworth . . . *Gay*: William Wordsworth (1770–1850), poet and essayist who admired the work of the Countess of Winchilsea and chose a selection of her poetry for an album (1819). *Windsor Forest* (1713), a topographical poem by Alexander Pope. *Paradise Lost* (1667), an epic poem by John Milton (1608–74). John Gay (1685–1732), poet. His poem *Rural Sports* (1713) was based on Pope's *Windsor Forest*.

Lady Grisell Baillie . . . *Mrs Hannah More*: Lady Grisell Baillie (1665–1746), poet and songwriter. Jean Adams (1710–65), nursery governess and popular songwriter. Isobel Pagan (1741–1821), owner of an illegal alehouse, and singer. Hester Lynch Thrale (1741–1821), poet and friend of Dr Johnson. Anne Hunter (1742–1821), Scottish poet. Her husband was the anatomist John Hunter (1728–93). Anna Laetitia Barbauld (1743–1825), poet, children's writer, and editor. Hannah More

(1745–1833), dramatist and member of the Blue Stocking Circle, a formal group of intellectual women in London in the eighteenth century.

88 *Miss Anna Seward . . . Mrs Browning*: Anna Seward (1742–1809), poet, essayist, and letter-writer, known as the 'Swan of Lichfield' because she grew up in Lichfield. Dr Erasmus Darwin (1731–1802), botanist, poet, and grandfather of Charles Darwin (1809–82). Seward wrote a memoir of Erasmus Darwin in which she accused him of plagiarizing one of her poems. Lady Anne Barnard (1750–1825), poet and author of 'Auld Robin Gray' (1771). She did not reveal her authorship of the poem until encouraged to do so by Sir Walter Scott two years before her death. Sir Walter Scott (1771–1832), poet, novelist, and publisher. Corydon is a shepherd who features in Theocritus' *Idylls*. His name has become conventional in pastoral poetry. In Greek mythology, Phyllis killed herself and was turned into a tree. Jean Glover (1758–1811), Scottish singer. Joanna Baillie (1762–1851), poet and dramatist. Mary Tighe (1772–1810), Irish poet and author of *Psyche* (1805). Frances Anne Kemble (1809–93), actress and poet. Mrs Sarah Siddons (1755–1831), actress. Letitia Elizabeth Landon (1802–38), poet, journalist, and novelist who wrote under her initials 'L. E. L.'. Sappho (seventh century BC), a Greek lyric poet whose subject matter was always love. Helen Selena, Lady Dufferin (1807–67), poet and granddaughter of Sheridan. The Hon. Mrs Caroline Norton (1808–77), poet, novelist, and editor who was involved in the revision of the laws relating to married women's property. Emily Jane Brontë (1814–48), novelist and poet who set her poems in an imaginary world called Gondal. Wilde makes an interesting change in his comment on Brontë for 'English Poetesses'. In 'Literary and Other Notes', Brontë's poems are described as being 'instinct with tragic power and quite terrible in their bitter intensity of passion'. In 'English Poetesses', Wilde describes them as 'instinct with tragic power, and seem often on the verge of being great'. Eliza Cook (1818–89), poet whose work appealed strictly to popular uncultured tastes. George Eliot, or Marian Evans (1819–80), novelist and poet. Jane Baillie Welsh Carlyle (1801–66), poet and letter-writer. Elizabeth Barrett Browning (1806–61), poet who was widely regarded as suitable to be the next Poet Laureate after the death of Wordsworth.

89 *Christina Rossetti . . . Lady Charlotte Elliot*: Christina Georgina Rossetti (1830–94), poet and essayist. Augusta Webster (1837–94), poet and local government activist. Harriet Eleanor Baillie Hamilton-King (1840–1920), poet and author. Wilde wrote to her on a number of occasions while he was editing *The Woman's World* to request work from her (*Letters*, pp. 316–17, 332–3). Mary Robinson (1758–1800), poet and actress whose work was admired by Coleridge. Dinah Maria Mulock Craik (1826–87), prolific writer of novels, poems, children's books, and short stories. Mrs Craik gave Wilde the idea of changing the name of his magazine from *The Lady's World* to *The Woman's World*. Jean Ingelow (1820–97), poet. Emily Jane Pfeiffer (1827–90), poet. May Probyn

(*c.* 1880s), poet. Edith Nesbit (1858–1924), poet and children's writer. Rosa Mulholland (1841–1921), Irish prose-writer and poet. Katharine Tynan (1859–1931), Irish poet and novelist who was involved in the Celtic Revival. Lady Charlotte Elliot (1839–80), poet. Wilde reuses most of this list for 'English Poetesses'.

Dame Juliana Berners . . . Puttenham: Dame Julians Barnes or Dame Juliana Berners was thought to be the author of a treatise on hunting in *The Book of St Albans* (1497). Anne Askew (1521–46), English Protestant martyr who was burned at the stake. Queen Elizabeth I (1533–1603), queen of England (1558–1603) and poet. Her poem on the conspiracies of Mary Stuart, Queen of Scots (1542–87), 'The doubt of future foes', was used as an example of rhetoric in George Puttenham's (*c.* 1529–91) book *The Arte of English Poesie* (1589). Exargasia is the repetition of the same idea in different ways.

Countess of Pembroke: Mary Herbert, Countess of Pembroke (1561–1621), poet and translator.

Sidney's: Sir Philip Sidney (1554–86), poet and essayist. His *Arcadia* (1581) was written at the house of his sister, the Countess of Pembroke.

Lady Mary Wroth . . . the 'Alchemist': Lady Mary Wroth (*c.* 1586–1562), poet and niece of Sir Philip Sidney. Ben Jonson (1572/3–1637), dramatist, poet, and scholar. His comic play *The Alchemist* (1610) is widely considered to be his finest.

Diana Primrose . . . of glorious memory: Diana Primrose (*c.* 1630), poet. Her *A Chain of Pearl* (1630) was a nostalgic poem about the Protestant Queen, aimed at King Charles I's pro-Catholic policies.

Mary Morpeth . . . Drummond of Hawthornden: Mary Oxlie of Morpeth, Scottish poet (*c.* 1600). William Drummond of Hawthornden (1585–1649), poet and essayist.

Princess Elizabeth . . . Duchess of York: Princess Elizabeth Stuart (1596–1662), daughter of James I (1566–1625), King of England and Ireland (1603–25) and, as James VI, King of Scotland (1567–1625). Anne Killigrew (1660–85), poet and maid of honour to Mary Beatrice d'Este of Modena (1658–1718), second wife of James II.

90 *Marchioness of Wharton . . . Amelia Opie*: Anne Lee, Marchioness of Wharton (1659–85), poet. Edmund Waller (1606–87), poet. Lady Mary Chudleigh (1656–1710), poet. Her poem *The Ladies Defence* (1656–1710) argues about the need for female education and the damaging effects of male contempt. Rachel Evelyn, Lady Russell (1826–98), poet. Constantia Grierson (1705–32), poet and translator of Roman ancient histories. Mary Barber (1690–1757), poet. Laetitia Pilkington (1709–50), Irish autobiographer and poet. Eliza Haywood (1693–1756), actress, poet, and novelist. Alexander Pope denounced her in *The Dunciad* (1728) as 'a shameless scribbler'. Henrietta Knight, Lady Luxborough, poet and letter-writer (1699–1756). Henry St John Bolingbroke (1678–1751), philosopher, journalist, and essayist. Lady Mary Wortley Montagu

(1689–1762), poet and letter-writer who introduced smallpox vaccinations into England. Anna, Countess Temple (d. 1777), poet. Horace Walpole (1717–97), novelist and printer. Mary Robinson, 'Perdita' (1758–1800), actress, poet, and novelist. Georgiana, Duchess of Devonshire (1757–1806), poet and socialite. Edward Gibbon (1737–94), essayist and author of *The History of the Decline and Fall of the Roman Empire*. Ann Ratcliffe or Radcliffe (1764–1823), Gothic novelist. Hester Chapone (1727–1801), poet. Amelia Opie (1769–1853), novelist and poet.

90 *'A Village Tragedy'* . . . *Guy de Maupassant*: *A Village Tragedy* (1887), a novel by Margaret Louise Woods (1856–1945). Fyodor Mikhailovich Dostoevsky (1821–81), Russian prose writer and novelist. Wilde reviewed Dostoevsky's *Injury and Insult* for the *Pall Mall Gazette* (2 May 1887). In the review Wilde admires Dostoevsky's 'fierce intensity of passion and concentration of impulse'. Guy de Maupassant (1850–93), French short story writer and novelist. Wilde criticizes Maupassant for his realism in the same way as he disparages Zola. In 'The Decay of Lying' (1889), Wilde describes Maupassant as writing 'lurid little tragedies in which everybody is ridiculous; bitter comedies at which one cannot laugh for the very tears'.

'twaddling about trees': in his letters, Byron was disparaging of the descriptive writing of some of his contemporaries. In a letter to the publisher John Murray in September 1821, Byron noted: 'Campbell is lecturing, Moore idling, Southey twaddling, Wordsworth drivelling, Coleridge muddling, Joanna Baillie piddling, Bowles quibbling, squabbling and snivelling.' Wilde also uses this quotation from Byron in his review of Roden Noel's *Essays on Poetry and Poets* for the *Pall Mall Gazette* in December 1886.

91 *Nothing in the United States* . . . *literature and art*: the differences between America and Britain is a subject which Wilde explores in more detail in two of his articles for *The Court and Society Review*. One of the American women who edited and owned newspapers was Mrs Frank Leslie (1836–1914), who would enter a brief marriage with Wilde's brother Willie in 1891.

M Sarcey: Francisque Sarcey (1827–99), French journalist and theatre critic.

92 *M Félix's*: fashion designer. Wilde mentions him again in his column of December 1887.

93 *John Halifax, Gentleman*: a novel by Mrs Craik published in 1856. The title character, John Halifax, achieves his status as a gentleman through his integrity and worth rather than through wealth and position.

'a palpable intention upon one': in a letter to J. H. Reynolds of February 1818, Keats states: 'We hate poetry that has a palpable design upon us.' It is possible that Wilde is alluding to this quotation and uses it as a criticism in the same way that Keats does.

Charlotte Brontë . . . 'Ruth': Charlotte Brontë's most famous work is *Jane Eyre* (1847). Elizabeth Cleghorn Gaskell (1810–65), novelist and biographer of Charlotte Brontë. Mrs Gaskell's *Ruth* was published in 1853. Wilde is mistaken in his observation that these two novels were published at the same time as *John Halifax, Gentleman* in 1849.

94 *Lady Brassey*: Lady Annie Allnutt Brassey (1839–87), traveller, collector, amateur photographer, and writer. Her travels aboard her boat, the *Sunbeam*, were recorded in a number of best-selling books. It is noteworthy that Wilde does not mention the immense contribution made by Lady Brassey to travel-writing, instead drawing attention to her involvement in more traditional female pursuits of the time such as cookery and charitable work.

Lady Bellairs: Lady Blanche St John Bellairs (*c.*1880), author.

Charybdis . . . Scylla: in classical mythology Charybdis is a ship-devouring monster, while Scylla is a sea nymph transformed into a sea monster who was believed to guide sailors to their deaths. Charybdis is also associated with a whirlpool off the north coast of Sicily lying opposite a rock named after Scylla on the Italian coast. Steering away from Charybdis would therefore put sailors at risk from Scylla.

96 *Miss Constance Naden*: Constance Naden (1858–99), poet and philosopher. Naden contributed a poem, 'Rest', to *The Woman's World* in March 1888. Wilde alluded to Naden's involvement in the philosophical movement Hylo-Idealism in his subtitle for 'The Canterville Ghost: A Hylo-Idealistic Romance' in the revised 1891 edition. See Josephine Guy, 'Self-Plagiarism, Creativity and Craftsmanship in Oscar Wilde', *English Literature in Transition 1880–1920*, 41 (1998), 6–23.

97 *Phyllis Browne . . . Robert Stephenson*: Phyllis Browne, pseudonym of Sarah Sharp Hamer (1839–1927), biographer. Mary Fairfax Somerville (1780–1872), Scottish mathematician and scientist. Joseph Mallord William Turner (1775–1851), landscape painter. Wilde mentions Turner in his famous passage on the fogs of London added to the version of 'The Decay of Lying' included in *Intentions* (1891). He remarks that 'Sunsets are quite old-fashioned. They belong to the time when Turner was the last note in art.' Richard Cobden (1804–65), MP and foremost leader of the Anti-Corn Law League. George Frideric Handel (1685–1759), composer. Sir Titus Salt (1803–76), manufacturer and inventor. Robert Stephenson (1803–59), engineer noted for his construction of railway bridges, especially the tubular bridge over the Menai Straits.

Laplace's La Mécanique Céleste: Pierre-Simon, Marquis de Laplace (1749–1827), French mathematician, physicist, and astronomer. He developed the theories of probability and the nebular hypothesis. His *La Mécanique céleste* was translated by Mrs Somerville and appeared under the title *Mechanism of the Heavens* (1831).

98 *'Recollections'*: Mrs Somerville's daughter Martha published her

mother's *Recollections* in 1873. Wilde draws frequently from this book for his review.

99 *George Sand . . . Countess of Albany*: George Sand, pseudonym of Aurore Dupin, Baronne Dudevant (1804–76), French novelist. Wilde reviewed a collection of Sand's letters for the *Pall Mall Gazette* on 6 March 1886. He remarked of Sand that 'she never shrieks and she never sneers. She is the incarnation of good sense.' Louisa, Countess of Albany (1752–1824), wife of Charles Edward Stuart, the Young Pretender (1720–88).

100 *Miss Mary Carpenter*: (1807–77), philanthropist and educator who devoted her life to the establishment of schools and the promotion of educational reform.

101 *Macbeth*: a tragedy by Shakespeare (1606).

Bacon's opinion: Wilde used this same point by Bacon in 'A Handbook to Marriage' (p. 10). He also reuses it in 'The Portrait of Mr W. H.' (1889), this time suggesting that Bacon's idea is taken from Plato's *Symposium*.

Charles Lamb: (1775–1834), essayist, journalist, critic, and poet.

'Ismay's Children' . . . 'Flitters, Tatters, and the Counsellor': Ismay's Children (1887) was published anonymously but was written by the Irish novelist Mrs May Hartley (1849–1916). Her novel *Flitters, Tatters, and the Counsellor* was published in 1881.

103 *Miss Edgeworth . . . 'Castle Rack-rent'*: Maria Edgeworth (1768–1849), Irish novelist. Her novel *Castle Rackrent* (1800) was praised for its portrayal of Irish regional life.

Tourgénieff: Ivan Sergeevich Turgenev (1818–83), Russian novelist and dramatist. Wilde admired Turgenev, noting in a review for the *Pall Mall Gazette* of 2 May 1887, 'Of the three great Russian novelists of our time [Tolstoy, Dostoevsky, and Turgenev] Tourgénieff is by far the finest artist.' He also mentioned Turgenev in another anonymous review for the *Pall Mall Gazette* identified by John Stokes. See John Stokes, 'Wilde on Dostoevsky', *Notes and Queries*, 27 (1980), 215–16. Wilde translated Turgenev's short story 'A Fire at Sea' from its original French and it was published anonymously in *Macmillan's Magazine* in May 1886. Wilde's first play, *Vera; Or, the Nihilists* (1880) shows a clear debt to Turgenev in its presentation of nihilism.

'In order . . . thereof!': Michel Eyquem de Montaigne (1533–92), French moralist and essayist. In the New Testament, Gehenna is a place where the wicked are punished after death.

104 *Il faut souffrir . . . pour souffrir*: 'One must suffer to be beautiful. One would have to be stupid to suffer.'

105 *Sarah Bernhardt tea-gown . . . Postillion costume*: Sarah-Marie-Henriette Bernhardt (1844–1923), French actress. Wilde admired Bernhardt and published a sonnet to her in *The World* in June 1879. In 1892 Bernhardt agreed to take the leading role in *Salomé* (1893) but the production was

cancelled when the Lord Chamberlain refused to give the play a licence. Bernhardt was supportive to Wilde during his imprisonment, and on his release he went to see her and described their tearful reunion in a letter to Robert Ross (*Letters*, p. 1116). Bernhardt's stage clothes were often copied and worn off-stage, hence Wilde's reference to the tea-gown. The Postillion costume was that worn by the person riding the horse at the front of a team of horses.

On tue une littérature . . . humaine: 'A literature is killed when it is forbidden human truth.'

M Spuller . . . Racine: Eugene Spuller (1835–96), French politician and writer. Jean Racine (1639–99), French tragic dramatist.

106 *Boileau . . . Athalie*: Nicholas Boileau-Despréaux (1636–1711), French critic and poet. Françoise d'Aubigné or Madame de Maintenon (1636–1719), teacher and wife of Louis XIV. Together with her husband, she founded a school called the Demoiselles de St Cyr in 1686 for the education of two hundred daughters of the poor nobility. Racine's 1691 drama *Athalie* was based on the Old Testament story of Athaliah, queen of Judah.

Goethe's aphorism: Wilde perhaps refers here to Goethe's aphorism from *Paolopost Futuri* (1784) which reads: 'If your father cannot do it, by your mother, 'twill be done.'

'Il me semble . . . avec son mari': 'It seems to me that the wife of the engineer of the Brooklyn Bridge has fulfilled Goethe's theory, and that not only has she become a father to her children but also a father to an admirable piece of work, a truly unique piece of work, which has immortalized the name that she shares with her husband.' Wilde assumes that his reading audience share his knowledge of French.

'Il ne s'agit . . . la société moderne': 'It's not a question of forming "femmes savantes" here. "Femmes Savantes" have been marked forever with a light taint of ridicule by one of the greatest geniuses of our race. No, it's not "femmes savantes" that we want, it's simply women, dignified women from this country of France which is the patron of good sense, measure, and grace, women having a fair notion and a sharp sense of the role which is given to them in modern society.'

Les Précieuses Ridicules: a satirical drama (1659) by Jean-Baptiste Poquelin, Molière (1622–73), based on the refined salon of Madame de Scudéry (1607–1701).

Miss Ramsay: Agatha Ramsay was the only student at Cambridge University to be in the first division of the first class of the Classical Tripos in 1887.

107 *Empress of Japan*: Itsuko Haruko (1857–1914).

M Worth: Charles Frederick Worth (1825–95), fashion designer and founder of Paris couture.

English Rational Dress Society: the society was formed in 1881 for the

promotion of rational dress for women. The primary aims of the society
were to draw attention to the restrictive corsetry of the day and to
encourage women to wear a maximum of 7 lb. of underwear. Most
women during this period wore at least 14 lb. of underwear. Wilde and
his wife were both members of the Rational Dress Society and Constance
Wilde edited the society's journal, the *Rational Dress Society's Gazette*,
1888–9.

107 *Ministering Children's League*: the Countess of Meath founded the
League in 1887.

Lady Meath: Mary Jane Maitland Brabazon, Countess of Meath (d.
1918). Wilde published a short article by Lady Meath about the Ministering Children's League in *The Woman's World* in December 1887.

Madame Ristori . . . Lady Martin: Adelaide Ristori (1822–1906), Italian
actress celebrated for her portrayal of tragic parts. Helen Faucit, Lady
Martin (1817–98), actress and author of *On Some of Shakespeare's Female
Characters* (1885).

108 *author of 'Obiter Dicta' . . . Garrick*: Augustine Birrell (1850–1933),
author of a volume of lightweight essays *Obiter Dicta* (1884) and Chief
Secretary for Ireland (1907–16). Wilde described Birrell in 'The True
Function and Value of Criticism II' (1890) as 'the charming and graceful
writer who has lately deserted the turmoil of literature for the peace of
the House of Commons'. David Garrick (1717–79), actor, dramatist, and
theatre manager.

Reynolds . . . David: Sir Joshua Reynolds (1723–92), painter who become
the most successful portraitist of his day. François-Joseph Talma (1763–
1826), French actor. Jacques Louis David (1748–1825), French neoclas-
sical painter.

109 *'The sensual life of verse . . . honeyless'*: this quotation comes from Keats's
article about Kean published in *The Champion* magazine of December
1817. Hybla is a Sicilian mountain famous for its honey. Keats quotes
Shakespeare's *Julius Caesar* (1599) here: 'But for your words, they rob the
Hybla bees, | And leave them honeyless' (*Julius Caesar*, v. i).

Salvini: Tommaso Salvini (1829–1915), Italian actor.

Phèdre: Racine's tragic play *Phèdre* (1677). Phèdre was one of Bernhardt's most famous roles.

Silvio Pellico's Francesca da Rimini . . . Marie Stuart: *Francesca da Rimini*
(1815), by the Italian patriot and dramatist Silvio Pellico (1789–1845).
Marie Stuart (1800), a drama by the German poet and dramatist Johann
Christoph Friedrich von Schiller (1759–1805).

110 *'J'ai voulu fondre . . . subir des transformations'*: 'I wanted to fuse the two
sides because I felt that as all things are susceptible to progress so
dramatic art was also called upon to undergo transformations.'

Gregory in Romeo and Juliet . . . St Peter's bark: Gregory, a character in
Shakespeare's tragedy *Romeo and Juliet* (1595). 'Here I have a pilot's
thumb . . .' comes from Shakespeare's *Macbeth* (i. iii). St Peter (*c*. AD 67),

a fisherman of Bethesda who became the leader of the apostles and is regarded by Roman Catholics as the first Pope.

Dogberrys: Dogberry, a constable in Shakespeare's *Much Ado About Nothing* (1598–9). He and his fellow constable Verges, despite their stupidity, manage to uncover the evil plot of Don John. Dogberry is a term sometimes used to describe a person prone to malapropisms.

Myrrha . . . Alfieri's: Myrrha is a character in *Mirra* (1784) by the Italian poet and dramatist Vittorio Alfieri (1749–1803).

Jules Janin . . . Rachel: Jules-Gabriel Janin (1804–74), French dramatic critic and journalist whose opinion was feared by the actors of his time. The Emperor of France was Charles Louis Napoleon Bonaparte (1808–73). Rachel or Éliza Félix (1820–58), French actress who specialized in tragic roles. Her range was very similar to that of Mme Ristori, hence Rachel's anxiety, as Wilde puts it, 'for her laurels'.

111 *Ary Scheffer . . . the Niobe*: Ary Scheffer (1795–1858), French painter. The marble statue of the Niobe in the Uffizi Gallery depicts the grief of Niobe, the wife of Amphion, King of Thebes. In Greek myth, Niobe's children were slain after she boasted of them and she was turned to stone. Even when turned to stone, she continued to weep.

handmaidens of Creusa: Creusa is another name for Glauce, a character in *Medea*.

'Ce n'est pas . . . se terminer en farce': 'This was not the first time that I had to prevent, by an effort of will, the tragedy from ending in farce.'

Montanelli's Camma: Guiseppe Montanelli (1813–62), Italian statesman and author of the tragedy *La Camma* (1857).

112 *'Aurora Leigh'*: Elizabeth Barrett Browning's poem (1857) about the life of a woman writer.

'Sordello' . . . Gigadibs: *Sordello* (1840) and *The Ring and the Book* (1868–9), poems by Robert Browning (1812–89). 'Ode on a Grecian Urn' (1819), a poem by John Keats. Blougram and Gigadibs are both characters in Browning's poem 'Bishop Blougram's Apology' (1855).

'Pippa Passes' . . . 'Red-cotton Night-cap Country': *Pippa Passes* (1841), *Men and Women* (1855), *Red-cotton Night-cap Country* (1873), poems by Robert Browning.

113 *'The Grammarian's Funeral'*: a poem by Browning (1855).

114 *'Dans l'art comme . . . fils de quelqu'un'*: this phrase and the ideas Wilde suggests about originality appear also in 'The Poet's Corner' (p. 17). It is probable that Wilde thought that his readers from the *Pall Mall Gazette* would be unlikely to read *The Woman's World* and vice versa.

Judas of Cherioth . . . Ysabel the wife of Ahab: Judas Iscariot (meaning man of Cherioth) was the apostle who betrayed Jesus for thirty pieces of silver. Nero, emperor of Rome (AD 37–68), was famous for his despotism and cruelty. Ysabel or Jezebel, wife of Ahab, King of Israel, tried to

introduce the worship of false idols and to destroy the prophets of Israel
(1 Kings 16–22).

114 *Flaubert*: Gustave Flaubert (1821–80), French novelist whose *Madame
Bovary* (1857) was deemed offensive to public morals with its depiction
of the adulteries and suicide of Emma Bovary. Wilde admired Flaubert,
writing to W. E. Henley in 1888 that 'Flaubert is my master' and that he
hoped to be 'Flaubert II, *Roi par grâce de Dieu*' (*Letters*, p. 372).

the perpetual curate of Pudlington Parva: here Wilde draws a comparison
between Trollope and his character Septimus Harding from *The Warden*
(1855). Harding is driven, by the public-spirited outcry of a local surgeon
(and his own sense of moral duty), to retire from his wardenship of
Hiram's Hospital to his old curacy of Crabtree Parva (*parva* being Latin
for small). By suggesting that Trollope is the perpetual curate of Pudlington Parva, Wilde is implying that his stature is similarly minor and
provincial.

As for George Meredith . . . except articulate: this passage about Meredith
is repeated nearly exactly in 'The Decay of Lying' (1889).

the author of 'Richard Feverel': *The Ordeal of Richard Feverel* (1859), a
novel by Meredith which caused a scandal when it was published.

115 *Theseus . . . Œdipus*: Greek myths: Theseus was celebrated for his slaying
of the minotaur in the labyrinth, while Oedipus killed his father, unaware
of his father's identity, and then unwittingly married his mother and had
four children with her. When the truth was revealed, Oedipus put out his
own eyes and his mother killed herself.

Lady Augusta Noel: (1838–1902), novelist.

An industrious Bostonian: Wilde is probably referring to one of his favourite authors, Edgar Allan Poe, who was born in Boston. Poe's 1827 poetry
collection, *Tamerlane and Other Poems*, was published under the pseudonym 'The Bostonian'. Wilde suggests here that a writer like Poe would
have made more of the ideas used by Lady Noel in *Hithersea Mere*.

116 *the Sagas*: Medieval narrative compositions from Iceland and Norway.

Dryad: a nymph or divinity of the woods.

Miss Alice Corkran's: Alice Abigail Corkran (d. 1916), author and journalist. Wilde was a friend of Corkran's family and asked her to contribute to
The Woman's World (*Letters*, p. 370).

Darwin: Charles Robert Darwin (1809–82), naturalist who formulated
the theory of evolution in *On the Origin of Species* (1859).

117 *Sir George Trevelyan*: Sir George Otto Trevelyan (1838–1928), writer
and British statesman.

Professor Romanes: George John Romanes (1848–94), scientist. Professor
Romanes's article, 'Mental Differences between Men and Women', was
published in *The Nineteenth Century* in May 1887.

118 *Defoe . . . Essay upon Projects*: Daniel Defoe (1660–1731), novelist and
journalist. His *An Essay upon Projects* was published in 1697.

Lord Tennyson's 'Princess': Alfred, Lord Tennyson (1809–92), poet. His poem *The Princess, a Medley* was published in 1847.

Mrs Fawcett: Millicent Garrett Fawcett (1847–1929), writer and suffragist.

119 *'The Deserted Village'*: 'The Deserted Village' (1770), a poem by Oliver Goldsmith.

120 *The most perfect and the most poisonous ... a sonnet*: this paragraph is copied nearly completely from Wilde's review, 'Dinners and Dishes' (p. 8).

Mrs Marshall ... 'Economical French Cookery for Ladies': Agnes Bertha Marshall (1855–1905), celebrity cook, cookery school owner, lecturer, and inventor of the ice-cream cone. Emilie Lebour Fawssett (active *c.*1880), 'Cordon Bleu', published *Economical French Cookery for Ladies* in April 1887.

Michael Field: Michael Field was the pseudonym of Katharine Bradley (1846–1914) and her niece Edith Cooper (1862–1913) who jointly wrote poetry and verse drama. Bradley and Cooper were acquaintances of Wilde and asked for his advice about the Independent Theatre production of their play *A Question of Memory* (1893).

122 *Knutlinga Saga*: Snorri Sturluson's *Heimskringla* (1230) saga included the reign of Canute.

Faun of 'Callirhöe': a character in *Callirhöe, and the Fair Rosamund*, a play by Michael Field (1884).

123 *Miss Frances Martin's 'Life of Elizabeth Gilbert'*: Frances Martin (*c.*1880), writer. Elizabeth Gilbert (1826–84), founder of the General Welfare of the Blind charity in 1854.

125 *Mrs Louise Chandler Moulton*: Ellen Louise Chandler Moulton (1835–1908), American poet, author, and journalist. Wilde met Moulton during his tour of America and asked her to contribute to *The Woman's World* (*Letters*, p. 302). She later reviewed 'The Decay of Lying' (1889) in the Boston *Sunday Herald*, calling Wilde a 'prodigal and charming talker'.

Castaly: a spring on Mount Parnassus sacred as the fount of inspiration. Wilde refers to Castaly in his poem 'Amor Intellectualis' (1881).

126 *We are often told that we are a shallow age ...*: Wilde admires the shallow because 'only the shallow know themselves' ('Phrases and Philosophies for the Use of the Young', 1894). Yet, at the same time, shallowness is not something he values. Dorian Gray, for example, eventually falls out of love with Sybil Vane because she is 'shallow and unworthy' (*The Picture of Dorian Gray*, 1891). As Wilde remarks in *De Profundis* (1897), 'The supreme vice is shallowness. Whatever is realised is right.'

Mrs De Courcy Laffan ... Mrs Leith Adams: Bertha Jane Laffan (d. 1912), novelist.

Jubilee Odes: it was Queen Victoria's Golden Jubilee in 1887, hence the rash of Jubilee poems.

126 *Madame de Staël . . . John H. Ingram*: Anne-Louise-Germaine Necker, Madame de Staël (1766–1817), French writer who was a major precursor to French Romanticism. John Henry Ingram (1842–1916), biographer and editor.

De Broglie family: Albertine, Madame de Staël's daughter, married the duc de Broglie and his family controlled de Staël's papers.

127 *'Corinne'*: Madame de Staël's 1807 novel that proposed the idea of women as independent artists.

Sorrows of Werther: Goethe's *The Sorrows of Young Werther* (1774) was a huge success throughout Europe. The hero, Werther, commits suicide in the novel because of his dissatisfaction with the world and himself.

128 *Heine*: Heinrich Heine (1797–1856), German poet.

Mr Harcourt . . . John Evelyn's 'Life of Mrs Godolphin': Sir William George Granville Venables Vernon Harcourt (1827–1904), English statesman. John Evelyn (1620–1706), diarist and biographer. His *Life of Mrs Goldolphin* was published in 1647.

Archbishop of York . . . Samuel Wilberforce: Edward Venables Vernon Harcourt (1757–1847), Archbishop of York (1808–47). Samuel Wilberforce (1805–73), Bishop of Oxford (1845–69).

Margaret Godolphin . . . Court of Charles II: Margaret Godolphin (1652–78), maid of honour to Catherine of Braganza (1638–1705). Charles II (1630–85), king of England, Scotland, and Ireland (1660–85).

129 *Buckingham . . . Sedley*: George Villiers, Duke of Buckingham (1628–87), writer and Charles II's chief minister. John Wilmot Rochester (1647–80), poet and satirist. Sir George Etheridge (*c.*1636–92), dramatist. Henry Killigrew (1613–1700), dramatist. Sir Charles Sedley (*c.*1639–1701), dramatist and poet.

Frances Jennings . . . Duchess of Marlborough: Frances Jennings, 1647–1731. Sarah Jennings, Duchess of Marlborough (1660–1744), maid of honour to Queen Anne (1665–1714).

author of the 'Mémoires de Grammont' . . . James II: Anthony Hamilton (*c.*1646–1720), Irish writer who published *Mémoires de la vie du comte de Grammont* in 1713. Richard Talbot (1630–91), Irish Jacobite. James II (1633–1701), king of England, Ireland, and (as James VII) of Scotland (1685–8).

William's successful occupation of Ireland: James II's pro-Catholic sympathies and arbitrary rule caused the Whigs and Tories to unite in inviting William of Orange to take the throne. James was defeated by the Protestant army of William at the Battle of the Boyne in 1690. It is noteworthy that Wilde refers to William of Orange's reign as the 'occupation' of Ireland, implying William should not be there.

Miss Emily Faithfull . . . Galignani: Emily Faithfull (1835–95), editor, campaigner for women's rights, and typesetter. *Galignani's Messenger* was a newspaper printed in Paris that was widely circulated amongst English residents on the Continent.

130 *Saltaire*: village designed and built by Titus Salt.

Lady Shrewsbury ... Mrs Joyce's: Lady Anne Theresa Shrewsbury's (1836–1912) article questions what will happen if women are given the jobs that men should have. She ends her article by stating her wish that 'women may become more and more guardian angel of the Englishmen's hearth and home, instead of becoming his rival in the labour market, college, and professions' ('Our Girl Workers', *The Woman's World* (Feb. 1888), 154–5). Lady Shrewsbury holds an opinion diametrically opposite to Emily Faithfull's on this subject so Wilde can be seen to be attempting to straddle both positions by 'entirely' agreeing with Faithfull but feeling 'that there is something to be said' for the views of Lady Shrewsbury. Ellen Joyce argues that the 'wisely arranged and thoroughly protected' emigration of women and children 'would greatly affect the condition of the unemployed in Britain' ('Emigration', *The Woman's World* (Feb. 1888), 173–6).

Mr Walter Besant: Sir Walter Besant (1836–1901), critic and novelist. His novel *Children of Gibeon* (1888) discussed the plight of seamstresses in Hoxton.

Miss Beatrice Crane: daughter of Walter Crane (see n. to p. 34).

131 *Professor Dowden ... Mr Watts'*: Edward Dowden (1843–1913), professor of English at Trinity College, Dublin and critic. G. F. Watts (1817–1904), artist and sculptor. Two of his most famous pictures were *Hope* and *Psyche*.

132 *Mr William Rossetti ... Messrs Hills and Saunders*: William Michael Rossetti (1829–1919), art critic and man of letters. Christina Rossetti's *Goblin Market* was published in 1862. George Mars Launder (1858–1922), professionally known as Mr George Lafayette (1858–1922), Irish photographer. He took a portrait of Alexandra, Princess of Wales (1844–1925) when she was awarded an honorary degree. Messrs Hills and Saunders were photographers based in Eton.

Princess Emily Ruete of Oman and Zanzibar: Princess Salamah bint Saïd (1844–1924), who became Emily Ruete when she married German trader Rudolph Heinrich Ruete. She was forced to flee her homeland when she became pregnant by Ruete. She then settled in Germany. Emily Ruete was the first Arab woman to write an autobiography and her memoirs gave unprecedented insights into the lives of Muslim women.

136 *Mrs Oliphant's*: Margaret Oliphant (1828–97), Scottish novelist and biographer.

Dante: Dante Alighieri (1265–1321), Italian poet and philosopher. He was born in Florence hence the reference to his indelible presence there.

137 *Petrarch ... Byron*: Francesco Petrarch (1304–74), Italian poet and humanist. Venice was sometimes known as Mistress of the Seas because

of its position at the head of the Adriatic Sea. In 1816 Byron left England, where doubts had been cast on his sanity and there were suggestions that he had had an incestuous relationship with his half-sister. He settled on the Continent and spent a great deal of time in Venice.

137 *two Bellinis ... Tintoret*: Wilde is probably referring to the two generations of the talented Italian painting family, the Bellinis. Jacopo Bellini (*c.*1400–70) taught his two sons, Giovanni (*c.*1430–1516) and Gentile (*c.*1429–1507), in the Venetian school of painting. Tiziano Vecellio or Titian (*c.*1490–1576), Italian painter of the Venetian school noted for his religious and mythological works. Jacopo Robusti or Tintoretto (1518–94), Italian painter of the Venetian school.

138 *Harriet Waters Preston*: (1836–1911), American poet.

Lady Beaumont: Margaret Beaumont (*c.*1758–1829), wife of Sir George Howland Beaumont (1753–1827), patron of Wordsworth and Coleridge.

139 *'an awful truth ... securely virtuous'*: this quotation comes from a letter from Wordsworth to Lady Beaumont of 21 May 1807.

140 *Miss May Morris*: (1862–1938), textile and wallpaper designer, editor of the writings of her father, William Morris. May Morris was in charge of the embroidery shop at Morris and Co. and a successful designer in her own right.

141 *Mr Henley*: it is not known when Wilde first met W. E. Henley but, typically for Henley, their relationship was a difficult one. At first close (Henley recommended Wilde for the exclusive Savile Club), their friendship began to deteriorate in 1889 when Henley's newspaper, the *Scots Observer*, criticized Wilde's 'The Portrait of Mr W. H.' (1889). Wilde wrote to Henley complaining: 'To be exiled to Scotland to edit a Tory paper in the wilderness is bad enough, but not to see the wonder and beauty of my discovery of the real Mr W. H. is absolutely dreadful' (*Letters*, p. 409). Matters became worse when the *Scots Observer* reviewed *The Picture of Dorian Gray*, famously labelling Wilde a writer for 'outlawed noblemen and perverted telegraph boys' (*Scots Observer*, 5 July 1890). Wilde at first assumed that the review was by Henley, when in fact it was not. It is likely, though, that the real culprit, Charles Whibley (1860–1930), was encouraged by Henley to attack Wilde. When Henley published a critical review of *The Ballad of Reading Gaol* (1898), Wilde decided not to respond, noting that Henley was 'so proud of having written *vers libres* on his scrofula that he is quite jealous if a poet writes a lyric on his prison' (*Letters*, p. 1032). This review was Wilde's only one of Henley's work.

Marsyas ... 'Rhymes and Rhythms in Hospital': Marsyas was a mortal who challenged Apollo to a musical competition to be judged by King Midas. After the competition, Apollo flayed Marsyas alive for his presumption. In 'The Decay of Lying' (1889), Wilde refers to Marsyas as 'the singer of life'. In classical myth, Apollo is the god of light, poetry, music, healing, and prophecy. Henley's 'Hospital Sketches' (1875) were written while he was in Edinburgh Royal Infirmary receiving treatment for tubercular arthritis from Joseph Lister (1827–1912). Henley had lost one foot as a child from the same condition but an extended period of painful treatment from Lister saved his other foot.

143 *Toyokuni colour-print*: Henley's 'Ballade of the Toyokuni Print' drew its inspiration from a colour woodblock by Otagawa Kunisada (1786–1865), who worked under the name Toyokuni III.

145 *reeds and pipes*: Wilde often uses this pastoral image of poetry being piped or played.

146 *Sordello*: (*c.*1200–69), Italian poet famous for his love poetry. He was the subject of Robert Browning's poem *Sordello* (1840).

If he took . . . his work would become trivial: the juxtaposition of triviality and seriousness is a common one throughout Wilde's work. It is used of course to greatest effect in *The Importance of Being Earnest* (1895), which Wilde subtitled 'A Trivial Comedy for Serious People'. As Wilde told Robert Ross of the play in 1895, 'It is exquisitely trivial, a delicate bubble of fancy, and it has its philosophy—that we should treat all the trivial things of life very seriously, and all the serious things with sincere and studied triviality.'

Mr William Sharp: Sharp published Wilde's 'On the Sale by Auction of Keats's Love Letters' (1886) in his edition, *Sonnets of this Century* (1886). This did not seem to enamour Sharp to Wilde as Wilde was reported as saying that Sharp's motto should be '*Acutus descensus averni* (Sharp is the descent into Hell)' (*Letters*, p. 270). Wilde admitted to some shame at his review of Sharp in a letter of 1888: 'Poor Sharp! He is really irresistible—he is so serious and foolish' (*Letters*, p. 375).

"Thomas the Rhymer" . . . *Clerk Saunders*: Thomas Erceldoune, known as Thomas the Rhymer (*c.*1220–97), seer and poet. His work is the source for a number of traditional tales. 'The Ballad of Clerk Saunders' was first recorded in 1776. Its author is unknown.

147 *at the beginning of the century by Wordsworth*: Wordsworth's Preface to *Lyrical Ballads* (1800) set out his views on the role of poetry and poetical diction. In the Preface he famously calls for poetry to use the common language of men and to take nature for its subject matter.

the Queen in 'Alice in Wonderland': in Lewis Carroll's *Alice's Adventures in Wonderland* (1865), the Queen of Hearts famously demands execution for everyone who upsets her. Her orders, however, as Wilde humorously puts it, were 'never carried into execution'.

'Sir Patrick Spens': an early Scottish ballad, included in Thomas Percy's *Reliques of English Poetry* (1765). Sir Walter Scott later rewrote the ballad.

148 *Chatterton's 'Ballad of Charity'* . . . *'Sister Helen' of Rossetti*: Thomas Chatterton (1752–70), poet and forger. His 'An Excelente Balade of Charitie: As Written bie the Gode Prieste Thomas Rowley 1464' was

published in 1777. Wilde admired Chatterton and had lectured about him earlier in 1888. However, the Chatterton lecture given by Wilde is famous for rather more unusual reasons. The manuscript of the lecture shows that Wilde not only plagiarizes two biographies of Chatterton but also has actually cut passages out of the books and pasted them into his lecture text. His intervening sentences suggest that he intended to pass these ideas off as his own. Samuel Taylor Coleridge (1772–1834), poet and critic. *The Rime of the Ancient Mariner* was first published in 1798 in *Lyrical Ballads*. Keats's ballad 'La Belle Dame Sans Merci' was published in 1820. Wilde suggests that the 'Ballad of Charity', *The Rime of the Ancient Mariner*, and 'La Belle Dame Sans Merci' contain the 'soul of Christ' in *De Profundis* (1897). Dante Gabriel Rossetti's 'Sister Helen' was first published in 1870.

150 *Miss Mary Robinson*: Agnes Mary Frances Robinson (1857–1944), poet.

Antiphons to the Unknowable: an antiphon is a short passage recited or sung after certain parts of a liturgical service. In philosophy, the Unknowable is the ultimate reality that underlies all phenomena but cannot be known. Wilde is suggesting that Robinson turn her attention to less complex poetical tasks.

the Sphinx . . . Dürer's 'Melencolia': in Greek myth, the Sphinx was a monster with a woman's head and a lion's body. She lay outside Thebes, asking travellers a riddle and then killing them if they failed to answer it. Oedipus answered her correctly and she killed herself. Wilde's poem, *The Sphinx* (1894), combined the Sphinx's mythical story with the presence of sphinxes (usually male) in Egypt. He also used the idea of secretive women being like sphinxes in his short story 'The Sphinx without a Secret: An Etching' (1891). Albrecht Dürer (1471–1528), German painter, art theorist, and draughtsman. His *Melencolia* was created in 1514.

Darwinism and 'The Eternal Mind': Darwinism is the theory of the origins of animal and plant species by evolution through a process of natural selection. The philosopher John Locke's *An Essay Concerning Human Understanding* (1690) argues that there is no innate idea of God and that the idea of God is acquired through sensation and reflection. He uses the phrase 'the eternal mind' to refer to the idea that God's existence is implied by the existence of a continuing orderly universe. By bringing together Locke and Darwin, Robinson brings together two ways of thinking about the creation of mankind. However, Wilde suggests that it is entirely inappropriate to leave these kinds of discussion in the hands of shepherdesses and thus, by extension, in poetry.

151 *Daphne*: Daphne was the daughter of the river god Peneus. Apollo pursued her for her love, having been shot with an arrow of love and lust by Eros. To enable her to escape, Peneus turned Daphne into a laurel tree. Apollo loved the tree and adorned himself with laurel.

There is an element of imitation . . .: here again Wilde sets forth his ideas about the reinterpretation of old ideas in poetry. See 'The Poet's Corner' (pp. 16–18).

153 *Philip Bourke Marston . . . Balaclava*: Philip Bourke Marston (1850–87), poet. The Great Exhibition of the Works of Industry of All Nations took place in Crystal Palace in 1851. The Crimean War (1853–6) was fought mostly in the Crimean region between Russia on one side and a coalition of Great Britain, France, Sardinia, and Turkey on the other. The Battle of the Alma took place on 20 September 1854. The allies cleared the way to Sebastopol in a major victory over the Russians. The Battle of Bala-clava (25 October 1854) was an inconclusive battle probably best known for the charge of the Light Brigade, a cavalry charge by the allies which went wrong due to a misunderstanding, resulting in heavy casualties. The battle was immortalized only weeks later by Tennyson in his poem 'The Charge of the Light Brigade' (1854).

155 *Mr W. B. Yeats*: William Butler Yeats (1865–1939), Irish poet, dramatist, and essayist. Yeats first met Wilde at W. E. Henley's house in 1888 where Wilde impressed him with his 'perfect sentences'. Wilde reviewed Yeats's *Wanderings of Oisin* (1889) in *The Woman's World* (March 1889) and for the *Pall Mall Gazette* (12 July 1889). He was probably led to review *Fairy and Folk Tales of the Irish Peasantry* because it contained stories taken from his mother's anthology, *Ancient Legends of Ireland* (1887).

Croker and Lover: Thomas Crofton Croker (1798–1854), Irish antiquar-ian and collector of Irish folklore. Samuel Lover (1797–1868), Irish novelist, painter, and anthologist of Irish legends.

Carleton: William Carleton (1794–1869), Irish novelist who wrote stories of Irish life. He was born the son of a peasant farmer, hence Yeats's reference to him as a 'peasant born'.

156 *Kennedy*: Patrick Kennedy (1801–73), Irish author of *Legendary Fictions of the Irish Celts* (1866).

'The Pretty Girl Milking the Cow': an Irish folk song.

Blake: William Blake (1757–1827), poet, artist, visionary, and essayist. Allan Cunningham (1784–1842) records in his *Lives of Eminent British Painters* (1829–33) Blake's claim of having seen a fairy's funeral.

158 *'The Parochial Survey of Ireland'*: also known as William Shaw Mason's (1774–1853) *A Statistical Account of Ireland*.

Giraldus Cambrensis: Giraldus Cambrensis de Barri (*c*.1146–1220), Welsh churchman and historian of Ireland.

Allingham's: William Allingham (1824–89), diarist and poet. His most famous poem, 'The Fairies', was published in 1850.

159 *'The Priest's Soul'*: the stories of 'The Horned Women' and 'The Priest's Soul' were taken by Yeats from Lady Wilde's *Ancient Legends of Ireland*, hence Wilde's enthusiasm for them.

'Gyp': Sybille Gabrielle de Mirabeau, Comtesse de Martel de Janville (1850–1932), novelist who wrote under the pseudonym 'Gyp'.

160 *'Autour du Mariage'* . . . *'Le Petit Bob'*: *Autour du Mariage* (1883), *Autour du Divorce* (1886), and *Le Petit Bob* (1882) are all novels by Gyp.

Violet Fane's 'Edwin and Angelina Papers': the poet Mary Montgomerie Lamb wrote under the pseudonym Violet Fane that she took from Disraeli's novel *Vivian Grey* (1826). Wilde met Fane early in the 1880s. She provided a poem, 'Hazely Heath', for the opening number of *The Woman's World* and an article on the Stuarts for the May 1888 number. Wilde asked her to write something about her vegetarianism on the grounds that 'even vegetarianism, in your hands, would make a capital article'. He went on to comment that 'the most violent republicans I know are all vegetarians: Brussels Sprouts seem to make people bloodthirsty, and those who live on lentils and artichokes are always calling for the gore of the aristocracy, and for the severed heads of kings' (*Letters*, p. 334). Fane sent Wilde a copy of *The Story of Helen Davenant* (1889) to review at his request (*Letters*, p. 389). Fane's *Edwin and Angelina Papers* was published in 1878.

Thackeray . . . *Dean Stanley's*: William Makepeace Thackeray (1811–63), novelist. Wilde notes of Thackeray in 'The Soul of Man Under Socialism' (1891) that 'at times, he is too conscious of the public, and spoils his work by appealing directly to the sympathies of the public, or by directly mocking at them'. For Bishop Samuel Wilberforce, see note to p. 128. Arthur Penrhyn Stanley, Dean of Westminster (1815–81).

161 *Bulwer Lytton* . . . *'The Pilgrims of the Rhine'*: Edward George Earl Lytton, first Baron Lytton (1803–73), MP, novelist, and editor. His collection *The Pilgrims of the Rhine* was published in 1834.

162 *Dr Anna Kingsford*: Anna Bonus Kingsford (1846–88), doctor, theosophist, and vegetarian campaigner.

Jamblichus . . . *Agathocles*: Jamblichus or Iamblichus (*c.* AD 330), Syrian philosopher and leading exponent of Neoplatonism. Agathocles (361–289 BC), tyrant of Syracuse and self-styled King of Sicily.

'Kubla Khan': Samuel Taylor Coleridge's 'Kubla Khan: A Vision in a Dream' (1816) was written after an opium-induced sleep. Coleridge awoke and wrote most of the poem and then was interrupted and failed to remember the remainder.

163 *Swedenborg* . . . *Hans Christian Andersen*: Emanuel Swedenborg (1688–1772), Swedish philosopher, mystic, and scientist. He began to experience visions in later life and to converse with angels, while awake as well as asleep. His works heavily influenced Blake's notions of spirituality. Hans Christian Andersen (1805–75), Danish playwright and novelist, most famous for his fairy stories.

164 *Hermes*: in Greek myth, the messenger and herald of the gods.

John the Baptist: in the New Testament, the son of Zachariah and Elizabeth and the forerunner of Jesus, whom he baptized. Wilde dramatizes Herod's murder of John the Baptist in *Salomé* (1896).

Mr Maitland . . . 'The Perfect Way': Edward Maitland (1824–97), editor and theosophist. *The Perfect Way; Or, The Finding of Christ* (1882) by Kingsford and Maitland set out to re-establish truth by comparing major world religions.

Miss Amy Levy: (1861–89), poet, novelist, and feminist. Levy was the first Jewish woman to enter Newnham College, Cambridge. She published a number of pieces in *The Woman's World* including a short story, 'The Recent Telepathic Occurrence at the British Museum' (November 1887), an article about Christina Rossetti (March 1888), and two poems. Wilde wrote in 1887 that Levy's first story for the magazine was 'a real literary gem' by someone 'who has a touch of genius in her work' (*Letters*, p. 325).

The Oxford World's Classics Website

www.worldsclassics.co.uk

- Information about new titles
- Explore the full range of Oxford World's Classics
- Links to other literary sites and the main OUP webpage
- Imaginative competitions, with bookish prizes
- Peruse the Oxford World's Classics Magazine
- Articles by editors
- Extracts from Introductions
- A forum for discussion and feedback on the series
- Special information for teachers and lecturers

www.worldsclassics.co.uk